Jeanne Jones'

Homestyle Cooking

MADE HEALTHY

Jeanne Jones'
Homestyle Cooking

200 Classic American Favorites
Low in Fat with All the Original Flavor!

MADE HEALTHY

Jeanne Jones
columnist, "Cook It Light"

Rodale Press, Inc.
Emmaus, Pennsylvania

Front Cover Recipes: Southern Fried Chicken (page 199),
Mashed Potatoes with Gravy (page 128), and Old-Fashioned
Green Beans (page 101)
Back Cover Recipe: Velvet Cake with Seven-Minute
Frosting (page 328)

Printed in the United States of America on acid-free ∞,
recycled paper ♼

Interior and Cover Designer: Christina Gaugler
Illustrator: Annie Gusman
Photographer: Thom DeSanto
Food Stylist: Andrea Swenson
Prop Stylist: Debrah Donahue

Library of Congress Cataloging-in-Publication Data

Jones, Jeanne.
    [Homestyle cooking made healthy]
    Jeanne Jones' homestyle cooking made healthy : 200 classic
American favorites, low in fat with all the original flavor! /
Jeanne Jones.
        p.   cm.
    Includes index.
    ISBN 0–87596–466–4 hardcover
    1. Low-fat diet—Recipes.   2. Cookery, American.   I. Title.
RM237.7.J66   1999
641.5'638—dc21   98–44630

Distributed to the book trade by St. Martin's Press

2 4 6 8 10 9 7 5 3 1 hardcover

─── OUR PURPOSE ───

*"We inspire and enable people to improve
their lives and the world around them."*

To my mother, Kathryn Fishback,

and my husband, Donald Breitenberg,

who served as the official

taste-testing panel for this book—

and never wanted their assignment to end!

In all Rodale Press cookbooks, our mission is to provide delicious and nutritious low-fat recipes. Our recipes also meet the standards of the Rodale Test Kitchen for dependability, ease, practicality, and, most of all, great taste. To give us your comments, call 1-800-848-4735.

Contents

Acknowledgments

In grateful acknowledgment to all those who contributed their time and talents to make this cookbook a reality.

JoAnn Brader
Tracy DeMas
Thom DeSanto
Debrah Donahue
Anne Egan
Kathy Everleth
Kathryn Fishback
Christina Gaugler
William Hansen
Karen Hatt
Marilyn Hauptly
Vicky Holly
Pat Mast
Margret McBride
Tom Ney
Eric Nutt
Melinda B. Rizzo
Jean Rogers
Sharon Sanders
Darlene Schneck
Andrea Swenson
John Vitollo

Introduction

For nearly three decades, I have worked to dispel the myth that food has to be either good or good for you because it can't be both. In my first book, *The Calculating Cook*, published in 1972, my goal was to prove that gastronomy, or the art of eating food, could be successfully combined with nutrition, the science of utilizing food. With all of the other advancements that have been made in improving quality of life, it only makes sense that the true enjoyment of fine food and the proper fueling of the body should be given equal status in recipe development and menu planning.

In my first few books, I focused on revising all of my own favorite dishes. However, for the past 15 years, I have been revising other people's recipes in my weekly newspaper column, "Cook It Light."

I have often been described as the "Dear Abby" of the food section because I write what is called an interacting column. In other words, my readers send me their problem recipes and I print them, along with my solutions, every week.

Hearing from so many thousands of people from all over the country has certainly been both a rewarding and an extremely educational experience. It has also helped to keep me on the cutting edge of knowing what kinds of recipes people are really looking for. It should come as no surprise that great-tasting homestyle food is tops on everyone's list. With the flavorful revisions in this book, homestyle cooking can be the food that's as good for your body as it is for your soul.

Everything Old Is New Again

In this book I have revisited and revised traditional recipes from friends and readers, old regional cookbooks, community cookbooks, and my own family. In these makeovers, I have kept two goals constantly in mind: The revised dish must taste *as good as* the original, and the revised dish must meet current nutritional guidelines for healthy eating.

I have worked diligently to retain the flavor appeal and textural integrity of the original recipes. I'm a realist. I reduce fat and sodium only as low as is palatable. I know that the lowest-fat dish in the world isn't going to help anyone if it's unappetizing.

Many of the makeovers are truly dramatic. A single serving of Chicken-Fried Steak with Country Gravy, for example, plummets from 720 calories and 45 grams of fat to just 308 calories and 3 grams of fat. Two tablespoons of Guacamole drops from 100 calories and 10 grams of fat to a mere 34 calories and 2.8 grams of fat.

Other equally awesome makeovers you'll want to taste are Deviled Eggs, Creamy Potato Salad, Twice-Baked Potatoes, Macaroni and Cheese, Chicken Kiev, Chicken Cordon Bleu, Beef Stroganoff, Stuffed Pork Chops, Cinnamon–Sour Cream Coffee Cake, and Black-Bottom Pie.

I loved the challenge of transforming these dishes. In the process, I've discovered how much I adore these old-time comfort foods. I don't think I've had a gelatin salad since I was a girl, and I had forgotten how satisfying it can be. I have also avoided fried foods and cream sauces because they are so high in fat and calories. Not anymore.

With the techniques in this book, I am again enjoying Fried Shrimp, Tuna Noodle Casserole, and Creamed Onions. In fact, my husband loved these dishes so much during recipe testing that he wished I could keep working on this book forever.

My hope is that these makeovers will inspire you to tinker with your own recipes. Even with the more than 200 recipes included here, I know there are scores of other classic American homestyle recipes in kitchens all across the country. Beginning on page 13, I outline the process you can use to do this satisfying task yourself. You can convert high-fat, high-calorie dishes into nutritional assets that taste just as good as the originals.

The process isn't difficult. In fact, once you get started, it's a fun challenge to streamline your family's favorites without altering the taste or texture. Sometimes, the people who love the dish the most can't even detect any difference.

A Healthy Revolution
in American Cooking

What is American homestyle cooking? It's scores of down-home dishes quilted together to make a distinctive national style of eating. It's Southern Fried Chicken, Chicken Potpie, Lasagna, Fried Shrimp, Cioppino, Cobb Salad, Caramel-Pecan Sticky Buns, Strawberry Shortcake, and Devil's Food Cake with Fudge Frosting. It's the foods we grew up with—from the place we call home.

American homestyle cooking has always been rich and nurturing. As a wealthy nation, we celebrated our good fortune at the table. But with abundance came overabundance and a subsequent host of diet-related ailments, such as heart disease, diabetes, cancer, and obesity. Health experts stepped in and dictated, "No more fried foods, no more cream sauces, no more fatty cheeses, no more desserts."

We tried dietary denial and suffered through meals of broiled skinless chicken, steamed vegetables, and salads dressed with lemon juice. But this just isn't the American dream!

American home cooks are rebelling against stringent health mandates that ignore the importance of taste in appetite satisfaction. Instead of saying no to the foods we love, we're saying no to foods that don't taste good—no matter how good they are for us. We're reclaiming the wonderful dishes that are our birthright. But that doesn't mean we are willing to pay the consequences of excess calories, fat, cholesterol, and sodium.

I sense a new American attitude about a healthy diet. We genuinely want to eat well for better health, but we also want food to taste great. The good news is that it is now possible to have both.

Planning Homestyle Meals for Health

Before you start cooking, please take a moment to look over the recipes in this book. Each recipe has a "Homestyle Makeover" sidebar that shows at a glance how the calories and total fat in the revised recipe compare to the original. In addition, I share tips in the recipe head notes on the methods and ingredients I used to adjust the nutritional profile of each dish. These recommendations can easily be applied to other recipes.

Following each recipe, you'll find a listing of nutrients. This information is valuable in planning your nutrient intake—particularly calories and fat—for one meal, an entire day, or a whole week. But, it is important to keep in mind that these figures are approximate. Like all living things, foods vary in the amount of fat and other nutrients they contain. The salmon or avocado you buy at your market will not have exactly the same amount of calories and fat as the salmon or avocado that was analyzed in a laboratory.

The flexible and sensible approach to all meal planning is to balance moderately high-fat dishes with *naturally* low-fat (and nutrient-rich) vegetables, fruits, and whole grains. The U.S. Department of Agriculture's dietary guidelines for Americans recommend an eating plan in which no more than 30 percent of calories come from fat. This doesn't mean, however, that every dish or even every meal you eat has to conform to this fat level. Rather, it means you can balance low-fat dishes with ones that are a bit higher in fat over a period of a day or several days. An average intake of fat and calories should be your goal.

Watching portion sizes is another technique that can enable you to enjoy your favorite dishes more often. By serving smaller portions of dishes that tend to be higher in fat, such as animal protein main dishes like Peppered Steak, complemented by lots of vegetables and grains, you can have your steak and eat it, too. Consult the chart on page 7 to determine your daily fat intake and the number of portions from each food group you should be eating daily, according to your ideal calorie intake.

And, finally, a word on sodium. In adapting these classic dishes, I have reduced the sodium content in most of them dramatically. I've done this by using sodium-reduced products and naturally low-sodium ingredients whenever feasible.

However, many reduced-fat and fat-free foods, particularly dairy products, tend to be high in sodium. So, if you are an individual who has a sensitivity to sodium, check the nutritional listing to determine how these dishes can fit into your daily sodium quota. Often, you can still enjoy a portion of a higher-sodium dish and then compensate by eating sodium-free foods the rest of the day.

Homestyle Meals for Special Days

Every year over the holidays, I get lots of fan mail from readers thanking me for saving their traditional meals. They thank me for revising their most decadent dishes to be healthy enough for everyone to enjoy without feeling guilty. In Party Menus (page 363), you'll find party plans for a variety of events. You can celebrate good health along with good times.

In recipes throughout the book, I've included notes on advance preparation and serving ideas that will help you include these healthier dishes in both your casual and fancier entertaining. If healthier recipes are to become a normal part of our entertaining style, I firmly believe that they have to be easy to do and convenient. Do-ahead dishes are often the best choice, leaving the cook free to enjoy the party.

Shopping for Healthy Convenience

Just as we don't wear the same style of clothing we did 20 years ago, we don't shop for food and cook it the same way either.

Convenience products have played a major role in how easy it is to cook healthy meals. Although some convenience foods contain high amounts of fat, added sugar, and salt, there are also a host of healthy convenience foods—prewashed spinach leaves, shredded cabbage, sliced fresh pineapple, and skinless, boneless chicken breasts, to name a few—that take the time and effort out of prep work. They make healthy cooking much faster and easier.

Other products such as turkey bacon and fat-free cream cheese make lowering the fat in traditional recipes more feasible. Ingredients such as these inspire me to create techniques to further intensify their flavors and bring them closer to the higher-fat products they are replacing.

For example, I've learned that cooking turkey bacon in a very small amount of vegetable oil prior to adding it to sauces, side dishes, or entrées greatly improves the flavor of the finished dish.

I also know from experience that fat-free cream cheese by itself will

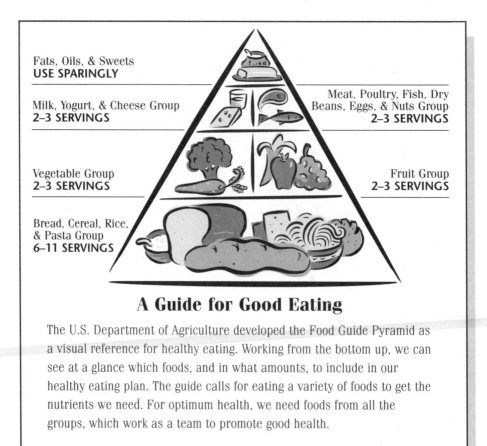

A Guide for Good Eating

The U.S. Department of Agriculture developed the Food Guide Pyramid as a visual reference for healthy eating. Working from the bottom up, we can see at a glance which foods, and in what amounts, to include in our healthy eating plan. The guide calls for eating a variety of foods to get the nutrients we need. For optimum health, we need foods from all the groups, which work as a team to promote good health.

never pass for full-fat. But if you blend fat-free cream cheese with two eggs, sugar, and vanilla extract, you can make a cheesecake that rivals one with *five* times the amount of fat. See page 327 for the luscious proof.

What Fat Does—And How to Do It with Less

Fat performs three main functions in cooking.

- Fat is a flavoring agent, either lending its own distinct flavor—as with butter or olive oil—or carrying the flavors of other ingredients throughout a dish.
- Fat is a cooking medium. Frying or sautéing foods in hot fat transforms their composition and taste.
- Fat acts as a texturizer, tenderizing baked goods in particular. Because fat is a relatively inexpensive and easy-to-use ingredient, it

has long been relied upon to perform these functions. But a bit of basic cooking knowledge is all you need to turn to other equally flavorful, but healthier, options to achieve the same good tastes and textures.

Flavor with Less Fat

The secret to enhancing the flavor of any dish is actually to boost the aroma. We actually perceive only four tastes: sweet, salt, sour, and bitter. These four basic tastes are in bands of tastebuds on our tongues.

Most of what we perceive as taste—as much as 90 percent by one expert's estimate—is actually smell. As we chew foods, odor molecules are released and travel up a passageway from the back of our throats to our nose. These many and varied aromas are what we perceive as flavors.

Many people say they can't taste when they have a cold. The truth is

---

Sized for Fitness

To guarantee a nutritional fit that's sized just right for you, consult the table that follows. Based on the U.S. Department of Agriculture's Dietary Guidelines for Americans, each calorie level indicates the recommended number of servings from a variety of healthful foods, plus the recommended daily intake of dietary fat. The lower level is right for many sedentary women and older adults; the moderate level is right for many active women, sedentary men, children, and teenage girls; and the higher level is right for many very active women, active men, and teenage boys.

Sample Daily Eating Plans at Three Calorie Levels

	Lower 1,600	Moderate 2,200	Higher 2,800
Bread, Cereal, Rice, and Pasta Group Servings	6	9	11
Vegetable Group Servings	3	4	5
Fruit Group Servings	2	3	4
Milk, Yogurt, and Cheese Group Servings*	2–3	2–3	2–3
Meat, Poultry, Fish, Dry Beans, Eggs, and Nuts Group Servings (ounces)	5	6	7
Total Fat (g.)	53	73	93

*Women who are pregnant or breastfeeding, teenagers, and young adults to age 24 need 3 servings.

---

that they can taste just fine but they can't smell the wonderful aromas released by foods.

The successful balancing of flavor in any dish is achieved by combining sweet, salt, and sour tastes (bitter is one we'd all rather avoid) with the aromas of both the ingredients and seasonings. To achieve maximum flavor in a dish from which you've removed fat, you need to pump up the aroma of every other ingredient you use.

Most fats—except for butter, extra-virgin olive oil, and roasted nut oils—taste neutral and don't have much aroma. As such, they don't contribute a distinctive flavor to a dish but, rather, they transport the aromas from other ingredients. That is why you can't just simply remove some or all of the fat from a dish and expect it to taste the same as the original. However, when you understand the powerful role that aroma plays in our enjoyment of foods, you can easily compensate for a lesser amount of fat.

Season for great taste by using plenty of herbs and spices that contain practically no calories or fat. Use them liberally to compensate for fat, as well as salt. Chop or crush fresh herbs before adding them to any recipe. When using dried herbs, choose whole-leaf herbs rather than powdered, and always crush them when you add to a dish, to release their essential oils. You can do this in a mortar and pestle, or simply rub them between your fingers until you can smell their aroma.

Black pepper retains its pungency for months if you buy the peppercorns whole and store them in a cool, dark spot. Grind black pepper in a pepper grinder just before using it for best flavor.

Marinate to make flavor soar by soaking fish, poultry, meats, fruits, vegetables, or tofu in a liquid before cooking. This technique adds enormously to the final flavor of the dish. A marinade can be as simple as plain lemon juice or as complex as a teriyaki or barbecue sauce. Simple buttermilk makes a remarkable marinade in my revision of Southern Fried Chicken (page 199), producing unbelievably moist chicken. Also, many salad dressings make great marinades. In addition, marinating can tenderize small pieces of tough meat by helping to break down the fibers.

Brown foods to intensify flavors in a skillet on the stove top, in a roasting pan in the oven, in the broiler, or on the barbecue grill. Browning meats and some vegetables, such as onions, creates wonderful new flavor compounds that add richness to many dishes. For some slow-cooking recipes, such as stews, the meat and/or vegetables are browned first to develop flavor and then slow-cooked to tenderize.

Toasting, another form of browning, is wonderful for nuts, which are naturally high in fat. The process enhances the flavor so much that you can actually cut the amount of nuts used almost in half and still end up with a tasty dish.

Toasting intensifies the flavor of both whole and ground spices. Place the spice in a heavy skillet and cook over medium heat, stirring occasionally, for 3 to 4 minutes, or until fragrant. You can toast batches of your favorite spices and then store them in a moisture-proof container in the freezer for several months.

Sizzle garlic when you want to add excitement to sauces, salad dressings, soups, stews, casseroles, and salads. Combine minced garlic and a small amount of oil in a sauté pan and heat just until the garlic sizzles. This technique can be used as a first step in many recipes, or you can sizzle up a batch of garlic and keep it in a jar in the refrigerator for up to one week as a convenient condiment for many savory dishes.

Intensify flavors by using less liquid when you simmer uncovered sauces, allowing the liquid to evaporate and the flavors to become more concentrated. Reduction sauces are used frequently in healthful cooking to achieve intense flavor and to thicken sauces and gravies without a fat-laden binder.

Sharpen flat flavors by adding a dash of acid—such as lemon juice, lime juice, or vinegar—for balance.

Enhance flavors with fresh ginger, horseradish, mustard, hot-pepper sauce, chili oil, ground red pepper, or crushed red-pepper flakes. These hot additives stimulate the tastebuds with what I call painful pleasure. Hot additives are used in many cuisines to add bite or sparkle to main dishes as well as condiments.

Sprinkle a small amount of high-fat ingredients on top of a dish for greatest impact. The aroma will dominate and fool you into thinking there is more of the ingredient than there really is.

If you choose the highest-quality, most aromatic cheeses available—such as Parmigiano-Reggiano, Pecorino Romano, or sharp Cheddar—you can often get away with using a scant amount to achieve superior flavor. These cheeses taste best if grated just before using. For greater convenience, however, you can grate a chunk and store the grated cheese, tightly covered, in the refrigerator for up to one month or in the freezer for up to six months. You can also buy prepackaged, good-quality grated Italian cheeses in many supermarket delicatessens or cheese departments.

Wait for good tastes by making stews, soups, and curries a day ahead of time. This gives the flavors a chance to blend overnight. Many of these saucy dishes are much better when they are made the day before they are eaten.

A wonderful side benefit is that any excess fat in the dish will rise to the top and harden, making it easy to remove and discard before serving.

Use fat in the starch instead of the sauce for a richer taste. For example, the flavor of a splash of extra-virgin olive oil tossed with the cooked pasta, not added to the sauce, will really pop because the pasta itself is so bland.

Choose reduced-fat or fat-free ingredients when the flavor of the dish will not be adversely affected—generally, in dishes with a lot of other ingredients. You may not like the taste of fat-free mayonnaise on a sandwich, or fat-free sour cream on a baked potato, because in these cases the flavor is showcased. But in some recipes, where all these ingredients have to do is carry other flavors, they may be the ideal choice.

Select a nutritious ingredient as a high-fat replacement if it won't adversely affect the flavor. I use tofu, for example, in the recipe for Guacamole (page 41) to carry flavor and to extend volume. It works equally well in many cream sauces, salad dressings, and creamy desserts.

Cook with Less Fat

Technology is helping to make healthy cooking truly easy. Nonstick spray and nonstick pans have revolutionized healthy meal preparation, making it painless to cut fat as well as the time and effort needed for clean up. By choosing the right cooking pans and incorporating a few simple techniques, you can cook with drastically less fat than you ever thought possible.

Nonstick cookware has improved dramatically from the old days when the surface would come off the pan along with the scrambled eggs. As with any cookware, invest in the best quality you can afford for durability and good performance.

Nonstick spray virtually eliminates the need for butter, margarine, or oil as a cooking medium. It can save literally thousands of fat grams a year if used consistently. For best results in browning foods, it is better to spray the food rather than the cooking pan. The spray has a tendency to bead up on a nonstick pan and prevent even browning.

Glazing with a liquid such as stock or broth is another way to color foods (and add flavor) without cooking in fat. Bring fat-free, reduced-sodium broth to a boil in a skillet or sauté pan and cook it until it has almost completely evaporated before adding the ingredient to be cooked. This glazing technique works particularly well for boneless chicken breasts or fish steaks because by the time they are nicely browned, they are perfectly cooked.

Sweat chopped onion by cooking it without any fat in a heavy pan, covered, over low heat for about 10 minutes, or until the onion is soft and translucent. You can add a few teaspoons of water, if necessary, to prevent scorching. This is a great alternative to many classic sauce recipes that usually begin directions with "heat 2 tablespoons of oil before adding the onion." Nobody will miss that extra *28* grams of fat.

Oven-fry thinly sliced fish, poultry, meat, or root vegetables for a short time in a very hot oven to crisp the outside without overcooking the inside. Coat the potatoes or onions with nonstick spray to produce a crisp texture.

Texturize with Less Fat

Texture can best be described as mouth feel. It is also associated with the viscosity, or body, of preparations such as salad dressings and gravy. In baked goods and desserts, texture often implies moisture and tenderness. Fat is often the ingredient that creates body, smooths out the consistency, creates a creaminess, or provides moisture. But other methods or ingredients can achieve these results in healthy cooking.

A pinch of plain gelatin powder whisked into fat-free and low-fat dressings can create the slightly creamy texture associated with high-fat dressings.

Fruit can replace moisture that is usually trapped by fat in baked goods and some desserts. Use drained applesauce, pureed cooked prunes, baby-food prunes, or a jarred fruit-based fat replacement (shelved with the cooking oils in the supermarket), such as Lighter Bake, to replace half of the fat in the recipe. Fruit-based replacements work best in baked goods that are moist and dense by nature—such as carrot cake or zucchini bread—or those that are made with intense flavorings such as cocoa powder.

Reduced-fat or fat-free dairy products can add volume and creaminess to many dishes. Replace whipping cream with fat-free evaporated milk in soups and sauces for nearly identical results. Use reduced-fat or fat-free sour cream in place of fatty cream sauces in casseroles.

Replace each whole egg with two egg whites in almost all recipes. This is of particular importance for people who are on low-cholesterol diets because each egg yolk contains 213 milligrams of cholesterol. Liquid egg substitute, which is mainly composed of egg whites, contains no fat or cholesterol and may be used in place of whole eggs. Use ¼ cup of liquid egg substitute for each large egg called for in a recipe.

Homestyle Cooking Has a Healthy Future

From my perspective, the outlook for healthful home cooking has never been more promising. The next few decades are bound to bring even more healthy convenience food products into our supermarkets and kitchens, enabling us to control the amounts of fat, sodium, sugar, and other ingredients in the meals we prepare. What could be more satisfying than to combine our love of good health and good taste right in our own kitchens?

It is my hope that in updating the homestyle recipe favorites that have stood the test of time, you will be able to nurture your family with these healthy, comforting dishes for many years to come.

How to Revise a Recipe

You've already read about some of the exciting ingredients and methods I use daily in streamlining recipes. If you're the type who responds to a challenge, what could be more fun than heading into your kitchen with the mission of making your family's favorite dishes healthier?

The first step I take in revising a recipe is to prepare the original so I have a benchmark for the taste and texture I want to duplicate. You're luckier. You're already *very* familiar with the original since you probably make it dozens of times a year.

The chart on page 14 diagrams Tuna Noodle Casserole as a blueprint for healthful change. I've noted each step, but don't be intimidated by that. Much of the process is common sense. The important thing is to trust your own tastebuds. You know what your family will and won't eat. You may be able to cut only 5 to 10 grams of fat per serving on a dish. But, if it's something your family eats frequently, multiply the fat reduction by the number of times you serve it per year, and the savings can be significant. A lot of small savings can add up to big health benefits.

Be Wise—Just Revise

Tuna Noodle Casserole is a dramatic example of a formerly high-fat, high-sodium dish transformed into a healthy re-creation with all the flavor and savor of the original.

This side-by-side comparison of the "Before" and "After" ingredient lists illustrates the methods I use to make dishes healthier. You can apply this approach to any recipe to lower the calories, fat, sodium, and cholesterol without sacrificing any of the taste, texture, or appearance.

When I was reading the original recipe, I identified eight ingredients that sent up red flags. They were too high in empty calories, cholesterol, fat, or sodium. Some could be eliminated, others had to be reduced or

Tuna Noodle Casserole *Makes 4 servings*

Original Recipe		Nutritional Concerns	Functions	Solutions/Improvements
8	ounces egg noodles	Cholesterol and fat	Adds texture and volume	No-yolk noodles eliminate 280 mg. cholesterol and 6 g. fat
2	tablespoons butter	Calories, fat, and cholesterol	Adds flavor and makes a base for the sauce	Use half the amount to cut 100 calories, 11 g. fat, and 31 mg. cholesterol
4	ounces mushrooms, sliced			Thinly slicing the mushrooms increases volume
¼	cup flour	Fat and calories	Makes a thick sauce to moisten and add volume	Condensed soup and yogurt make a rich sauce that eliminates 13 g. fat and 175 calories
2½	cups whole milk			
1	cup (4 ounces) shredded Monterey Jack cheese	Fat	Adds flavor and creaminess	Reduced-fat cheese eliminates 16 g. fat
¼	cup chopped onion			Use scallions—and increase the amount—to pump up flavor and color
1	can (12 ounces) oil-packed tuna, drained	Fat and calories	Adds flavor and protein	Water-packed tuna saves 23 g. fat and 270 calories
½	cup crushed potato chips	Fat	Adds texture and flavor	Eliminate 10 g. fat with reduced-fat crackers
½	cup (2 ounces) grated Parmesan cheese	Calories, fat, and sodium	Adds flavor and creaminess	Use half the amount to cut 129 calories, 8 g. fat, and 528 mg. sodium

Homestyle Makeover
Each serving contains

	Before	After
Calories	1,038	622
Fat g.	41	14

Add seasonings to boost flavor

Broccoli adds flavor, nutrients, fiber, and color

replaced. The revised recipe shows the happy results. I urge you to taste this particular dish to sample how truly satisfying a makeover can be.

When converting your own recipes, consider these issues.

Scan the ingredients list for problems. With practice, it takes only seconds to spot potential problem ingredients—full-fat dairy, fatty cuts of meat or poultry, processed foods, fats and oils, and sugar. You can give a green light to unprocessed vegetables, fruits, and whole-grain products—ingredients that are your nutrient-rich friends.

Determine the function of each problem ingredient. To make recipe changes intelligently, you need to understand what the ingredient contributes to the dish. Does it add flavor, tenderize, create volume, or serve as a cooking medium? Make a list of all the functions in order of their importance.

Come up with solutions and make improvements. If a lot of butter is called for as a cooking medium, you can probably drastically reduce the amount. Or substitute canola oil, which contains very little saturated fat. Another option is to eliminate the butter altogether and use only stock. Note in the revised recipe that I have added more seasonings to boost flavor.

Taste and analyze the results. How does the recipe taste? How many calories and how much fat did you save? This is the payoff. The rewards are plain to see. You really can have it all.

Revised Recipe

8	ounces no-yolk noodles
1	tablespoon butter or margarine
4	ounces mushrooms, thinly sliced
1	can (10¾ ounces) fat-free, reduced-sodium condensed cream of mushroom soup
8	ounces fat-free plain yogurt
1	cup (4 ounces) shredded reduced-fat Monterey Jack cheese
½	cup sliced scallions
1	can (12 ounces) water-packed chunk light tuna, rinsed, drained, and flaked
½	cup crushed reduced-fat snack crackers
¼	cup (1 ounce) grated Parmesan cheese
½	teaspoon ground black pepper
¼	teaspoon celery seeds
¼	teaspoon crushed red-pepper flakes
1	package (16 ounces) frozen broccoli florets, thawed

Recipes

Appetizers, Dips, and Spreads

A party is only as good as its appetizers. Delectable, savory nibbles send a signal that good times will follow.

American appetizers are versatile, adapting to all sorts of tastes and entertaining styles. They can be served hot like Buffalo Wings with Blue Cheese Dip, Swedish Meatballs, or Spanakopita. They can be eaten cold like Deviled Eggs, Pimiento Cheese–Stuffed Celery Ribs, or Smoked Salmon Mousse.

Depending on the occasion, appetizers can be passed on trays, set out on a buffet or sideboard, or served more formally on plates as a course preceding the main dish.

But by far the easiest appetizer for the cook to make and serve (and the favorite of most guests) is the dip—the quintessential American party food. Baked Artichoke Dip, Clam Dip, Guacamole, Onion Dip, and other favorites are lightened here for your enjoyment and health—so the party never has to end.

Cheese Ball

Photograph on page 24

Delight your fitness-conscious friends with this zesty appetizer cheese ball that is not only lower in fat than the original but also lower in calories. Serve it on a large platter surrounded by reduced-fat crackers or a rainbow of cut raw vegetables.

Homestyle Makeover
Each serving contains

	Before	After
Calories	65	37
Fat g.	5.5	1.7

2 cups (8 ounces) shredded fat-free Cheddar cheese

2 cups (8 ounces) shredded American processed cheese

3 ounces fat-free cream cheese, softened

3 tablespoons buttermilk

1 tablespoon Worcester-shire sauce

½ teaspoon hot-pepper sauce

⅛ teaspoon garlic powder

¾ teaspoon chili powder

¾ teaspoon paprika

1. In a food processor, combine the Cheddar, processed cheese, cream cheese, buttermilk, Worcestershire sauce, hot-pepper sauce, and garlic powder. Process until smooth. Remove the mixture and pat into a ball. Cover in plastic wrap and refrigerate for at least 2 hours, or until firm.

2. Combine the chili powder and paprika on a plate. Mix well. Unwrap the cheese ball and roll it in the mixture until well-coated.

Makes 32 servings

Per serving: 37 calories   1.7 g. fat   7 mg. cholesterol
173 mg. sodium   1.3 g. carbohydrates   3.6 g. protein

Cook's Notes

• To make a cheese log, simply shape the mixture into a cylinder. Roll it in ground toasted walnuts or almonds to add a special flavor touch.

• You can wrap the finished cheese ball in plastic wrap and store it in the refrigerator for 1 to 2 days before serving.

Pimiento Cheese–Stuffed Celery Ribs

This is not only a marvelous filling for celery but also a tasty dip for other vegetables, chips, or crackers. I also like it as a sandwich filling, either spread on toasted whole-grain bread or rolled up in soft lavash or whole-wheat tortillas.

6 ounces fat-free cream cheese, softened

1 jar (2 ounces) sliced pimientos, drained

¼ cup (1 ounce) shredded fat-free Cheddar cheese

2 tablespoons grated onion

1 tablespoon chili sauce

1 tablespoon lemon juice

½ teaspoon sugar

¼ teaspoon salt

8 large ribs celery

1. In a medium bowl, combine the cream cheese, pimientos, Cheddar, onion, chili sauce, lemon juice, sugar, and salt. Mix into a smooth paste.

2. Spoon 2 tablespoons of the mixture into each celery rib. Arrange on a dish. Cover tightly with plastic wrap. Refrigerate for 2 hours, or until the flavors blend. To serve, cut each celery rib into 8 pieces.

Makes 64

Per 4 pieces:	12 calories	0 g. fat	1 mg. cholesterol
	99 mg. sodium	1.6 g. carbohydrates	1.4 g. protein

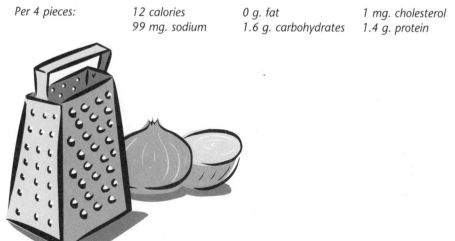

Mexican Pinwheels

These tasty Southwestern (by way of Mexico) appetizers can also be served in larger portions as an entrée and make great roll-up sandwiches for picnics and tailgate parties.

Photograph on page 25

Homestyle Makeover

Each serving contains

	Before	After
Calories	387	207
Fat g.	26	4.7

12 ounces fat-free cream cheese, softened

½ cup finely chopped chives or scallion tops

2 tablespoons taco sauce (see note)

1 can (4 ounces) diced green chile peppers, drained (optional)

8 flour tortillas (10" diameter)

2 cups (8 ounces) shredded reduced-fat Monterey Jack cheese

2 cups loosely packed fresh cilantro leaves

4 plum tomatoes, thinly sliced

1. In a medium bowl, combine the cream cheese, chives or scallion tops, taco sauce, and peppers (if using). Mix well. Spread evenly over the top of each tortilla. Sprinkle each tortilla with ¼ cup of the Monterey Jack. Scatter the cilantro and tomatoes over the cheese, leaving a ½" border around the edges. Roll the tortillas tightly and wrap in plastic wrap. Refrigerate for at least 1 hour.

2. To serve, cut each roll diagonally in quarters.

Makes 32

Per 2 pinwheels:	207 calories	4.7 g. fat	11 mg. cholesterol
	290 mg. sodium	28 g. carbohydrates	14 g. protein

Cook's Note

• Taco sauce is available in mild, medium, and hot, so select the heat range you like best. For a still hotter sensation, add a few drops of your favorite hot-pepper sauce.

Swiss Cheese–Fondue Canapés

Back in the 1960s, cheese fondue was in style for romantic dinners. These sensational hors d'oeuvres are based on the classic fondue but are served like canapés. No mess—and no burned tongues!

1 tablespoon unbleached or all-purpose flour

1 cup dry white wine or fat-free milk

2 cups (8 ounces) shredded Swiss cheese

2 cups (8 ounces) shredded part-skim mozzarella cheese

½ teaspoon salt

⅛ teaspoon ground white pepper

Dash of ground nutmeg

2 French baguettes

1. Coat a 13" × 9" baking dish with nonstick spray. Set aside.

2. Place the flour in a medium saucepan. Gradually add the wine or milk, whisking continually, until smooth. Cook over medium heat until almost to the boiling point. Gradually add the Swiss and mozzarella, stirring constantly, until the mixture boils. Remove from the heat. Add the salt, pepper, and nutmeg. Stir to mix. Pour into the prepared baking dish. Cool to room temperature. Cover tightly and refrigerate for several hours.

3. To serve, cut the cheese mixture into 72 (1" × 1½") rectangular pieces. Cut each baguette into 36 thin slices. Place a cheese rectangle on each bread slice.

Makes 72

Per canapé:

24 calories	1.4 g. fat	5 mg. cholesterol
40 mg. sodium	0 g. carbohydrates	1.8 g. protein

Refried Bean Dip

This Southwestern dip is perfect for unexpected guests. You can whip it up in minutes using pantry staples. Serve it with fat-free baked tortilla chips.

1 can (16 ounces) fat-free refried beans

1 can (4 ounces) diced green chile peppers

2 cups (8 ounces) shredded fat-free Cheddar cheese

1½ teaspoons chili powder

¼ teaspoon ground cumin

Hot-pepper sauce

1. In a medium bowl, combine the beans, peppers (with liquid), Cheddar, chili powder, cumin, and 2 drops of the hot-pepper sauce. Mix to combine. Season to taste with the hot-pepper sauce, if needed.

Makes 24 servings

Per serving:

35 calories	0 g. fat	1 mg. cholesterol
181 mg. sodium	4.8 g. carbohydrates	3.7 g. protein

Deviled Eggs (page 44) 23

24   **Cheese Ball (page 18)**

Mexican Pinwheels (page 20)   25

Baked Artichoke Dip (page 45)

Cheddar Cheese Soup (page 65) 27

French Onion Soup (page 64)

Lobster Bisque (page 66)

29

30　*Grilled Cheese Sandwich (page 151) and Cream of Tomato Soup (page 59)*

Cobb Salad (page 76)

32   *Warm Spinach Salad (page 82)*

Seven-Layer Salad (page 80)   33

Classic Baked Beans (page 98)

Roasted Tomatoes (page 133)

Twice-Baked Potatoes (page 127)

Green Bean Casserole (page 100)

Macaroni and Cheese (page 137)

Clam Dip

Clam dip is one of the most popular and easy-to-make hors d'oeuvres. Accompanied by baked chips, low-fat crackers, or fresh vegetables, it is also one of the lowest in calories and fat.

4 ounces fat-free cream cheese

4 ounces fat-free sour cream

2 tablespoons lemon juice

1 tablespoon grated onion

1 clove garlic, pressed or minced

1 teaspoon Worcestershire sauce

¼ teaspoon salt

2 cans (6 ounces each) minced clams, rinsed and drained

1. In a medium bowl, combine the cream cheese, sour cream, lemon juice, onion, garlic, Worcestershire sauce, and salt. Stir to combine. Add the clams. Mix well.

Makes 24 servings

Per serving: 27 calories / 0 g. fat / 10 mg. cholesterol / 77 mg. sodium / 2 g. carbohydrates / 4 g. protein

Cook's Note

• Store, tightly covered, in the refrigerator for up to 1 day.

Hot Crab Dip

Ever since our forefathers discovered crabs, "goin' crabbing" has been a favorite pastime in coastal areas of this country. From Louisiana comes this spicy dip that is usually served hot and accompanied by toast or crackers.

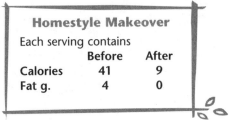

Homestyle Makeover

Each serving contains

	Before	After
Calories	41	9
Fat g.	4	0

8 ounces fat-free cream cheese, softened

1 small onion, finely chopped

2 tablespoons prepared horseradish

2 teaspoons Worcestershire sauce

¼ teaspoon hot-pepper sauce

3 cans (6 ounces each) white crabmeat, drained and rinsed

1 tablespoon dry bread crumbs

⅛ teaspoon paprika

1. Preheat the oven to 350°F. Coat a 1-quart baking dish with nonstick spray. Set aside.

2. In a large bowl, beat the cream cheese until smooth. Add the onion, horseradish, Worcestershire sauce, and hot-pepper sauce. Stir to mix thoroughly. Fold in the crab. Spoon the mixture into the prepared dish.

3. In a small bowl, combine the bread crumbs and paprika. Stir to mix well. Sprinkle over the crab mixture. Bake for 15 to 20 minutes, or until hot and bubbly.

Makes 48 servings

Per serving: 9 calories 0 g. fat 6 mg. cholesterol
37 mg. sodium 0 g. carbohydrates 2 g. protein

Cook's Note

• This crab dip tastes great cold. Try spreading it on a split French baguette for a Louisiana crab po' boy sandwich.

Guacamole

Homestyle Makeover		
Each serving contains		
	Before	After
Calories	100	34
Fat g.	10	2.8

Avocados are high in vitamins and minerals but also contain a great deal of fat. To lower the fat by more than two-thirds, I've added volume with tofu. Your guests will enjoy the taste of this guacamole so much, they'll never know that it is not the "real thing"!

¾ cup silken tofu, drained (see note)

1 tablespoon lemon juice

1 tablespoon Worcester- shire sauce

1 clove garlic, crushed

½ teaspoon salt

1 large ripe avocado, peeled and pitted

3 dashes of hot-pepper sauce (optional)

¾ cup salsa

1. In a blender or food processor, combine the tofu, lemon juice, Worcestershire sauce, garlic, and salt. Blend or process until smooth. Spoon into a bowl. Add the avocado and hot-pepper sauce (if using). Mash coarsely with a fork. Add the salsa. Stir to mix well.

Makes 16 servings

Per serving:	34 calories	2.8 g. fat	0 mg. cholesterol
	88 mg. sodium	1.7 g. carbohydrates	1.1 g. protein

Cook's Notes

• Any consistency of silken tofu—firm, extra-firm, or soft—is fine for this dip.

• If refrigerating the guacamole before serving, make sure it's tightly covered to prevent browning. The most effective way to keep the guacamole green is to place the plastic wrap directly on the surface. Store in the refrigerator for up to 2 hours.

Onion Dip

Lipton can truly be given the credit for starting America dipping. I've retained the spirit of the classic California onion dip, while trimming the fat and sodium. Instead of 1 envelope of soup mix and 2 cups of full-fat sour cream, I've used half the soup mix and fat-free sour cream.

Homestyle Makeover		
Each serving contains		
	Before	After
Calories	39	14
Fat g.	4	0

8 ounces fat-free sour cream

4 ounces 1% cottage cheese

2 tablespoons (½ envelope) dry onion soup mix

1. In a medium bowl, combine the sour cream, cottage cheese, and soup mix. Mix well.

2. Place, tightly covered, in the refrigerator for at least 2 hours to blend the flavors.

Makes 24 servings

Per serving:

14 calories	0 g. fat	0 mg. cholesterol
87 mg. sodium	2 g. carbohydrates	1.2 g. protein

Cook's Note

• To lower the sodium even further, replace 1 tablespoon of the soup mix with 1 tablespoon dried chopped onion.

Smoked Salmon Mousse

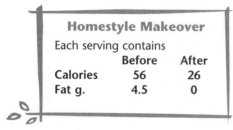

Homestyle Makeover

Each serving contains

	Before	After
Calories	56	26
Fat g.	4.5	0

For entertaining, this mousse makes a stunning impression molded into a fish shape and presented on a platter surrounded by sprigs of fresh dill and cocktail rye bread.

1 envelope (¼ ounce) unflavored gelatin

2 tablespoons cold water

⅓ cup boiling water

8 ounces fat-free sour cream

½ cup fat-free mayonnaise

1 package (4 ounces) sliced smoked salmon

1 scallion, quartered

2 tablespoons lemon juice

2 tablespoons chopped fresh parsley

1 tablespoon chopped fresh dill

½ teaspoon paprika

Sprigs of fresh dill (optional)

1. In a small bowl, combine the gelatin and the cold water. Set aside for 5 minutes. Add the boiling water. Stir until the gelatin is completely dissolved.

2. In a blender or food processor, combine the sour cream, mayonnaise, salmon, scallion, lemon juice, parsley, dill, paprika, and the dissolved gelatin. Blend or process until smooth. Spoon into a 1-quart mold. Store, tightly covered, in the refrigerator for several hours or overnight.

3. Unmold onto a serving plate. Garnish with sprigs of dill (if using).

Makes 32 servings

Per serving:　26 calories　0 g. fat　1 mg. cholesterol

75 mg. sodium　2.4 g. carbohydrates　3.6 g. protein

Cook's Note

• For an easy pasta accompaniment, toss any leftover mousse with drained cooked pasta and 1 to 2 tablespoons reserved pasta cooking water. Garnish with chopped fresh dill or fennel leaves.

Deviled Eggs

Photograph on page 23

To lower the cholesterol and fat, I've used only half of the egg yolks in the filling. To make up for the loss in volume, I've increased the amount of fat-free ingredients. This recipe also makes a fine egg salad sandwich filling. Just chop up the whites and add them to the filling mixture.

Homestyle Makeover		
Each serving contains		
	Before	After
Calories	329	70
Fat g.	29	3

8 **hard-cooked eggs, shelled**

¼ **cup fat-free mayonnaise**

2 **ounces fat-free sour cream**

2 **tablespoons spicy brown mustard**

⅛ **teaspoon ground black pepper**

Paprika and/or chopped fresh parsley (optional)

1. Cut the eggs in half lengthwise and remove the yolks, being careful not to tear the whites. Place the whites on a serving dish and set aside.

2. In a small bowl, combine the mayonnaise, sour cream, mustard, pepper, and 4 of the yolks. Mash with a fork until smooth.

3. Spoon the filling into the egg whites. Sprinkle with the paprika and/or parsley, if using.

Makes 8

Per deviled egg:	*70 calories*	*3 g. fat*	*106 mg. cholesterol*
	189 mg. sodium	*4 g. carbohydrates*	*6 g. protein*

Baked Artichoke Dip

Photograph on page 26

Homestyle Makeover

Each serving contains

	Before	After
Calories	71	28
Fat g.	6.5	1

I revised this recipe for a reader several years ago and liked it so much because all of the ingredients are shelf staples, which makes it convenient to whip up on a moment's notice. It can be served warm, at room temperature, or cold.

1 can (14 ounces) artichoke hearts, rinsed, drained, and chopped

¾ cup fat-free mayonnaise

1 can (4 ounces) diced green chile peppers, drained

¾ cup (3 ounces) grated Parmesan cheese

1. Preheat the oven to 350°F.

2. In a medium ovenproof baking dish, combine the artichokes, mayonnaise, peppers, and all but 2 tablespoons of the Parmesan. Mix well. Sprinkle the remaining Parmesan evenly over the top. Bake for 40 to 50 minutes, or until the top is a rich golden brown.

Makes 24 servings

Per serving:

28 calories	1 g. fat	3 mg. cholesterol
164 mg. sodium	2 g. carbohydrates	1.7 g. protein

Spanakopita

Most recipes for these Greek-style cheese-stuffed pastries are outrageously high in fat because they call for brushing melted butter on the phyllo sheets. In this lighter version, I coat the sheets with nonstick spray.

Homestyle Makeover		
Each serving contains		
	Before	After
Calories	55	21
Fat g.	4	0

1 teaspoon olive oil

1 medium onion, minced

1 package (10 ounces) frozen chopped spinach, thawed and squeezed dry

½ cup (2 ounces) crumbled feta cheese

1 egg, lightly beaten

¼ teaspoon ground black pepper

8 sheets (17" × 11") frozen phyllo dough, thawed

1. Heat the oil in a medium saucepan over medium heat. Add the onion and cook, stirring frequently, for about 5 minutes, or until translucent. Remove from the heat. Add the spinach, feta, egg, and pepper. Stir to mix.

2. Preheat the oven to 425°F. Lightly coat 2 large baking sheets with nonstick spray. Set aside. Cut the phyllo sheets lengthwise into 5 equal strips. Place the strips on a piece of waxed paper, then cover with another piece of waxed paper. Cover with a damp towel.

3. Place 4 strips of phyllo at a time on work surface. Coat lightly with nonstick spray. Place 1 scant tablespoon of the spinach mixture at the end of each strip. Fold one corner of each strip diagonally over the filling so that the short edge meets the long edge of each strip, forming a right angle. Continue folding over at right angles, as you would fold a flag, until you reach the end of each strip, forming 4 triangular pastries per batch. Place the pastries, seam side down, on a prepared baking sheet. Coat them lightly with nonstick spray. Repeat with the remaining phyllo strips and spinach mixture.

4. Bake the pastries, in two batches if necessary, for about 10 minutes, or until golden brown. Serve hot.

Makes 40

Per pastry:

21 calories	0 g. fat	7 mg. cholesterol
41 mg. sodium	3 g. carbohydrates	0 g. protein

Angels on Horseback

To lighten this popular old-timey recipe, I've used turkey bacon, which has 65 percent less fat than ordinary bacon and doesn't shrink appreciably during cooking.

Homestyle Makeover		
Each serving contains		
	Before	After
Calories	130	96
Fat g.	9.6	3.7

8 shucked oysters, rinsed and drained

8 slices turkey bacon, cooked and drained

4 slices whole-wheat bread, toasted and halved diagonally

1. Pat the oysters dry and set aside.

2. Wrap a slice of the bacon around each oyster and carefully place them in a large nonstick skillet. Cover and cook over low heat for 5 minutes. Uncover and turn the heat up to high. Cook for 1 to 2 minutes, or until any liquid in the skillet is completely evaporated and the oysters are opaque. Place each bacon-wrapped oyster on a toast triangle.

Makes 8

Per appetizer:	*96 calories*	*3.7 g. fat*	*22 mg. cholesterol*
	320 mg. sodium	*10 g. carbohydrates*	*5 g. protein*

Cook's Notes

• To vary the presentation, cut the Angels on Horseback in half diagonally and skewer with toothpicks.

• For a light entrée, serve the Angels on Horseback on lightly seasoned couscous or rice.

• To make *Devils on Horseback*, sprinkle with a few drops of hot-pepper sauce.

Buffalo Wings with Blue Cheese Dip

Now that chicken wing sections are available precut in supermarkets, this appetizer is a snap to make. It's every bit as rich and zesty as the original but with a fraction of the fat.

Homestyle Makeover		
Each serving contains		
	Before	After
Calories	375	90
Fat g.	33	3

Dip

¾ teaspoon cider vinegar

½ teaspoon steak sauce

½ teaspoon Worcestershire sauce

¼ teaspoon sugar

¼ teaspoon salt

¼ teaspoon ground black pepper

1 small clove garlic, pressed or minced

1 tablespoon finely chopped onion

¼ cup (1 ounce) crumbled blue cheese

2 ounces 1% cottage cheese

¼ cup buttermilk

6 tablespoons fat-free mayonnaise

Wings

½ cup unbleached or all-purpose flour

24 chicken wing drummettes, skinned and trimmed of all visible fat

1 tablespoon butter or margarine

1 tablespoon white vinegar or cider vinegar

1 teaspoon hot-pepper sauce

¼ teaspoon salt

1. *To make the dip:* In a medium bowl, combine the vinegar, steak sauce, Worcestershire sauce, sugar, and salt. Stir until the sugar and salt are completely dissolved.

2. Add the pepper, garlic, and onion. Mix well. Stir in the blue cheese, cottage cheese, and buttermilk. Add the mayonnaise and stir until completely blended. Cover and refrigerate for at least 1 hour before serving.

3. *To make the wings:* Preheat the oven to 425°F. Coat a 13" × 9" baking dish with nonstick spray.

4. Put the flour in a large paper bag and add the chicken drummettes. Holding the top closed, shake until the drummettes are completely coated. Remove the drummettes one at a time, shaking to remove any excess flour before placing in the prepared dish. Bake for 30 minutes, turning once, or until the drummettes are golden brown and no pink remains. Check by inserting the tip of a sharp knife into 1 drummette.

5. In a large skillet, combine the butter or margarine, vinegar, hot-pepper sauce, and salt. Place over medium heat to melt the mixture. Add the drummettes and toss for 1 to 2 minutes, or until evenly coated with the sauce. Remove with tongs to a serving platter. Serve with the Blue Cheese Dip.

Makes 12 servings

Per serving:	*90 calories*	*3 g. fat*	*29 mg. cholesterol*
	240 mg. sodium	*3 g. carbohydrates*	*19 g. protein*

Swedish Meatballs

These wonderful hors d'oeuvres are also delicious served as an entrée over pasta or rice. Leftover meatballs are a good addition to soups and make satisfying sandwiches.

Meatballs

½ tablespoon butter or margarine

1 onion, finely chopped

1 cup fresh rye bread crumbs

¾ teaspoon ground allspice

½ teaspoon ground nutmeg

¼ teaspoon ground black pepper

1 pound very lean ground round beef

½ pound ground turkey breast

2 egg whites, lightly beaten

⅓ cup fat-free evaporated milk

Gravy

1½ tablespoons butter or margarine

2 tablespoons unbleached or all-purpose flour

½ cup fat-free, reduced-sodium beef broth or chicken broth

¼ teaspoon ground allspice

¼ teaspoon ground nutmeg

¼ teaspoon ground black pepper

1 cup fat-free evaporated milk

1. *To make the meatballs:* Melt the butter or margarine in a large nonstick skillet over low heat. Add the onion. Cover and cook for 8 to 10 minutes, or until translucent. If needed, add a few teaspoons of water to the skillet to prevent the onion from scorching. Uncover and increase the heat to medium. Cook the onion, stirring constantly, for 2 to 3 minutes, or until lightly browned.

2. Spoon the onion into a large bowl. Set the skillet aside for later use. Add the bread crumbs, allspice, nutmeg, and pepper. Stir to mix well. Add the beef, turkey, egg whites, and evaporated milk. Mix thoroughly. Shape into 36 meatballs.

3. Heat the skillet over medium heat. Place the meatballs in the skillet in a single layer. (If necessary, cook in two batches to avoid crowding.) Cook, turning as needed, for 10 minutes, or until browned on all sides. Reduce the heat to low. Cover and cook for 10 minutes, or until no pink remains. Check by inserting the tip of a sharp knife into 1 meatball.

4. *To make the gravy:* Meanwhile, melt the butter or margarine in a large saucepan over medium-low heat. Add the flour and cook, stirring constantly, for 2 minutes. Add the broth, allspice, nutmeg, and pepper. Mix well. Gradually add the evaporated milk, stirring constantly, until slightly thickened.

5. Place the meatballs in the gravy. Reduce the heat to low. Cook, covered, for 10 minutes to blend the flavors.

Makes 36

Per 2 meatballs:	85 calories	3 g. fat	22 mg. cholesterol
	96 mg. sodium	4 g. carbohydrates	10 g. protein

Cook's Note

• Serve hot in a chafing dish, or spear each meatball with a toothpick and pass on a serving plate.

Recipes

Chowders and Soups

Homemade soups, probably more than any other type of dish, remind us of the early American kitchen. The reassuring aroma of simmering soup is every bit as welcoming today as it was 100 or 200 years ago.

Our third president and noted gourmet Thomas Jefferson believed that soup tasted better the day after it was made—and I agree. When soups are made with many diverse ingredients, flavors do tend to blend or marry overnight. Patience makes a good soup even better. Split Pea Soup with Ham, Chili, and Beef Vegetable Soup are wonderful examples of this edible alchemy.

Its homespun virtues notwithstanding, soup can also put on the ritz for special occasions. Lobster Bisque, New England Clam Chowder, and Oyster Stew are but three examples of classic special-occasion American soups.

Corn and Vegetable Chowder

In American cooking, chowder originally referred to a chunky seafood soup that was very popular in the Northeast. The term has evolved, however, to include soups based on corn, chicken, or other ingredients. This chowder makes a satisfying vegetarian entrée if you double the ingredients.

Homestyle Makeover		
Each serving contains	Before	After
Calories	200	162
Fat g.	7	2

1 tablespoon butter or margarine

1 large red bell pepper, chopped

6 scallions, chopped

2 cups water

¾ pound red potatoes, diced

1 tablespoon chopped fresh thyme leaves or 1 teaspoon dried thyme

½ teaspoon salt

½ teaspoon ground black pepper

2 cans (14¾ ounces each) no salt added cream-style corn

1 can (12 ounces) fat-free evaporated milk

1. In a large pot or Dutch oven, melt the butter or margarine over medium heat. Add the bell pepper and scallions. Cook, stirring occasionally, for 5 minutes, or until softened. Add the water, potatoes, thyme, salt, and black pepper. Stir to mix well. Bring to a boil. Reduce the heat to low and simmer for 15 to 20 minutes, or until the potatoes can easily be pierced with a fork

2. Stir in the corn and milk. Cook for 3 to 4 minutes, or until heated through.

Makes 8 servings

Per serving:
162 calories
207 mg. sodium
2 g. fat
33 g. carbohydrates
5 mg. cholesterol
6 g. protein

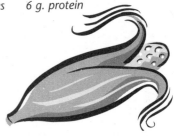

New England Clam Chowder

Homestyle Makeover

Each serving contains

	Before	After
Calories	321	292
Fat g.	12	6

Traditionally this rich, creamy soup is made with whole milk or half-and-half. However, to reduce the amount of fat without losing the marvelous richness, I have substituted fat-free evaporated milk. The velvety texture and rich flavor are remarkably close to the original.

1 teaspoon vegetable oil

4 slices turkey bacon, chopped

2 onions, chopped

2 cans (6½ ounces each) chopped clams

1 russet potato, peeled and diced

1½ cups fat-free, reduced-sodium chicken broth

1 can (12 ounces) fat-free evaporated milk

¼ teaspoon ground white pepper

1. Heat the oil in a large pot or Dutch oven over medium-high heat. Add the bacon and cook, stirring frequently, for 5 to 6 minutes, or until browned. Reduce the heat to low. Add the onions. Cover and cook for 8 to 10 minutes, or until the onions are translucent.

2. Drain the cans of clams, reserving the juice. To the pot, add the clam juice, potato, and broth. Increase the heat to high. Bring to a boil. Reduce the heat to low. Cover and cook, for 15 to 20 minutes, or until the potatoes can easily be pierced with a fork. Add the milk and pepper. Stir to mix well. Add the clams. Cook for 3 to 4 minutes, or until cooked through. Watch carefully so the chowder does not boil and toughen the clams.

Makes 6 servings

Per serving:

292 calories	*6 g. fat*	*80 mg. cholesterol*
890 mg. sodium	*23 g. carbohydrates*	*34 g. protein*

Manhattan Clam Chowder

Unlike creamy New England Clam Chowder, Manhattan Clam Chowder is broth-based. In this recipe, I have pureed part of the soup to slightly thicken it. However, if you prefer a thinner-textured chowder, you can omit this step.

Homestyle Makeover		
Each serving contains		
	Before	After
Calories	282	176
Fat g.	9	5

1 teaspoon vegetable oil

3 slices turkey bacon, chopped

½ onion, finely chopped

1 clove garlic, pressed or minced

1 potato, diced

¼ carrot, finely chopped

1 rib celery, finely chopped

¼ green bell pepper, finely chopped

2 bottles (8 ounces each) clam juice

1 can (14½ ounces) diced tomatoes

1 cup water

½ teaspoon dried thyme

¼ teaspoon ground black pepper

1 can (6½ ounces) chopped clams

1. Warm the oil in a large saucepan over medium heat. Add the bacon. Cook, stirring frequently, for 4 to 5 minutes, or until browned. Add the onion and garlic. Cook for 5 to 6 minutes, or until the onion is translucent. Add the potato, carrot, and celery. Stir to mix. Reduce the heat to low. Cover and cook for 10 minutes so the flavors marry. Add the bell pepper, clam juice, tomatoes (with juice), water, thyme, and black pepper. Increase the heat to high and bring to a boil. Reduce the heat to low. Simmer, uncovered, for 30 minutes, or until the flavor is developed. Remove from the heat.

2. Carefully remove 1 cup of the mixture and pour it into a blender or food processor. Blend or process until smooth. Return to the saucepan. Add the clams (with juice). Stir to mix well. Cook over medium heat for 2 to 3 minutes, or until heated to the desired temperature. Watch closely so the chowder does not boil and toughen the clams.

Makes 4 servings

Per serving:		
176 calories	5 g. fat	42 mg. cholesterol
476 mg. sodium	19 g. carbohydrates	16 g. protein

Gazpacho

I like to prepare this refreshing Spanish-style soup a day in advance so it's properly chilled and the flavors are really blended.

Homestyle Makeover

Each serving contains

	Before	After
Calories	104	27
Fat g.	5	0

2½ cups vegetable juice cocktail

1 large tomato, peeled and diced

½ red or green bell pepper, diced

½ onion, diced

½ small cucumber, peeled and diced

2 tablespoons lime juice or lemon juice

1 clove garlic, pressed or minced

¼ teaspoon ground black pepper

¼ teaspoon Worcestershire sauce

1 scallion top, finely chopped

1. In a large bowl, combine the vegetable juice cocktail, tomato, bell pepper, onion, cucumber, lime juice or lemon juice, garlic, black pepper, and Worcestershire sauce. Stir to mix thoroughly. Store, tightly covered, in the refrigerator overnight.

2. To serve, spoon ⅔ cup of the soup into each of 6 bowls. Sprinkle with the scallion tops.

Makes 6 servings

Per serving:	27 calories	0 g. fat	0 mg. cholesterol
	337 mg. sodium	6 g. carbohydrates	1 g. protein

Cook's Note

• By reducing the vegetable juice cocktail to ½ cup, you can make a fresh salsa dip for tortilla chips, or a cold or hot sauce for fish, chicken, or meat. I even like to use it as a fat-free salad dressing.

Cream of Mushroom Soup

For a more exotic soup, you can use wild mushrooms, such as chanterelles, shiitakes, or morels, in this recipe. Leftover soup makes a wonderful sauce for pasta or rice and is also delicious served over toast as a brunch entrée.

Homestyle Makeover		
Each serving contains		
	Before	After
Calories	336	149
Fat g.	29	4

1 pound mushrooms

1 tablespoon butter or margarine

3 tablespoons unbleached or all-purpose flour

1 can (12 ounces) fat-free evaporated milk

1½ cups fat-free, reduced-sodium chicken broth

1 tablespoon dry sherry (optional)

Ground black pepper (optional)

1. Slice enough mushrooms to measure 1½ cups. Finely chop the remaining mushrooms.

2. Melt the butter or margarine in a large saucepan over medium heat. Add all of the mushrooms and cook, stirring frequently, for 10 to 12 minutes, or until the mushrooms are soft and starting to brown. Sprinkle with the flour. Cook, stirring constantly, for 3 minutes.

3. Gradually add the milk and broth. Cook, stirring constantly, for 5 minutes, or until thickened slightly. Add the sherry (if using). Season to taste with pepper (if using).

Makes 4 servings

Per serving: 149 calories   4 g. fat   11 mg. cholesterol
                 364 mg. sodium   19 g. carbohydrates   10 g. protein

Cream of Tomato Soup

Photograph on page 30

Homestyle Makeover

Each serving contains

	Before	After
Calories	119	81
Fat g.	8	2

Nothing conjures up memories of childhood lunches better than a steaming bowl of cream of tomato soup with a Grilled Cheese Sandwiches (page 151).

4 large tomatoes, peeled and cored

1 tablespoon butter or margarine

½ onion, finely chopped

1 can (12 ounces) fat-free evaporated milk

¼ teaspoon salt

⅛ teaspoon ground black pepper

1. With a sharp knife, halve the tomatoes crosswise. Press the halves gently to squeeze out the seeds. Carefully remove any remaining seeds with a small spoon. Discard the seeds. Dice the tomatoes; set aside.

2. In a large pot or Dutch oven, melt ½ tablespoon of the butter or margarine over medium heat. Add the onion and cook for 4 to 5 minutes, or until translucent. Add the tomatoes. Cover and cook, stirring occasionally, for 25 to 30 minutes, or until the tomatoes are very soft.

3. Pour the tomato mixture into a blender or food processor. Add the milk, salt, and pepper. Blend or process until smooth. Pour back into the pot.

4. Cook over medium heat for 4 to 5 minutes, or until heated through. Just before serving, add the remaining ½ tablespoon of butter or margarine. Stir until the butter or margarine is melted.

Makes 4 servings

Per serving:	81 calories	2 g. fat	7 mg. cholesterol
	226 mg. sodium	11 g. carbohydrates	5 g. protein

Lentil Vegetable Soup

Lentils, often used as a meat substitute, are popular throughout Europe, the Middle East, and India. Brown lentils are the most commonly used type. Lentils will keep well for up to 6 months if stored at room temperature in an airtight container.

Homestyle Makeover

Each serving contains

	Before	After
Calories	201	143
Fat g.	9	2

1 tablespoon extra-virgin olive oil

1 onion, finely chopped

3 cloves garlic, pressed or minced

1 cup (8 ounces) dried brown lentils

4 cups fat-free, reduced-sodium chicken broth

1 bay leaf

¼ teaspoon ground black pepper

2 large ribs celery, chopped

1 cup chopped cabbage

1 large carrot, chopped

2 plum tomatoes, peeled and chopped

2 tablespoons lemon juice

2 tablespoons balsamic vinegar

1. Heat the oil in a large pot or Dutch oven over medium heat. Add the onion and garlic. Cook, stirring frequently, 10 to 12 minutes, or until the onion is translucent. Add the lentils, broth, bay leaf, and pepper. Stir to mix well. Bring to a boil. Reduce the heat to low. Cover and cook for 40 to 45 minutes, or until the lentils are tender.

2. Pour half of the mixture into a bowl. Set aside. Pour the remaining mixture into a blender or food processor. Blend or process until smooth. Return the puree to the pot. Add the celery, cabbage, and carrot. Cook over medium heat, stirring frequently, for 10 minutes, so the flavors blend. Add the tomatoes, lemon juice, vinegar, and the reserved lentil mixture. Cook, stirring frequently, for 10 to 12 minutes, or until heated through. Remove and discard the bay leaf.

Makes 8 servings

Per serving:	*143 calories*	*2 g. fat*	*0 g. cholesterol*
	398 mg. sodium	*21 g. carbohydrates*	*10 g. protein*

Tortilla Soup

Homestyle Makeover

Each serving contains

	Before	After
Calories	568	452
Fat g.	26	12

This is a marvelous soup to include in a South-western meal. To make it into a hearty main dish, add 2 cups of cooked beans, poultry, or meat near the end of the cooking time and heat through before serving.

1 onion, chopped

2 cloves garlic, pressed or minced

1½ teaspoons ground cumin

¼ teaspoon ground black pepper

2 cups fat-free, reduced-sodium chicken broth

1 can (14½ ounces) diced tomatoes

1 cup frozen corn kernels

1 can (4 ounces) diced green chile peppers

¼ cup chopped fresh cilantro

1 cup crushed fat-free baked corn tortilla chips

1 cup (4 ounces) shredded reduced-fat Monterey Jack cheese or sharp Cheddar cheese

½ avocado, chopped (optional)

1. Coat a large saucepan with nonstick spray. Add the onion, garlic, cumin, and black pepper. Cover and cook over low heat, stirring occasionally, for 10 to 15 minutes, or until the onion is translucent. Add the broth, tomatoes (with juice), corn, and chile peppers (with liquid). Stir to mix. Increase the heat to high; bring to a boil. Reduce the heat to low. Simmer, uncovered, for 8 minutes, for the flavors to blend. Stir in the cilantro.

2. To serve, place ¼ cup tortilla chips in each of 4 large soup bowls. Divide the soup over the chips in each bowl. Sprinkle each bowl with ¼ cup of the cheese and 2 tablespoons avocado (if using).

Makes 4 servings

Per serving:

452 calories	12 g. fat	30 mg. cholesterol
861 mg. sodium	64 g. carbohydrates	24 g. protein

Minestrone

This robust Italian soup, which usually contains pasta and beans, has been heartily adopted by Americans. Sprinkle it with grated Parmesan cheese and serve with bread and a light green salad on the side.

1 tablespoon extra-virgin olive oil

1 onion, chopped

½ pound fresh green beans, cut into 1" pieces

1 large potato, chopped

2 large carrots, chopped

2 large ribs celery, chopped

3 cups fat-free, reduced-sodium beef broth

3 cups water

½ small head cabbage, thinly sliced

1 can (14½ ounces) diced tomatoes

2 zucchini, chopped

1¼ cups baby spinach leaves

1 can (15 ounces) red kidney beans, rinsed and drained

½ cup (2 ounces) grated Parmesan cheese

1. Heat the oil in a large pot or Dutch oven over medium heat. Add the onion, green beans, potato, carrots, and celery. Cook for 10 to 12 minutes, or until the vegetables are lightly browned.

2. Add the broth, water, cabbage, tomatoes (with juice), zucchini, and spinach. Bring to a boil. Reduce the heat to low. Cover and simmer for 30 to 40 minutes, or until the potato and carrots are tender. Add the kidney beans. Cook for 15 minutes so flavors can blend.

3. To serve, ladle 1½ cups into each of 8 soup bowls. Sprinkle each serving with 1 tablespoon of the Parmesan.

Makes 8 servings

Per serving: 161 calories   4 g. fat   4 mg. cholesterol
649 mg. sodium   24 g. carbohydrates   9 g. protein

Potato Soup

This recipe is for an old-fashioned thick, creamy soup. If you prefer a thinner soup, just add a bit more chicken broth or milk. This versatile potage can be served hot or cold. Chopped leftover poultry or meat can be added to the hot soup to make a hearty main dish.

Homestyle Makeover

Each serving contains

	Before	After
Calories	199	105
Fat g.	15	2

2 teaspoons butter or margarine

4 slices turkey bacon, chopped

2 onions, chopped

3 potatoes, peeled and chopped

2 cups fat-free, reduced-sodium chicken broth

1 bay leaf

1 can (12 ounces) fat-free evaporated milk

¾ teaspoon ground black pepper

1. Melt the butter or margarine in a large saucepan over medium heat. Add the bacon and cook for 5 to 6 minutes, or until browned. Add the onions and stir to mix. Reduce the heat to low. Cover and cook for 8 to 10 minutes, or until the onions are translucent. Add the potatoes, broth, and bay leaf. Increase the heat to high; bring to a boil. Reduce the heat to low. Cover and simmer for 20 to 25 minutes, or until the potatoes can easily be pierced with a fork. Remove from the heat and allow to cool slightly. Remove and discard the bay leaf.

2. Ladle half the potato mixture into a blender or food processor to puree and the other half into a medium bowl. Blend or process until smooth. Pour the pureed soup into the saucepan. Repeat with the remaining soup. Add the milk and pepper to the saucepan. Cook over low heat for 4 to 5 minutes, or until heated through.

Makes 8 servings

Per serving: | 105 calories | 2 g. fat | 12 mg. cholesterol
| 443 mg. sodium | 14 g. carbohydrates | 6 g. protein

French Onion Soup

Even though this delicious baked soup originated in France, it has certainly become an American classic and is served in restaurants ranging from gourmet establishments to mom-and-pop coffee shops.

Photograph on page 28

Homestyle Makeover

Each serving contains

	Before	After
Calories	384	377
Fat g.	20	13

1 tablespoon butter or margarine

2 large onions, thinly sliced

¼ cup dry white wine or nonalcoholic white wine

4 cups fat-free, reduced-sodium beef broth

½ teaspoon ground black pepper

8 very thin slices French bread, dried

1 cup (4 ounces) shredded reduced-fat Swiss cheese

1. Preheat the oven to 325°F.

2. Melt the butter or margarine in a large pot over low heat. Add the onions. Cover and cook for 10 to 12 minutes, or until the onions are soft. Remove the lid and increase the heat to high. Cook the onions, stirring constantly so that they don't burn, for 5 to 7 minutes, or until browned. Decrease the heat to medium. Add the wine. Cook, stirring frequently, for 2 to 3 minutes, or until the wine is completely absorbed. Add the broth and pepper. Stir to mix well. Bring to a boil. Reduce the heat to low and simmer for 5 minutes so the flavors can blend.

3. Place 4 ovenproof bowls in a baking dish or sturdy baking sheet with sides. Evenly divide the soup among the bowls. Place 2 bread slices on top of each bowl of soup. Allow to stand for 5 minutes, or until the bread is saturated with soup and has expanded. Sprinkle ¼ cup Swiss over each serving.

4. Bake for 20 minutes, or until the bread puffs up and the cheese is lightly browned.

Makes 4 servings

Per serving:	*377 calories*	*13 g. fat*	*40 mg. cholesterol*
	1,026 mg. sodium	*32 g. carbohydrates*	*26 g. protein*

Cheddar Cheese Soup

Photograph on page 27

Homestyle Makeover

Each serving contains

	Before	After
Calories	462	346
Fat g.	33	16

This tangy soup is wonderful served with just a vegetable salad and crusty sourdough bread for lunch or a light supper. It can also serve double duty as a sauce. I especially like it on baked potatoes.

2 teaspoons butter or margarine

½ small onion, finely chopped

¼ cup unbleached or all-purpose flour

4 cups fat-free milk

1½ cups (6 ounces) shredded reduced-fat sharp Cheddar cheese

2 teaspoons finely chopped fresh oregano or ½ teaspoon dried

2 teaspoons Worcestershire sauce

½ teaspoon dry mustard

½ teaspoon ground black pepper

¼ teaspoon salt

1. In a large saucepan, melt the butter or margarine over medium heat. Add the onion and cook, stirring constantly, for 4 to 5 minutes, or until the onion is translucent. Add the flour; stir to mix well. Cook, stirring constantly, for 3 minutes. Add the milk, whisking until completely blended. Bring to just a boil, reduce the heat to low, and simmer for 10 to 12 minutes, stirring frequently to prevent scorching, or until thickened. Add the Cheddar, oregano, Worcestershire sauce, mustard, pepper, and salt. Cook, stirring constantly, for 1 to 2 minutes, or until the cheese is completely melted.

Makes 4 servings

Per serving:	346 calories	16 g. fat	70 mg. cholesterol
	891 mg. sodium	23 g. carbohydrates	33 g. protein

Lobster Bisque

Photograph on page 29

Ever since Fannie Merritt Farmer published *The 1896 Boston Cooking-School Cook Book*, bisques have been a popular soup in America. A bisque is a rich, creamy soup, usually consisting of cooked seafood and cream that are pureed just before serving.

Homestyle Makeover

Each serving contains

	Before	After
Calories	411	181
Fat g.	29	5

1 tablespoon butter or margarine

½ onion, chopped

½ carrot, chopped

½ rib celery, chopped

2½ cups fat-free, reduced-sodium chicken broth

½ cup dry white wine or nonalcoholic white wine

2 tablespoons long-grain white rice

1 bay leaf

Dash of ground red pepper

1 large tomato, peeled, cored, and diced

2 cups (½ pound) cooked, cubed lobster meat

1¼ cups 2% milk

1. In a large pot or Dutch oven, melt the butter or margarine over medium heat. Add the onion, carrot, and celery. Reduce the heat to low. Cover and cook for 10 to 12 minutes, or until the onion is translucent.

2. Add the broth, wine, rice, bay leaf, and pepper. Stir to mix. Bring the mixture to a boil over high heat. Reduce the heat to low. Cover and simmer for 15 minutes, or until the rice is tender.

3. Remove the pot from the heat. Remove and discard the bay leaf. Add the tomato and 1¾ cups of the lobster; stir to mix well. Spoon the mixture into a blender or food processor. Blend or process until smooth.

4. Return to the pot. Stir in the milk. Place over medium-low heat. Cook for 4 to 5 minutes, or until the bisque is heated through. Watch closely so the bisque does not boil and toughen the lobster. Garnish with the remaining ¼ cup lobster.

Makes 4 servings

Per serving:	181 calories	5 g. fat	54 mg. cholesterol
	748 mg. sodium	11 g. carbohydrates	16 g. protein

Oyster Stew

In researching this recipe, I wasn't able to solve the mystery of why this milk-based soup is named a stew. I decided that an oyster soup by any other name still tastes good.

Homestyle Makeover

Each serving contains

	Before	After
Calories	261	106
Fat g.	21	4

1 pint (2 cups) shucked fresh oysters

1 tablespoon butter or margarine

1 onion, finely chopped

1 rib celery, finely chopped

1 clove garlic, pressed or minced

2 tablespoons finely chopped fresh parsley

3 tablespoons unbleached or all-purpose flour

2 cups 2% milk

2 cups fat-free, reduced-sodium chicken broth

⅛ teaspoon ground white pepper

1. Chop 1 cup of the oysters; set aside. Melt the butter or margarine in a large saucepan over medium heat. Add all of the oysters. Cook, stirring constantly, for 3 to 5 minutes, or until the oysters turn opaque and the edges of the whole oysters start to curl. Remove all of the oysters with a slotted spoon to a bowl and set aside.

2. Add the onion, celery, garlic, and parsley; stir to mix well. Reduce the heat to low. Cover and cook for 10 to 15 minutes, or until the onion is translucent.

3. Add the flour. Increase the heat to medium and cook, stirring constantly, for 3 minutes. Add the milk, stirring constantly, until the mixture is smooth. Simmer, stirring frequently, for 8 to 10 minutes, or until slightly thickened. Add the broth, pepper, and the reserved oysters. Stir to mix well. Cook for 4 to 5 minutes, or until heated to the desired temperature. Watch carefully so the stew does not boil and toughen the oysters.

Makes 4 servings

Per serving:	106 calories	4 g. fat	39 mg. cholesterol
	400 mg. sodium	9 g. carbohydrates	7 g. protein

Chicken Noodle Soup

Chicken soup is thought to be a cure-all for colds, the flu, and assorted other illnesses. For most people, it conjures up a multitude of childhood memories. Chicken noodle soup is decidedly the most popular and frequently served version in most homes and restaurants.

Homestyle Makeover

Each serving contains

	Before	After
Calories	176	104
Fat g.	8	2

½ tablespoon butter or margarine

½ onion, finely chopped

1 rib celery, finely chopped

½ pound boneless, skinless chicken breast halves, chopped

4 cups fat-free, reduced-sodium chicken broth

⅛ teaspoon ground black pepper

¼ pound (2 cups) noodles

1. Melt the butter or margarine in a large nonstick skillet over low heat. Add the onion and celery. Cover and cook for 10 minutes, or until the onion and celery are translucent. Add the chicken. Cover and cook, stirring occasionally, for 10 to 12 minutes, or until the chicken turns opaque.

2. Meanwhile, bring the broth to a boil in a large saucepan over high heat. Add the pepper and noodles and return to a boil. Reduce the heat to medium and simmer for 7 minutes, or until the noodles are soft. Add the chicken mixture; stir to mix.

Makes 6 servings

Per serving: 104 calories   2 g. fat   32 mg. cholesterol
                377 mg. sodium   11 g. carbohydrates   10 g. protein

Chili

Homestyle Makeover

Each serving contains

	Before	After
Calories	327	224
Fat g.	21	3

Chili originated in Texas, where it's known as "a bowl of red" and was originally made without beans. The beans were cooked in a separate pot and served on the side. In this updated version, the beans are combined with the meat for an easy one-dish meal.

1 pound lean round steak, trimmed of all visible fat and cut into ½" cubes

2 onions, finely chopped

3 cloves garlic, pressed or minced

2 cans (15 ounces each) kidney beans

3 cups diced tomatoes or 2 cans (14½ ounces each) diced tomatoes, drained

1 can (7 ounces) diced green chile peppers

2 teaspoons chili powder

1 teaspoon dried oregano

1 teaspoon ground cumin

½ teaspoon ground black pepper

1. Coat a large pot or Dutch oven with nonstick spray and place over medium heat until hot enough for drops of water to dance on the surface. Add the beef and cook, stirring frequently, for 6 to 8 minutes, or until browned. Add the onions and garlic. Cover and cook, stirring occasionally, for 8 to 10 minutes, or until the onions are translucent.

2. Add the beans (with liquid), tomatoes, chile peppers (with liquid), chili powder, oregano, cumin, and black pepper. Stir to mix thoroughly. Reduce the heat to low. Cover and simmer for 10 to 15 minutes.

Makes 6 servings

Per serving:	224 calories	3 g. fat	29 mg. cholesterol
	847 mg. sodium	27 g. carbohydrates	20 g. protein

Cook's Note

• I like to serve chili with a variety of condiments—chopped fresh cilantro, onions, tomatoes, grated cheese, reduced-fat sour cream, and low-fat tortilla chips—to sprinkle over the top.

Split Pea Soup with Ham

Split pea soup is a standard of American coffee shops and diners. Few soups are more rib-sticking. I have purposely made this recipe for a larger amount because it freezes so well. Serve with a dash of sherry or hot-pepper sauce.

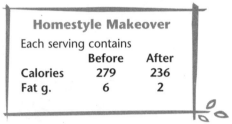

Homestyle Makeover

Each serving contains

	Before	After
Calories	279	236
Fat g.	6	2

1 **pound split peas, sorted and rinsed**

8 **cups water**

1 **fully cooked smoked ham hock**

1 **large onion, chopped**

2 **carrots, chopped**

2 **ribs celery, chopped**

1 **bay leaf**

3 **cups fat-free, reduced-sodium chicken broth**

1. In a large pot or Dutch oven, combine the peas, water, ham hock, onion, carrots, celery, and bay leaf. Bring to a boil over high heat. Reduce the heat to low. Cover and simmer for 2 to 3 hours. Cool to room temperature. Remove and discard the bay leaf. Refrigerate, uncovered, overnight.

2. Remove and discard all of the fat that has congealed on top of the soup. Remove the ham hock. Remove all of the ham meat; discard the bone. Trim all fat and gristle from the ham meat. Chop the ham meat and set aside.

3. Working in batches, ladle the soup into a blender or food processor to puree. Blend or process until smooth. Pour the pureed soup into a large saucepan. Add the broth and reserved ham. Stir to mix well. Cook over medium heat for 4 to 5 minutes, or until heated through.

Makes 8 servings

Per serving: *236 calories*   *2 g. fat*   *7 mg. cholesterol*
                       476 mg. sodium   *38 g. carbohydrates*   *18 g. protein*

Beef Vegetable Soup

This hearty, old-fashioned-tasting soup makes an ideal winter supper with just-toasted bread or crusty rolls. I often double this recipe because it takes very little additional time to make a bigger batch and the leftover soup freezes so well.

½ pound boneless beef stew meat, trimmed of all visible fat and cut into 1" cubes

1 onion, chopped

3 cups water

1 can (14½ ounces) diced tomatoes

1 potato, peeled and cubed

4 carrots, sliced ¼" thick

1 green bell pepper, chopped

2 ribs celery, chopped

½ teaspoon dried thyme

½ teaspoon dried basil

¼ teaspoon salt

¼ teaspoon ground black pepper

1 cup frozen peas

1 cup frozen green beans

1 cup frozen corn kernels

1. Coat a large nonstick skillet with nonstick spray and place over high heat until hot enough for drops of water to dance on the surface. Add the beef and cook, stirring frequently, for 5 to 7 minutes, or until well-browned. Remove from the skillet and place in a large pot; set aside.

2. Add the onion to the skillet. Cook, stirring frequently, over medium heat for 8 to 10 minutes, or until the onion is translucent. Add to the pot with the beef. Add the water and tomatoes (with juice). Bring to a boil over high heat. Reduce the heat to low; cook at a simmer for 30 minutes. Add the potato, carrots, bell pepper, celery, thyme, basil, salt, and black pepper. Increase heat to high and bring to a boil. Reduce the heat to low. Cover and cook at a simmer for 30 minutes, or until the potato and carrots can easily be pierced with a fork. Add the peas, green beans, and corn. Cover and cook for 5 to 10 minutes, or until the peas, green beans, and corn are heated through.

Makes 5 servings

Per serving:	223 calories	7 g. fat	30 mg. cholesterol
	513 mg. sodium	29 g. carbohydrates	14 g. protein

Recipes

Simple and Fancy Salads

American salads have always been substantial. In the days before widespread refrigeration, cooks didn't have year-round access to delicate seasonal greens so they fashioned marvelous cold dishes from sturdier vegetables. Carrot-Raisin Salad, Creamy Coleslaw, and Creamy Potato Salad are just three examples.

American salads have always been democratic. Fruits and gelatins—including Ambrosia, Waldorf Salad, and Cranberry Gelatin Salad—hold a time-honored place on the roster of favored salad specialties.

And finally, American salads are as abundant as our land. Cobb Salad, Seven-Layer Salad, Warm Spinach Salad, and Macaroni Salad provide plenty of appetite satisfaction. I've trimmed the fat from all of these delightful heirloom salads so you can enjoy them now more than ever.

Celery Victor

Celery Victor reminds me of my grandmother, who served it as a first course whenever she entertained her lady friends for lunch. It can easily be turned into a light luncheon salad by serving it on a bed of watercress or mixed salad greens, sprinkled with cooked shrimp.

Homestyle Makeover

Each serving contains

	Before	After
Calories	169	44
Fat g.	15	4

¼ cup red wine vinegar
1 teaspoon salt
1 teaspoon sugar
½ cup water
2 teaspoons lemon juice
1½ teaspoons dried tarragon
1 teaspoon Worcestershire sauce
1 clove garlic, pressed or finely chopped

½ teaspoon Dijon mustard
¼ teaspoon ground black pepper
2 tablespoons vegetable oil
8 hearts celery, with leaves (see note)
1 jar (2 ounces) sliced pimientos, drained
¼ cup capers, rinsed and drained

1. In a small bowl, combine the vinegar, salt, and sugar. Whisk to dissolve the salt and sugar. Add the water, lemon juice, tarragon, Worcestershire sauce, garlic, mustard, and pepper. Whisk until smooth. Slowly add the oil, whisking until smooth.

2. Place a vegetable steamer in a large saucepan over simmering water. Steam the celery hearts (in batches, if necessary) for 5 to 8 minutes, or until tender when pierced with a knife. With tongs, remove from the saucepan and immediately place under cold running water. Drain and pat dry. Place the celery hearts in a glass or ceramic rectangular dish. Pour the vinegar mixture over the celery hearts. Cover tightly and refrigerate all day or overnight.

3. To serve, remove the celery hearts and place each heart on a chilled plate. Drizzle with the vinegar mixture. Garnish each serving with pimientos and capers.

Makes 8 servings

Per serving: 44 calories   4 g. fat   0 mg. cholesterol
                  353 mg. sodium   3 g. carbohydrates 0 g. protein

Cook's Note

• Use just the inner light green ribs of celery, left attached at the base, for this salad. Plan on using the outer ribs of celery for another dish such as cream of celery soup.

Carrot-Raisin Salad

Homestyle Makeover

Each serving contains

	Before	After
Calories	279	196
Fat g.	22	0

All I had to do to lighten this salad was to replace regular mayonnaise with fat-free mayonnaise. To compensate for the absence of fat, I added a little lemon juice and honey. Also, I plumped the raisins in apple juice to moisten and flavor them.

½ cup apple juice

½ cup raisins

½ cup fat-free mayonnaise or mayonnaise-style salad dressing

2 teaspoons lemon juice

2 teaspoons honey

8 carrots, peeled and shredded

1. In a small saucepan, bring the apple juice and raisins to a boil over medium heat. Remove from the heat and allow to stand for at least 20 minutes, or until the raisins are plump.

2. In a large bowl, combine the mayonnaise or salad dressing, lemon juice, and honey. Whisk until smooth. Drain the raisins and add them to the bowl. Add the carrots. Stir well to mix. Cover tightly and refrigerate for several hours to blend the flavors.

Makes 4 servings

Per serving:	196 calories	0 g. fat	0 mg. cholesterol
	293 mg. sodium	48 g. carbohydrates	3 g. protein

Cobb Salad

Photograph on page 31

This irresistible American salad originated at the legendary Brown Derby Restaurant in Los Angeles. It arrived in a bowl with all of the ingredients arranged in pristine rows on the top of the lettuce. It was then dressed and tossed at your table before being served.

Homestyle Makeover		
Each serving contains		
	Before	After
Calories	702	352
Fat g.	57	18

Vinaigrette

½ cup water

¼ cup lemon juice

1 tablespoon red wine vinegar

2 teaspoons sugar

1 teaspoon Worcestershire sauce

1 clove garlic, minced

½ teaspoon salt

½ teaspoon dry mustard

2 tablespoons vegetable oil

Salad

1 small head lettuce, chopped

½ pound cooked boneless, skinless chicken breast, chopped

2 tomatoes, chopped

4 hard-cooked egg whites, chopped

1 small ripe avocado, chopped

¼ cup (1 ounce) crumbled blue cheese

4 slices turkey bacon, crisply cooked, drained, and crumbled

1. *To make the vinaigrette:* In a medium bowl, whisk together the water, lemon juice, vinegar, sugar, Worcestershire sauce, garlic, salt, and mustard. Slowly whisk in the oil. Cover and refrigerate for at least 1 hour.

2. *To make the salad:* Divide the lettuce on each of 4 large salad plates. Top with the chicken, tomatoes, egg whites, avocado, blue cheese, and bacon in rows. Spoon the vinaigrette over each serving.

Makes 4 servings

Per serving:	*352 calories*	*18 g. fat*	*86 mg. cholesterol*
	695 mg. sodium	*13 g. carbohydrates*	*35 g. protein*

Creamy Coleslaw

Photograph on page 106

Homestyle Makeover

Each serving contains

	Before	After
Calories	218	60
Fat g.	17	0

I did this recipe makeover years ago for a reader, and it remains my own favorite coleslaw. I like the addition of both the caraway seeds and the apple, neither of which is traditional. I confess that these days instead of shredding my own cabbage, I buy preshredded cabbage in the produce department of my supermarket.

¼ cup fat-free mayonnaise

2 tablespoons rice wine vinegar or white wine vinegar

1 tablespoon sugar

2 teaspoons Dijon mustard

½ teaspoon caraway seeds, crushed

⅛ teaspoon salt

½ head cabbage, shredded (1 pound)

1 large Granny Smith apple, chopped

½ small red onion, finely chopped

1. In a large bowl, combine the mayonnaise, vinegar, sugar, mustard, caraway seeds, and salt. Stir to mix thoroughly.

2. Add the cabbage, apple, and onion. Stir to mix well. Cover tightly and refrigerate for at least 4 hours to blend the flavors before serving.

Makes 4 servings

Per serving:

| 60 calories | 0 g. fat | 0 mg. cholesterol |
| 214 mg. sodium | 14 g. carbohydrates | 1 g. protein |

Creamy Potato Salad

Photograph on page 105

Summer cookouts and potato salad go together like fireworks and the Fourth of July. In fact, potato salad is often referred to as picnic salad. If you're taking it to a picnic, or a tailgate party, keep it in the cooler until serving time.

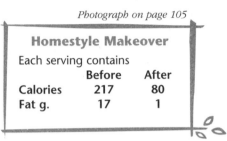

Homestyle Makeover

Each serving contains

	Before	After
Calories	217	80
Fat g.	17	1

6 medium potatoes

1 cup fat-free mayonnaise or mayonnaise-style salad dressing

1 tablespoon white vinegar

1 tablespoon brown mustard

½ teaspoon salt

¼ teaspoon ground black pepper

2 ribs celery, chopped

1 small onion, chopped

2 hard-cooked eggs, chopped

3 hard-cooked egg whites, chopped

1. Put the potatoes in a large saucepan and cover them with water. Bring to a boil over high heat. Reduce the heat to low. Simmer for 30 to 35 minutes, or until the potatoes can easily be pierced with a fork. Drain the potatoes and allow to cool enough until safe to handle. Peel the potatoes and cut them into 1" cubes.

2. In a large bowl, combine the mayonnaise or salad dressing, vinegar, mustard, salt, and pepper. Stir to mix well. Add the potatoes, celery, onion, eggs, and egg whites. Stir to mix well. Cover and refrigerate at least 4 hours to blend the flavors before serving.

Makes 12 servings

Per serving:		
80 calories	*1 g. fat*	*35 mg. cholesterol*
304 mg. sodium	*14 g. carbohydrates*	*3 g. protein*

Lettuce Wedges with Roquefort Dressing

Twenty-five years ago—before designer greens and exotic vinaigrettes—a wedge of iceberg lettuce topped with Roquefort dressing was considered opulent. Amazingly, this old-fashioned salad is staging a comeback on trendy menus and is considered new again.

2 tablespoons red wine vinegar

2 teaspoons lemon juice

⅛ teaspoon salt

½ cup fat-free mayonnaise

¼ cup fat-free sour cream

1 clove garlic, pressed or finely chopped

¼ teaspoon ground black pepper

¼ cup chopped scallions

½ cup (2 ounces) Roquefort cheese, crumbled

1 head iceberg lettuce, quartered

1 small tomato, chopped (optional)

1. In a medium bowl, combine the vinegar, lemon juice, and salt. Stir until the salt has completely dissolved. Add the mayonnaise, sour cream, garlic, and pepper. Stir to mix well. Add the scallions and Roquefort. Cover tightly and refrigerate for several hours or overnight to allow flavors to blend (see note).

2. To serve, place each wedge of lettuce on a chilled plate and top with ¼ cup of the dressing. Garnish with the tomato, if using.

Makes 4 servings

Per serving:	112 calories	5 g. fat	13 mg. cholesterol
	577 mg. sodium	12 g. carbohydrates	6 g. protein

Cook's Note

• The flavor of the dressing really benefits from overnight chilling. In a pinch, this dressing can be served right after making. It is also good on many other salads, as a sauce for poultry and meat, or as a tasty topping for a baked potato.

Seven-Layer Salad

Photograph on page 33

I like to make this salad in a clear glass trifle dish and bring it to the table so that my guests can see how attractive the individual layers are before I toss and serve it. In revising this recipe to lower the fat, I used turkey bacon and fat-free mayonnaise.

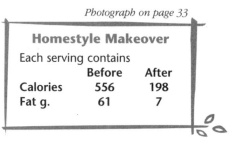

Homestyle Makeover

Each serving contains

	Before	After
Calories	556	198
Fat g.	61	7

1 package (6 ounces) assorted young greens, torn into bite-size pieces

2 large ribs celery, thinly sliced

½ pound trimmed radishes, sliced

2 scallions, sliced

6 slices turkey bacon, cooked and drained

1 package (10 ounces) frozen green peas, thawed

1½ cups fat-free mayonnaise

½ cup (2 ounces) shredded extra-sharp Cheddar cheese

1. Place the greens in the bottom of a large glass bowl. Add the celery, radishes, scallions, bacon, and peas in individual layers. Carefully spread the mayonnaise over the peas, covering the top completely and sealing to the edge of the bowl. Sprinkle with the Cheddar. Cover the salad tightly and refrigerate at least 2 hours but no longer than 12 hours to blend the flavors before serving.

2. To serve, toss the salad and spoon on each of 6 chilled salad plates.

Makes 6 servings

Per serving:	*198 calories*	*7 g. fat*	*25 mg. cholesterol*
	761 mg. sodium	*23 g. carbohydrates*	*10 g. protein*

Three-Bean Salad

This popular picnic salad is even better if made a few hours, or even a few days, before serving because the flavors blend more completely.

½ cup red wine vinegar

1 teaspoon sugar

½ teaspoon dry mustard

¼ teaspoon salt

¼ cup water

½ teaspoon dried oregano

½ teaspoon dried tarragon

½ teaspoon Worcestershire sauce

¼ teaspoon ground black pepper

½ small red onion, finely chopped

1 package (10 ounces) frozen cut green beans, thawed (see note)

1 can (15 ounces) wax beans, rinsed and drained

1 can (15 ounces) kidney beans, rinsed and drained

1. In a large bowl, combine the vinegar, sugar, mustard, and salt. Stir until the salt and sugar are completely dissolved. Add the water, oregano, tarragon, Worcestershire sauce, and pepper. Stir to mix well. Add the onion, green beans, wax beans, and kidney beans. Stir to mix well. Cover and refrigerate for at least 2 hours to blend the flavors before serving.

2. To serve, stir to redistribute the dressing.

Makes 6 servings

Per serving:	94 calories	0 g. fat	0 mg. cholesterol
	602 mg. sodium	20 g. carbohydrates	5 g. protein

Cook's Note

• You can also use fresh green beans for this salad. Remove the ends and place them on a vegetable steamer set over simmering water in a saucepan. Steam them just until crisp-tender. Place them under cold running water to stop the cooking. Drain thoroughly.

Warm Spinach Salad

Popeye would love the convenience that bags of prewashed and trimmed spinach leaves provide. Available in almost all supermarkets, this spinach is ready to serve, without all the time-consuming washing and trimming formerly required.

Photograph on page 32

Homestyle Makeover		
Each serving contains		
	Before	After
Calories	307	188
Fat g.	22	11

2 packages (6 ounces each) prewashed baby spinach leaves

1 small red onion, chopped

½ cup cider vinegar

⅓ cup water

1 tablespoon sugar

¼ teaspoon salt

¼ teaspoon ground black pepper

1 tablespoon vegetable oil

8 slices turkey bacon, chopped

2 hard-cooked eggs, chopped

1. In a large bowl, combine the spinach and onion. Set aside.

2. In a small bowl, combine the vinegar, water, sugar, salt, and pepper. Stir until the salt and sugar have completely dissolved. Set aside.

3. Heat the oil in a large skillet over medium heat. Add the bacon and cook, stirring frequently, for 3 to 4 minutes, or until browned. Add the vinegar mixture. Increase the heat to high. Cook, stirring, until the mixture boils. Spoon over the spinach mixture. Toss for about 1 minute to slightly wilt the spinach.

4. To serve, place 2 cups of the salad on each of 4 salad plates. Top each serving with the eggs.

Makes 4 servings

Per serving: 188 calories 11 g. fat 136 mg. cholesterol
594 mg. sodium 12 g. carbohydrates 10 g. protein

Cook's Note

• This salad is also good made with red-leaf lettuce. It can be topped with chopped tomatoes instead of eggs.

Warm German Potato Salad

Homestyle Makeover

Each serving contains

	Before	After
Calories	217	158
Fat g.	9	3

Stephan Griebels, the talented executive chef of the Caribbean cruise ship Wind Spirit, *shared this delicious warm German potato salad recipe with me. The only change I had to make in his already light salad was to use a bit less olive oil.*

3 medium russet potatoes, scrubbed and halved

1 tablespoon olive oil

1 onion, chopped

1 cup fat-free, reduced-sodium chicken broth

½ cup white vinegar

1 tablespoon Dijon mustard

1 teaspoon caraway seeds, crushed

½ teaspoon ground black pepper

4 scallions, chopped

1. Place the potatoes in a medium saucepan and cover with water. Bring to a boil over high heat. Reduce the heat to low. Cover and simmer for 20 to 25 minutes, or until the potatoes can easily be pierced with a fork. Drain the potatoes and allow to cool just enough until safe to handle.

2. Meanwhile, heat the oil in a large skillet over medium heat. Add the onion and cook, stirring frequently, for 8 to 10 minutes, or until translucent. Add the broth and vinegar. Stir to mix well. Simmer for 5 minutes, or until slightly reduced. Remove from the heat. Add the mustard, caraway seeds, and pepper. Stir to mix. Set aside.

3. Peel, if desired, and dice the warm potatoes. Put them in a large bowl. Add the onion mixture and the scallions. Toss to mix. Serve warm.

Makes 6 servings

Per serving:	158 calories	3 g. fat	0 mg. cholesterol
	238 mg. sodium	31 g. carbohydrates	4 g. protein

Cook's Note

• This salad can be served at room temperature.

Macaroni Salad

This is a lighter version of a recipe I found in a 1920s cookbook. I purposely kept just the ingredients called for in that recipe. You can add other vegetables such as tomatoes, bell peppers, chives, and pimientos to this traditional pasta salad for more color and texture.

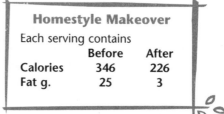

Homestyle Makeover

Each serving contains

	Before	After
Calories	346	226
Fat g.	25	3

1 package (8 ounces) elbow macaroni

1 cup fat-free mayonnaise

2 tablespoons cider vinegar

1 tablespoon brown mustard

½ teaspoon salt

½ teaspoon celery seeds

4 large ribs celery, sliced

2 radishes, sliced

1 small scallion, sliced

2 hard-cooked eggs, chopped

3 hard-cooked egg whites, chopped

1. Bring a large covered pot of water to a boil over high heat. Add the macaroni and cook according to package directions. Rinse well under cool running water. Drain and allow to cool.

2. In a large bowl, combine the mayonnaise, vinegar, mustard, salt, and celery seeds. Stir to mix well. Add the macaroni. Stir to mix well. Add the celery, radishes, scallion, eggs, and egg whites. Serve immediately, or cover tightly and refrigerate for several hours.

Makes 6 servings

Per serving: 226 calories   3 g. fat   106 mg. cholesterol
663 mg. sodium   37 g. carbohydrates   10 g. protein

Fruit Salad

The toasted walnuts add a wonderful crunchiness to this salad. You can toast nuts either by putting them in a skillet over medium heat and stirring them constantly until lightly browned or by placing them on a pan in a 350°F oven for about 8 to 10 minutes, stirring occasionally.

Dressing

1 can (20 ounces) pineapple chunks in juice

¾ cup frozen apple juice concentrate

2 tablespoons cornstarch

2 tablespoons lemon juice

2 cups reduced-fat ricotta cheese

⅓ cup fat-free plain yogurt

Salad

4 large Red Delicious apples, chopped

1 can (11 ounces) mandarin orange sections, drained

2 large bananas, sliced

½ cup coarsely chopped walnuts, toasted

1. *To make the dressing:* Drain the pineapple and measure ¾ cup of the juice into a small saucepan. Save the remainder for another use. Add the apple juice concentrate, cornstarch, and lemon juice. Cook over medium heat, whisking constantly, for 3 to 4 minutes, or until thickened. Remove from the heat; allow to cool.

2. Spoon the cooled mixture into a blender or food processor. Add the ricotta and yogurt. Blend or process until smooth. Set aside.

3. *To make the salad:* In a large bowl, combine the reserved pineapple chunks, apples, oranges, and bananas. Pour in the dressing. Stir to mix well. Cover tightly and refrigerate for 2 to 3 hours.

4. To serve, add the walnuts and fold to mix.

Makes 8 servings

Per serving:	270 calories	9 g. fat	18 mg. cholesterol
	84 mg. sodium	40 g. carbohydrates	10 g. protein

Waldorf Salad

As created at New York's famed Waldorf-Astoria Hotel in 1890, this apple salad originally did not contain walnuts. Later, however, walnuts became part of the standard ingredient list. This version is a makeover of a reader's recipe that departs from tradition by using almonds and also by adding some spices.

Homestyle Makeover		
Each serving contains		
	Before	After
Calories	324	109
Fat g.	30	6

Dressing

1 cup soft silken tofu
1 tablespoon lemon juice
1 tablespoon vegetable oil
1 teaspoon sugar
¾ teaspoon curry powder

½ teaspoon salt
¼ teaspoon ground cinnamon
⅛ teaspoon ground ginger

Salad

1 cup coarsely chopped almonds
4 Red Delicious apples, cored and chopped
8 large ribs celery, sliced

½ cup raisins
½ cup chopped chives or scallion tops

1. *To make the dressing:* In a blender or food processor, combine the tofu, lemon juice, oil, sugar, curry powder, salt, cinnamon, and ginger. Blend or process until smooth.

2. *To make the salad:* Place the almonds in a dry skillet over medium heat, stirring constantly, for 8 to 10 minutes, or until lightly browned. Remove from the heat. Set aside to cool.

3. In a large bowl, combine the almonds, apples, celery, raisins, and chives or scallion tops. Add the dressing. Toss to mix.

Makes 16 servings

Per serving:

109 calories	*6 g. fat*	*0 mg. cholesterol*
108 mg. sodium	*12 g. carbohydrates*	*3 g. protein*

Cook's Notes

• If possible, make the Waldorf Salad dressing a day or two in advance to let flavors blend.

• You can assemble the salad—except for adding the nuts—several hours in advance of serving. Store, tightly covered, in the refrigerator. Add the nuts just before serving so they stay crunchy.

• If desired, you can serve the salad on a bed of greens.

Ambrosia

Homestyle Makeover

Each serving contains

	Before	After
Calories	332	125
Fat g.	7	0

In this lighter version of the classic fruit salad, I replace the highly saturated shredded coconut with fat-free coconut extract. Be sure to measure the extract precisely. A small amount is wonderful, but too much can produce an unpleasant taste.

3 tablespoons orange juice

2 tablespoons sugar

¾ teaspoon coconut extract

2 large navel oranges, cut into small chunks

2 bananas, cut into small chunks

1. In a medium bowl, combine the orange juice, sugar, and coconut extract. Add the oranges and bananas. Stir to mix well. Serve immediately, or cover tightly and store in the refrigerator for up to 2 days before serving.

Makes 4 servings

Per serving: *125 calories*   *0 g. fat*   *0 mg. cholesterol*
    1 mg. sodium   *32 g. carbohydrates*   *1 g. protein*

Cook's Note

• If you like marshmallows, simply mix ½ cup into the salad before serving.

Shrimp Rémoulade

Rémoulade is a French mayonnaise sauce that inspired this spicier version that became popular in New Orleans. Because the original recipe called for mayonnaise made with egg yolks and oil, the fat was much higher than it is in this revised recipe.

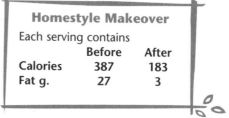

Homestyle Makeover

Each serving contains

	Before	After
Calories	387	183
Fat g.	27	3

½ cup fat-free mayonnaise

2 tablespoons Dijon mustard

2 tablespoons horseradish

2 hard-cooked egg whites, finely chopped

1 shallot, finely chopped

1 tablespoon Worcestershire sauce

⅛–¼ teaspoon ground red pepper

1 pound peeled cooked small shrimp

2 heads Boston or Bibb lettuce, torn into bite-size pieces

1. In a large bowl, combine the mayonnaise, mustard, horseradish, egg whites, shallot, Worcestershire sauce, and ⅛ teaspoon of the pepper. Stir to mix well. Stir in the shrimp. Cover tightly and refrigerate for at least 2 hours to blend the flavors before serving.

2. To serve, arrange the lettuce on each of 4 chilled salad plates. Taste the shrimp mixture and add up to ⅛ teaspoon of the pepper if you want a hotter sauce. Stir to mix. Spoon a quarter of the shrimp mixture on top of the lettuce on each plate.

Makes 4 servings

Per serving: 183 calories   3 g. fat   173 mg. cholesterol
562 mg. sodium   12 g. carbohydrates   27 g. protein

Cook's Notes

• For a milder version, increase the fat-free mayonnaise by 1 tablespoon and decrease the horseradish by 1 tablespoon.

• This versatile sauce works equally well with other seafood or chicken.

Shrimp Louis

This traditional seafood dish is still a popular salad on luncheon menus. It can be made with any type of cold seafood, such as crab or lobster, or a combination of them. You can add chives, green bell peppers, and capers to this salad, if you wish. Either mix them into the dressing or sprinkle them over the top.

Dressing

½ cup fat-free mayonnaise

¼ cup chili sauce

2 tablespoons sweet pickle relish

2 tablespoons lemon juice

¼ teaspoon sugar

⅛ teaspoon salt

⅛ teaspoon ground black pepper

Salad

1 head iceberg lettuce, shredded

1 pound peeled cooked medium shrimp

4 ribs celery, cut into 3" sticks

4 tomatoes, quartered

2 hard-cooked egg whites, quartered

4 sprigs parsley

1. *To make the dressing:* In a medium bowl, combine the mayonnaise, chili sauce, relish, lemon juice, sugar, salt, and pepper.

2. *To make the salad:* Arrange 2 cups lettuce on each of 4 large chilled salad plates. Place one-quarter of the shrimp in the center of the lettuce. Arrange one-quarter of the celery sticks, 4 tomato quarters, and 2 egg white quarters around the shrimp. Top each serving with ¼ cup of the dressing and a sprig of parsley.

Makes 4 servings

Per serving:	212 calories	3 g. fat	173 mg. cholesterol
	596 mg. sodium	19 g. carbohydrates	27 g. protein

Curried Chicken Salad on Greens

This unforgettable curried chicken salad is an adaptation of the one served at the Come On In café in La Jolla, California, by Leslie and Kelvin Deboer. In revising the dish, I used fat-free mayonnaise and slightly increased the amount of the spices to compensate for the lack of fat.

Homestyle Makeover		
Each serving contains		
	Before	After
Calories	561	363
Fat g.	40	9

Salad

¾ cup white wine or apple juice

½ cup golden raisins

6 tablespoons slivered almonds

¾ pound boneless, skinless chicken breast halves, trimmed of all visible fat

2 Granny Smith apples, cored and chopped

4 large ribs celery, finely chopped

1 package (6 ounces) assorted young greens, torn into bite-size pieces

Dressing

½ cup fat-free mayonnaise

1 tablespoon lime juice

1 tablespoon curry powder

2 teaspoons ground ginger

1. *To make the salad:* In a small saucepan, combine ½ cup of the wine or apple juice and the raisins. Bring to a boil over medium heat. Remove from the heat and allow to stand 20 to 30 minutes or longer, because marinating improves the flavor of the raisins.

2. Meanwhile, place the almonds in a large skillet. Cook over medium-high heat, stirring occasionally, for 4 to 6 minutes, or until golden. Remove from the heat and set aside to cool.

3. Pour the remaining ¼ cup of wine or apple juice into the skillet. Bring to a boil. Add the chicken. Reduce the heat to low. Cover and simmer for 8 to 10 minutes. Check for doneness by inserting the tip of a sharp knife into the center of 1 breast half to make sure that no pink remains. An instant-read thermometer inserted in the center of a breast, not touching the skillet, should register 160°F. (Do not overcook the chicken or it will become tough and dry.) Remove the chicken from the skillet

and place on a cutting board. Using 2 forks, pull the chicken apart into bite-size strips. Place in a large bowl.

4. Drain the raisins, discarding the liquid. Add the raisins, apples, and celery to the chicken. Toss to mix. Set aside. Arrange the greens equally on each of 4 chilled salad plates. Set aside.

5. *To make the dressing:* In a small bowl, combine the mayonnaise, lime juice, curry powder, and ginger. Pour the dressing over the salad. Toss to mix.

6. To serve, spoon 1½ cups of the chicken salad on each plate of lettuce. Sprinkle with the almonds.

Makes 4 servings

| *Per serving:* | 363 calories | 9 g. fat | 49 mg. cholesterol |
| | 325 mg. sodium | 49 g. carbohydrates | 25 g. protein |

Cook's Notes

• For a simpler presentation, you can toss the chicken salad in a bowl with the greens and the almonds just before serving.

• For the ultimate curried chicken salad sandwich, spread a little of this salad between two slices of toasted whole-grain bread.

Tomato Aspic with Artichokes

This savory gelatin salad is an American favorite that complements many types of dishes. This revision cuts the amount of sodium nearly in half. For an even lower-sodium count, you can omit the salt.

Homestyle Makeover

Each serving contains

	Before	After
Calories	110	103
Fat g.	0	0

3 envelopes (¼ ounce each) unflavored gelatin

5½ cups tomato juice

⅓ cup lemon juice

1 tablespoon grated onion

1 clove garlic, minced

¼ teaspoon salt

2 teaspoons dried dillweed

1 teaspoon dried basil

1 teaspoon dried oregano

1 bay leaf

1 can (14 ounces) artichoke hearts, drained and halved lengthwise

Parsley or crisp greens

1. In a small bowl, combine the gelatin and ½ cup of the tomato juice. Set aside to soften.

2. In a medium saucepan, combine the lemon juice, onion, garlic, salt, dill-weed, basil, oregano, bay leaf, and the remaining 5 cups tomato juice. Bring to a boil over high heat. Reduce the heat to low. Simmer, stirring occasionally, for 10 minutes, to blend the flavors. Remove from the heat. Pour through a fine mesh strainer into a medium bowl. Add the softened gelatin and stir until completely dissolved. Set aside and allow to cool to room temperature.

3. Coat a 2-quart ring mold with nonstick spray. Arrange half of the artichokes in a decorative pattern in the bottom of the mold. Carefully spoon in enough of the tomato-juice mixture to measure about ¼" in the bottom of the mold. Refrigerate for 30 to 35 minutes, or until the gelatin is thickened. Carefully add the remaining artichoke hearts. Gently pour in the remaining tomato-juice mixture. Refrigerate for 3 hours, or until set.

4. To serve, unmold the aspic on a large plate. Garnish with parsley or greens.

Makes 12 servings

Per serving: 103 calories 0 g. fat 0 mg. cholesterol
576 mg. sodium 7 g. carbohydrates 20 g. protein

Salad Smarts

The widely held notion that all salads are low in calories is simply not true. Many salad ingredients and salad dressings are so high in fat that they can sink the good nutrition ship.

Salads that contain fatty processed meats, cheeses, and nuts can prevent the salad from being a healthy choice. Choose lean meats, poultry, and seafood as well as fat-reduced cheeses.

Nuts and seeds, although relatively high in fat and calories, provide valuable nutrients and add enormously to the flavor and texture of salads. Toasting nuts enhances their flavor so much that you only need to use half as much. Sprinkle nuts over salads just before serving so they stay crunchy.

Homemade croutons are another tasty low-fat addition for salads. To make croutons, cut good-quality bread into cubes. Spread on a baking sheet in a single layer. Coat with nonstick spray, then sprinkle with an herb mixture such as Italian seasoning. Toss and coat again with nonstick spray. Bake in a preheated 350°F oven for 10 to 12 minutes, or until golden.

Making your own reduced-fat or fat-free salad dressings is well worth the small amount of time it takes. They taste fresher and cost much less than commercial brands.

To achieve the same volume in a low-fat dressing as in the original recipe, replace part of the oil with broth, fruit or vegetable juice, fat-free sour cream, or fat-free plain yogurt. A pinch of plain gelatin powder whisked into the dressing will add body to thinner liquids. Mustard, honey, and horseradish are other options that can add flavor and body.

Season the dressing with your favorite herbs, spices, or sizzled garlic (page 9). I like to make my dressing at least two days before I plan to use it, allowing the flavors to blend.

Lemon Gelatin Fruit Salad

This lemon gelatin salad was easy to improve. I used pineapple chunks in juice rather than syrup, fat-free whipped topping in place of whipped cream, and reduced-fat Cheddar instead of full-fat. I toasted the walnuts to heighten their flavor so I only needed to use half the amount.

Homestyle Makeover		
Each serving contains		
	Before	After
Calories	290	220
Fat g.	14	5

1 package (6 ounces) lemon gelatin	2½ tablespoons flour
1½ cups boiling water	1 egg, lightly beaten
1 can (20 ounces) pineapple chunks in juice	1 carton (16 ounces) fat-free whipped topping
1 cup miniature marshmallows	1 cup (4 ounces) shredded reduced-fat Cheddar cheese
3 bananas	½ cup chopped walnuts, toasted
½ cup sugar	

1. In a large bowl, combine the gelatin and water. Stir to dissolve the gelatin. Place in the refrigerator for 30 minutes, or until slightly thickened.

2. Drain the pineapple chunks, reserving the juice to use in the topping. Remove the gelatin from the refrigerator. Add the pineapple and marshmallows. Slice and add the bananas. Stir to mix well. Spoon the mixture into a 13" × 9" glass or ceramic baking dish. Refrigerate for at least 3 hours, or until set.

3. In a medium saucepan, whisk the sugar and flour to combine. Add the reserved pineapple juice and egg. Whisk to combine. Cook over low heat for 5 to 7 minutes, or until thickened. Remove from the heat and let cool completely.

4. Add the whipped topping. Fold to mix. Spread the topping over the salad. Sprinkle the Cheddar and walnuts evenly over the top. Refrigerate for 1 hour.

Makes 16 servings

Per serving:	220 calories	5 g. fat	21 mg. cholesterol
	134 mg. sodium	38 g. carbohydrates	7 g. protein

Cranberry Gelatin Salad

This colorful holiday salad can easily be doubled for a large group and still be made in the same amount of time. For a more festive presentation on a buffet table, make it in a wreath mold and unmold it onto a bed of greens.

1 package (3 ounces) raspberry gelatin

1 package (3 ounces) strawberry gelatin

1½ cups boiling water

1 can (16 ounces) whole-berry cranberry sauce

1 can (8 ounces) crushed pineapples in juice, drained

½ cup chopped pecans, toasted

1. In a medium bowl, combine the raspberry and strawberry gelatin and water. Add the cranberry sauce and pineapple to the mixture. Stir until well-mixed. Pour into a 13" × 9" baking dish. Place in the refrigerator for 40 to 45 minutes, or until slightly thickened. Remove from the refrigerator and stir in the pecans. Refrigerate for at least 3 hours, or until set.

Makes 12 servings

Per serving:	*147 calories*	*3 g. fat*	*0 mg. cholesterol*
	48 mg. sodium	*30 g. carbohydrates*	*2 g. protein*

Recipes

Vegetables, Stuffings, and Side Dishes

Side dishes have always played an important role in a well-balanced American meal. What's the holiday turkey without all the trimmings—Sweet Potato Casserole, Herbed Bread Dressing, and Creamed Onions? Imagine Meat Loaf (page 260) without Old-Fashioned Green Beans or Mashed Potatoes with Gravy. Side dishes make the meal.

I have gathered recipes for a variety of cherished regional American vegetable dishes, as well as stuffings, dressings, grits, and other starches. Along with trimming nutritional profiles, I have streamlined techniques whenever possible to speed preparation.

I'm sure you remember, and often long for, the traditional tastes and aromas of your childhood. Certainly among these early edible memories are dishes such as Macaroni and Cheese, Scalloped Potatoes, and Classic Baked Beans. If you find you're not making these as often as you used to because of their high fat content, these delightful makeovers will convince your tastebuds that they can go home again.

Classic Baked Beans

Photograph on page 34

This recipe is my all-time favorite for this old-fashioned, soul-satisfying dish. The unhurried baking time allows the smoky Southern Ham Stock and the molasses, brown sugar, and spicy mustard to permeate the heart of each bean.

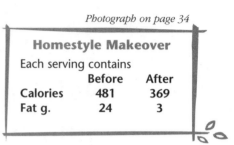

Homestyle Makeover

Each serving contains

	Before	After
Calories	481	369
Fat g.	24	3

1 **pound small dry white beans**

6 **cups Southern Ham Stock (page 99)**

⅓ **cup packed dark brown sugar**

3 **tablespoons molasses**

1 **tablespoon dry mustard**

1 **teaspoon salt**

¼ **teaspoon ground black pepper**

1. Pick out and discard any broken or discolored beans. Place the beans in a large pot. Add cold water to cover by at least 2". Bring to a boil over high heat. Remove from the heat. Cover and let stand for 1 hour. Drain and rinse the beans well. Return to the pot. Add cold water to cover by at least 2". Bring to a boil, then reduce the heat. Cover and simmer for 1 hour, or until the beans can easily be pierced with a fork.

2. Preheat the oven to 325°F. Coat a bean pot or a 2-quart baking dish with nonstick spray. Drain the beans thoroughly and return to the pot. Add the Southern Ham Stock, brown sugar, molasses, mustard, salt, and pepper. Stir to mix well. Spoon into the prepared bean pot or baking dish. Cover and bake for 4 hours, stirring once every hour, or until all the liquid is absorbed.

3. Uncover the beans and bake for 30 minutes, or until glazed.

Makes 8 servings

Per serving:	369 calories	3 g. fat	13 mg. cholesterol
	757 mg. sodium	63 g. carbohydrates	25 g. protein

Cook's Note

• The beans can also be covered with water and soaked overnight, if desired.

Southern Ham Stock

This rich, yet fat-free ham stock is wonderful as a smoky flavoring base for baked beans, vegetables, soups, and stews.

1–2 **pounds cured smoked ham hocks**

8–10 **cups water**

1. Place the ham hocks in a deep pot and add up to 10 cups of water, enough to cover. Bring to a boil over high heat. Reduce the heat to low. Cover and simmer for 3 to 3½ hours, or until the meat starts to fall off the bones.

2. Cool to room temperature and then refrigerate, uncovered, overnight. Remove and discard all the fat that has congealed on the top. Remove all the lean meat from the ham hocks, discarding the bones, skin, and all fat. Shred the lean meat and return it to the liquid. Mix well.

3. Refrigerate, tightly covered, for up to 1 week or freeze in plastic freezer containers for up to 3 months.

Makes 6 cups

Per ¼ cup:	8 calories	0 g. fat	3 mg. cholesterol
	86 mg. sodium	0 g. carbohydrates	2 g. protein

Cook's Note

• You can also spoon the mixture into ice-cube trays and freeze. Remove the cubes and store in plastic freezer bags. Two cubes equal about ¼ cup. Use to steam and flavor 1 pound of green beans or spinach in a tightly closed pot.

Green Bean Casserole

In the 1930s and 1940s this dish, made with canned green beans, was so popular that you could always find it at family reunions, barbecues, and church suppers. I like to use frozen green beans for better color and texture.

Photograph on page 37

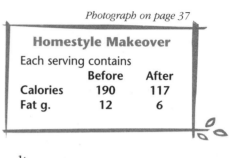

Homestyle Makeover

Each serving contains

	Before	After
Calories	190	117
Fat g.	12	6

2 packages (9 ounces each) frozen french-cut green beans, thawed and drained

1 onion, sliced into rings and separated

2 ounces Canadian bacon, cut into 1" strips

¼ cup sugar

¼ cup white vinegar

2 tablespoons canola oil

½ teaspoon salt

¼ teaspoon liquid smoke (see note)

¼ cup slivered almonds

1. In a 1½-quart baking dish, layer the beans, onion, and bacon. Set aside.

2. In a small bowl, combine the sugar, vinegar, oil, salt, and liquid smoke. Stir until the sugar and salt are completely dissolved. Pour over the bean mixture. Cover tightly and refrigerate overnight, or as long as several days, for the flavors to blend.

3. Preheat the oven to 350°F. Sprinkle the almonds over the bean mixture. Bake for 45 minutes, or until bubbly and the almonds are toasted.

Makes 6 servings

Per serving:

117 calories	6 g. fat	4 mg. cholesterol
305 mg. sodium	14 g. carbohydrates	4 g. protein

Cook's Note

• Liquid smoke, condensed smoke flavoring, is sold in supermarkets with the barbecue sauces.

Old-Fashioned Green Beans

Photograph on front cover

Old-fashioned kitchen wisdom, especially in the South, dictated that green beans simmer with sugar and bacon for a long time over low heat to magically transform their flavor.

1 tablespoon vegetable oil

12 slices turkey bacon, cut into ½" pieces

¼ cup packed dark brown sugar

1½ cups water

2 pounds green beans, trimmed and broken into 2" pieces

1. Heat the oil in a large skillet over medium heat. Add the bacon and cook, stirring frequently, for 5 to 7 minutes, or until browned. Add the brown sugar and water. Stir to mix well. Bring to a boil. Add the beans and reduce the heat to low. Cover and simmer for 50 to 60 minutes, or until the beans are soft and all of the liquid has been absorbed.

Makes 8 servings

Per serving: *103 calories*   *5 g. fat*   *8 mg. cholesterol*
    293 mg. sodium   *12 g. carbohydrates*   *5 g. protein*

Cauliflower au Gratin

You may want to make this recipe in individual au gratin dishes rather than one casserole. You can also make this recipe with broccoli or broccoflower.

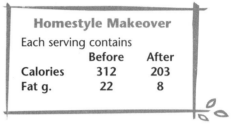

Homestyle Makeover

Each serving contains

	Before	After
Calories	312	203
Fat g.	22	8

1 head cauliflower (1½ pounds), cut into florets

2 teaspoons butter or margarine

1 clove garlic, minced

3 tablespoons unbleached or all-purpose flour

¾ cup fat-free, reduced-sodium chicken broth

½ cup 1% milk

1 cup (4 ounces) shredded reduced-fat sharp Cheddar cheese

⅓ cup fat-free mayonnaise

1 tablespoon lemon juice

½ teaspoon ground black pepper

1 slice fresh whole-wheat bread, crumbled

1. Preheat the oven to 375°F. Coat a 2-quart baking dish with nonstick spray. Set aside.

2. Place a steamer over simmering water in a large saucepan. Place the cauliflower on the steamer. Cover and steam for 3 to 5 minutes, or until crisp-tender. Remove the cauliflower and rinse under cold running water. Drain and pat dry. Place in the prepared baking dish.

3. In a medium saucepan, melt the butter or margarine over medium heat. Add the garlic and cook, stirring, just until it sizzles. Add the flour and stir for 1 minute, but do not brown. Slowly add the broth and milk. Cook, whisking constantly, until the mixture comes to a boil. Reduce the heat to low. Cook for 1 minute.

4. Stir in the Cheddar, mayonnaise, lemon juice, and pepper. Stir to melt the Cheddar. Pour over the cauliflower. Sprinkle with the bread. Bake for 40 to 45 minutes, or until bubbly.

Makes 6 servings

Per serving:	203 calories	8 g. fat	24 mg. cholesterol
	516 mg. sodium	20 g. carbohydrates	15 g. protein

Chicken Salad Sandwich (page 142)

103

Muffaletta (page 148)

Hamburger (page 152) and Creamy Potato Salad (page 78)   105

106 *Barbecued Beef Sandwich (page 154) and Creamy Coleslaw (page 77)*

Quiche Lorraine (page 161)

108 *Salmon Croquettes (page 173) and Creamed Spinach Casserole (page 131)*

Tuna Noodle Casserole (page 176)   109

110   **Crab Cakes (page 181)**

New England Clambake (page 182)

112   *Fried Shrimp (page 195)*

Chicken and Dumplings (page 202)   113

Chicken Cacciatore (page 204)

Chicken Cordon Bleu (page 211) and Rice Pilaf (page 138)   115

Chicken Paprika (page 208)

Spicy Turkey Sausage Patties (page 242)   117

118   ***Apple and Sage Rock Cornish Hens (page 244) and***
Wild Rice Dressing (page 139)

Corn Fritters

These lighter fritters are much tastier and more delicate than greasy deep-fried fritters. Be careful to turn them over gently when cooking because they can break easily. Serve them as a side dish for dinner or make them for brunch topped with maple syrup, honey, or fruit jam.

12 ears fresh corn on the cob or 6 cups frozen corn, thawed

1 cup 2% milk

2 tablespoons melted butter or margarine

1 teaspoon sugar

¾ teaspoon salt

¼ teaspoon ground black pepper

⅔ cup unbleached or all-purpose flour

2 teaspoons baking powder

1 egg

2 egg whites

1. With a sharp knife, cut the kernels from the ears of corn. Place in a large bowl. Discard the cobs. Crush the corn with the back of a large spoon. Stir in the milk, butter or margarine, sugar, salt, and pepper. Set aside.

2. In a small bowl, combine the flour and baking powder. Add slowly to the corn mixture, stirring constantly, to make a thin batter.

3. Using the small bowl again, add the egg and egg whites and lightly beat with a fork until smooth. Add to the corn mixture. Stir until well-mixed.

4. Coat a large nonstick griddle or skillet with nonstick spray. Place over medium heat until hot enough for drops of water to dance on the surface. Drop the batter, 2 tablespoons at a time, onto the griddle or skillet. Cook for 2 to 3 minutes, or until browned. Turn and cook for 1 to 2 minutes, or until browned. Cook the fritters in batches, if needed. Do not crowd the griddle or skillet. There should be enough batter for 48 fritters.

Makes 6 servings

Per serving:

258 calories	7 g. fat	49 mg. cholesterol
499 mg. sodium	43 g. carbohydrates	10 g. protein

Succotash

The name of this popular southern side dish of corn and lima beans is taken from the Native American word msickquatash, which means boiled whole kernels of corn. This dish is now usually cooked in milk and is often made more colorful with the addition of chopped red or green peppers.

Homestyle Makeover

Each serving contains

	Before	After
Calories	427	326
Fat g.	7	4

8 ears fresh corn on the cob or 4 cups frozen corn, thawed

2 cups shelled baby lima beans or 2 cups frozen baby lima beans, thawed

2 cups water

1 cup 2% milk

1 tablespoon butter or margarine

½ teaspoon salt

¼ teaspoon ground black pepper

1. With a sharp knife, cut the kernels from the ears of corn. Place in a large saucepan. Discard the cobs. Add the beans and water. Cook over medium heat, for 10 to 15 minutes, or until tender. Drain thoroughly. (If using frozen corn kernels and lima beans, prepare according to the package directions and drain thoroughly.) Return to the saucepan.

2. Add the milk, butter or margarine, salt, and pepper. Cook over medium heat for 4 to 5 minutes, or until heated through. Do not boil.

Makes 6 servings

| Per serving: | 326 calories | 4 g. fat | 8 mg. cholesterol |
| | 246 mg. sodium | 59 g. carbohydrates | 17 g. protein |

◆ VEGETABLES, STUFFINGS, AND SIDE DISHES ◆

Granny's Turnip Greens

Soul food dishes, such as these tasty turnip greens, once found on menus only in the South, have become popular in restaurants all over the country. I have named this recipe after my own Texas grandmother, Mena Jones, because the original recipe came from her collection.

Homestyle Makeover

Each serving contains

	Before	After
Calories	105	70
Fat g.	6	4

1 **pound fresh turnip greens or 1 package (16 ounces) frozen turnip greens, thawed**

1 **teaspoon vegetable oil**

6 **slices turkey bacon, chopped**

4 **cups water**

3 **scallions, chopped**

1 **tablespoon white vinegar**

1 **teaspoon sugar**

1 **teaspoon salt**

1 **teaspoon ground black pepper**

1. If using fresh greens, thoroughly rinse them under cool running water. Remove any tough stems and discard. Tear the leaves into bite-size pieces. Set aside.

2. Heat the oil in a Dutch oven or large pot over medium heat. Add the bacon and cook, stirring constantly, for about 5 minutes, or until browned. Add the water, scallions, vinegar, sugar, salt, and pepper. Bring to a boil.

3. Cover the pot and reduce heat to low. Simmer for 1 hour, or until the greens are very tender and the flavors are blended.

Makes 6 servings

Per serving:	70 calories	4 g. fat	15 mg. cholesterol
	395 mg. sodium	6 g. carbohydrates	3 g. protein

Cook's Note

• Select young, fresh turnip greens, which will be tender and not as bitter as older leaves. Turnip greens are sold year-round but are more readily available from October through February. If you can't find turnip greens, collard greens or kale makes a good substitute.

Creamed Onions

About 70 species of onions are native to North America. Many of them were used by the Native Americans and also the early European settlers. In fact, in 1624, French Jesuit missionary Jacques Marquette credited wild onions with sustaining him while exploring the southern shore of Lake Michigan.

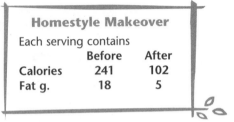

Homestyle Makeover

Each serving contains

	Before	After
Calories	241	102
Fat g.	18	5

6 onions, cut into ½" thick slices

1 cup water

3 tablespoons butter or margarine

3 tablespoons unbleached or all-purpose flour

¾ cup fat-free milk

½ teaspoon salt

¼ teaspoon ground white pepper

1 slice whole-wheat bread, crumbled

1. Preheat the oven to 350°F. Coat a 13" × 9" baking dish with nonstick spray. Set aside.

2. In a large saucepan, bring the onions and water to a boil. Reduce the heat to low. Cover and cook for about 10 minutes, or until the onions are tender. Reserve ½ cup of the cooking water. Drain the onions and place them in the prepared baking dish. Set aside.

3. In a medium saucepan, melt 2 tablespoons of the butter or margarine over medium-low heat. Add the flour and cook, whisking constantly, for 2 minutes. Do not brown.

4. Gradually add the milk and the reserved cooking water, whisking constantly. Cook, whisking constantly, for 4 to 5 minutes, or until the flour mixture comes to a boil and thickens. Add the salt and pepper. Stir to mix. Pour evenly over the onions. Set aside.

5. Place the bread in a small bowl. Drizzle with the remaining 1 tablespoon of the butter or margarine. Toss to mix well. Sprinkle over the onions. Bake for about 25 minutes, or until the sauce begins to bubble and the top is lightly browned.

Makes 8 servings

Per serving: *102 calories*   *5 g. fat*   *0 mg. cholesterol*
                         655 mg. sodium   *12 g. carbohydrates*   *3 g. protein*

Cook's Notes

• For a special occasion, it is pretty to replace the onions with 3 baskets or bags (12 ounces each) of pearl onions. To peel the onions, place them in a pot of boiling water for 30 seconds. Drain and rinse under cold running water. The skins should slip off easily.

• Try adding your favorite herbs or spices to vary this recipe. I like adding a little thyme or marjoram.

Fried Okra

The word okra comes from an African word meaning vegetable. African slaves from Ethiopia brought okra to the American South, where it is still popular in stews and soups.

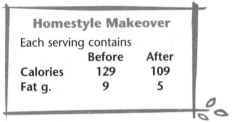

Homestyle Makeover

Each serving contains

	Before	After
Calories	129	109
Fat g.	9	5

1 **pound fresh okra, tips and stem ends trimmed, cut into ½" slices, or 1 package (16 ounces) sliced frozen okra, thawed (see note)**

½ **cup self-rising flour**
½ **cup cornmeal**
2 **tablespoons vegetable oil**
¼ **teaspoon salt**

1. Place the okra in a large bowl. Set aside. In a small bowl, combine the flour and cornmeal. Add to the okra and toss to coat.

2. Heat 1 tablespoon of the oil in a large skillet over medium heat until hot enough for drops of water to dance on the surface. Using a slotted spoon and shaking off excess flour and cornmeal, place the okra in a single layer in the skillet. Do not crowd the okra in the skillet or it will turn mushy and not brown properly. Cook, stirring constantly, for 6 to 8 minutes, or until well-browned. Remove with a slotted spoon to drain on paper towels. Add the remaining 1 tablespoon oil. Repeat cooking the remaining okra. Sprinkle with the salt.

Makes 6 servings

Per serving:	109 calories	5 g. fat	0 mg. cholesterol
	95 mg. sodium	14 g. carbohydrates	3 g. protein

Cook's Note

• If using fresh okra, moisten it before attempting to coat with the flour and cornmeal. It needs to be damp for the breading to stick.

Hash Brown Potato Casserole

<table>
<tr><td colspan="3">Homestyle Makeover</td></tr>
<tr><td colspan="3">Each serving contains</td></tr>
<tr><td></td><td>Before</td><td>After</td></tr>
<tr><td>Calories</td><td>221</td><td>199</td></tr>
<tr><td>Fat g.</td><td>15</td><td>5</td></tr>
</table>

This traditional midwestern favorite is truly delicious and very easy to make. I reduced the fat significantly by using frozen hash browns without frying them.

1 package (27 ounces) frozen hash brown potatoes, thawed

2 cups (8 ounces) shredded reduced-fat sharp Cheddar cheese

16 ounces fat-free sour cream

1 onion, finely chopped

1 can (10¾ ounces) low-fat condensed cream of mushroom soup

1 cup crushed fat-free potato chips

1. Preheat the oven to 375°F. Coat a 13" × 9" baking dish with nonstick spray. Set aside.

2. In a large bowl, combine the potatoes, Cheddar, sour cream, onion, and soup. Spoon into the prepared baking dish. Sprinkle with the potato chips.

3. Bake for 45 to 50 minutes, or until a deep golden brown.

Makes 12 servings

Per serving:	199 calories	5 g. fat	20 mg. cholesterol
	375 mg. sodium	18 g. carbohydrates	16 g. protein

Scalloped Potatoes

A lot of American dishes, especially in the Midwest, are scalloped, which means layered in a cream sauce in a casserole. Of all the scalloped dishes, potatoes are definitely the most popular throughout the country.

Photograph on page 221

Homestyle Makeover

Each serving contains

	Before	After
Calories	131	97
Fat g.	6	2

3 large potatoes, peeled and thinly sliced

2 tablespoons unbleached or all-purpose flour

1 teaspoon salt

1 teaspoon ground black pepper

2 onions, thinly sliced

1 tablespoon butter or margarine

1 can (12 ounces) fat-free evaporated milk

1. Preheat the oven to 350°F. Coat a 13" × 9" baking dish with nonstick spray.

2. Layer one-third of the potatoes in the bottom of the prepared dish and sprinkle with half of the flour and ½ teaspoon each of the salt and pepper. Top with half of the onions.

3. Repeat with another third of the potatoes and the remaining flour, salt, pepper, and onions.

4. Top with the remaining potatoes. Dot with the butter or margarine and pour the evaporated milk over the top. Bake for 1 hour. Increase the heat to 375°F and bake for 30 to 40 minutes, or until the potatoes are tender and golden brown.

Makes 6 servings

Per serving: 97 calories · 2 g. fat · 0 mg. cholesterol · 594 mg. sodium · 15 g. carbohydrates · 4 g. protein

Cook's Note

• To add a fresher note to Scalloped Potatoes, scatter ¼ cup of chopped fresh celery leaves or parsley over the onions.

Twice-Baked Potatoes

Photograph on page 36

Homestyle Makeover

Each serving contains

	Before	After
Calories	304	196
Fat g.	20	8

You can vary the flavor of this popular side dish by replacing the Cheddar cheese with Swiss, mozzarella, or Parmesan. Cold Twice-Baked Potatoes are good for picnics and in sack lunches.

2 large russet potatoes (1 pound)

⅓ cup 2% milk

1 tablespoon butter or margarine

¼ teaspoon salt

¼ teaspoon ground black pepper

1 cup (4 ounces) shredded reduced-fat sharp Cheddar cheese

4 tablespoons chopped fresh chives or scallion top

1. Preheat the oven to 425°F. Scrub the potatoes well and pierce each one with a fork to allow steam to escape. Place on a baking sheet. Bake for 1 hour, or until they can be easily squeezed. (Protect your hand with an oven mitt.) Remove from the oven. Set aside and allow to cool until safe to handle.

2. Reduce the oven temperature to 375°F. Cut the potatoes in half lengthwise. With a spoon, remove the flesh, leaving a ¼" shell. Put the flesh in a large bowl. Cover the shells and set aside.

3. With a potato masher or electric mixer, mash the potato flesh. Gradually add the milk, mashing or beating after each addition.

4. Add the butter or margarine, salt, and pepper. Beat until thoroughly blended. Add the cheese and 2 tablespoons of the chives or scallion. Fill each shell with the potato mixture and place on a baking sheet.

5. Bake for 20 to 25 minutes, or until hot and lightly browned. Sprinkle with the remaining chives or scallion.

Makes 4 servings

Per serving:	196 calories	8 g. fat	24 mg. cholesterol
	349 mg. sodium	23 g. carbohydrates	11 g. protein

Mashed Potatoes with Gravy

No side dish is more all-American than mashed potatoes and gravy. It's a hearty, ideal accompaniment to almost any entrée. For a vegetarian meal, simply replace the beef broth with vegetable broth.

Photograph on front cover

Homestyle Makeover

Each serving contains

	Before	After
Calories	486	99
Fat g.	37	4

Potatoes

2 pounds russet potatoes, peeled and cut into chunks

½ cup fat-free milk

2 tablespoons melted butter or margarine

½ teaspoon salt

¼ teaspoon ground black pepper

Gravy

4 cups fat-free, reduced-sodium beef broth or chicken broth

3 tablespoons cornstarch

¼ cup water

½ teaspoon dried thyme

¼ teaspoon ground black pepper

1. *To make the potatoes:* In a large saucepan, cover the potatoes with water and bring to a boil over high heat. Reduce the heat to low. Cook for 15 minutes, or until the potatoes can easily be pierced with a fork. Drain thoroughly. Place in a large bowl.

2. With a potato masher or electric mixer, mash the potatoes until all of the lumps are gone. Add the milk, butter or margarine, salt, and pepper. Mash or beat until smooth and fluffy.

3. *To make the gravy:* Bring the broth to a boil in a medium saucepan. Boil for about 10 minutes, or until reduced in volume by one-third.

4. In a small bowl, combine the cornstarch and water. Stir until completely dissolved. Gradually add to the hot broth, stirring constantly. Cook over low heat, stirring constantly, for 4 to 5 minutes, or until thickened. Add the thyme and pepper. Stir to mix.

5. To serve, spoon the mashed potatoes onto plates. Top with the gravy.

Makes 8 servings

Per serving:	99 calories	4 g. fat	9 mg. cholesterol
	334 mg. sodium	14 g. carbohydrates	3 g. protein

Cook's Note

• Sautéed fresh mushrooms are a wonderful addition to this gravy. Cook 4 ounces of sliced mushrooms with 1 teaspoon butter or margarine in a medium skillet over medium heat for 4 to 5 minutes, or until they can easily be pierced with a fork. Stir into the gravy just before serving.

Oven French Fries

Photograph on page 228

Homestyle Makeover

Each serving contains

	Before	After
Calories	210	90
Fat g.	14	0

These baked french fries have that crisp golden exterior and moist interior associated with this outrageously popular side dish. It boasts a phenomenal savings of 14 grams of fat per serving.

**2 russet potatoes (1 pound),
cut into ½"-thick strips**

1. Preheat the oven to 375°F. Coat a baking sheet with nonstick spray. Arrange the potatoes in a single layer so that they do not overlap. Coat them lightly with nonstick spray.

2. Bake for 1 hour, turning the potato strips every 15 minutes, until they are well-browned and can easily be pierced with a fork.

Makes 4 servings

Per serving:	90 calories	0 g. fat	0 mg. cholesterol
	7 mg. sodium	20 g. carbohydrates	2 g. protein

Sweet Potato Casserole

Photograph on page 223

The orange sweet potato is often confused with yams because that's what they're called in the South. In this recipe, you can use canned sweet potatoes to save time if you wish. However, this dish is considerably tastier and prettier when made with fresh sweet potatoes.

Homestyle Makeover		
Each serving contains		
	Before	After
Calories	202	163
Fat g.	9	5

1 **pound sweet potatoes**
½ **cup fat-free milk**
¼ **cup packed light brown sugar**
1 **egg**
2 **egg whites**

2 **tablespoons butter or margarine**
1½ **teaspoons vanilla extract**
1 **teaspoon ground cinnamon**
½ **teaspoon salt**

1. Preheat the oven to 400°F.

2. Prick the sweet potatoes with a fork and place them on a baking sheet. Bake for about 1 hour, or until they can easily be pierced with a fork. Remove from the oven. Set aside and allow to cool until safe to handle.

3. Reduce the oven temperature to 350°F. Coat an 11" × 7" baking dish with nonstick spray. Set aside.

4. Peel the sweet potatoes. Place the flesh in a large bowl. Mash or beat thoroughly with a potato masher or electric mixer. Add the milk, brown sugar, egg, egg whites, butter or margarine, vanilla, cinnamon, and salt. Mash or beat to mix well. Spoon into the prepared baking dish. Bake for 30 minutes, or until lightly browned.

Makes 6 servings

Per serving:	163 calories	5 g. fat	46 mg. cholesterol
	268 mg. sodium	26 g. carbohydrates	4 g. protein

Creamed Spinach Casserole

Photograph on page 108

Homestyle Makeover

Each serving contains

	Before	After
Calories	318	201
Fat g.	25	11

The easiest and fastest way to prepare this dish is to buy the packaged, prewashed baby spinach leaves, which eliminates the time-consuming task of washing the spinach and removing the stems.

1 tablespoon butter or margarine

½ onion, chopped

¼ teaspoon ground nutmeg

¼ teaspoon salt

¼ teaspoon ground black pepper

¾ cup 1% milk

6 ounces reduced-fat cream cheese

4 packages (6 ounces each) prewashed baby spinach leaves or 2 packages (10 ounces each) frozen chopped spinach, thawed and squeezed dry

2 egg whites

1. Preheat the oven to 350°F. Coat an 11" × 7" baking dish with nonstick spray. Set aside.

2. In a large saucepan, melt the butter or margarine over medium heat. Add the onion, nutmeg, salt, and pepper. Cook, stirring frequently, for about 5 minutes, or until the onion is translucent. Add the milk and cream cheese. Cook, stirring, for 3 to 4 minutes, or until the cream cheese is melted. Add the spinach and cook for 2 minutes, or until the fresh leaves are wilted or the thawed spinach is warm. Remove from the heat. Set aside.

3. Place the egg whites in a medium bowl. With an electric mixer, beat the egg whites until they hold firm peaks. Fold into the spinach mixture.

4. Spoon into the prepared baking dish. Bake for 20 to 25 minutes, or until slightly puffy. Serve immediately.

Makes 4 servings

Per serving: 201 calories 11 g. fat 29 mg. cholesterol 660 mg. sodium 14 g. carbohydrates 14 g. protein

Eggplant Parmesan

Thomas Jefferson is credited with introducing the eggplant to America. Eggplant has, in recent years, become more widely used in this country because of the growing popularity of Mediterranean and Asian cuisines.

Homestyle Makeover

Each serving contains

	Before	After
Calories	380	248
Fat g.	23	12

Salt

1 **large eggplant, peeled and cut lengthwise into ½" slices**

1 **slice whole-wheat bread, torn into small pieces**

¼ **cup (1 ounce) grated Parmesan cheese**

2 **cups low-fat pasta sauce**

½ **teaspoon dried oregano**

2 **cups (8 ounces) shredded reduced-fat mozzarella cheese**

1. Lightly salt the eggplant slices and place them in a bowl. Cover and allow to stand for 1 hour to draw out any bitter juices.

2. Preheat the oven to 350°F. Coat an 11" × 7" baking dish with nonstick spray. Set aside. Drain the liquid from the eggplant. Rinse under cold running water. Place a steamer over simmering water in a large saucepan. Place a single layer of eggplant on the steamer. Cover and steam for 2 to 3 minutes, or until the eggplant can easily be pierced with a fork. Remove and set aside. Continue until all the eggplant is cooked.

3. Place the bread and the Parmesan in a food processor and process until the bread is the consistency of fine gravel. Add the sauce and oregano. Process to mix. Spoon half of the sauce mixture into the prepared baking dish. Cover with half of the eggplant slices. Spoon on one-quarter of the remaining sauce. Spread evenly over the eggplant. Sprinkle with half of the mozzarella. Starting with the remaining eggplant, repeat the layers.

4. Bake for 25 to 30 minutes, or until bubbly and lightly browned. Remove from the oven. Allow to stand for 5 minutes before cutting.

Makes 4 servings

Per serving:	248 calories	12 g. fat	35 mg. cholesterol
	634 mg. sodium	17 g. carbohydrates	20 g. protein

◆ VEGETABLES, STUFFINGS, AND SIDE DISHES ◆

Roasted Tomatoes

Photograph on page 35

Homestyle Makeover		
Each serving contains		
	Before	**After**
Calories	91	81
Fat g.	4	2

Today, the tomato ranks as one of this country's favorite vegetables. This is amusing because it is actually a fruit. The U.S. government reclassified it, however, as a vegetable for trade purposes in 1893.

6 tomatoes

8 ounces fat-free plain yogurt

1 tablespoon unbleached or all-purpose flour

2 teaspoons finely chopped fresh thyme or 1 teaspoon dried

½ teaspoon salt

½ teaspoon ground black pepper

½ teaspoon finely chopped fresh sage or ¼ teaspoon dried

6 tablespoons (1½ ounces) grated Parmesan cheese

1. Preheat the oven to 400°F. Spray a 13" × 9" glass baking dish with nonstick spray. Set aside.

2. Cut a ¼"-thick slice off the stem end of each tomato. Gently squeeze each tomato to release its juice and seeds. Place each tomato, cut side up, in the prepared dish.

3. In a medium bowl, combine the yogurt, flour, thyme, salt, pepper, and sage. Spoon into each tomato and sprinkle with 1 tablespoon Parmesan. Bake for about 20 minutes, or until lightly browned.

Makes 6 servings

Per serving:	81 calories	2 g. fat	5 mg. cholesterol
	314 mg. sodium	11 g. carbohydrates	6 g. protein

Cook's Note

• Sprigs of fresh thyme and sage make a decorative garnish for the roasted tomatoes.

Herbed Bread Dressing

Photograph on page 215

Dressing is usually made of seasoned bread; however, it can also be made with rice or potatoes. It is sometimes called stuffing because it is also used to stuff poultry, fish, meat, and some vegetables.

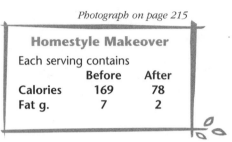

Homestyle Makeover

Each serving contains

	Before	After
Calories	169	78
Fat g.	7	2

10 slices whole-wheat bread, toasted and crumbled

1 teaspoon dried marjoram

½ teaspoon dried sage

½ teaspoon ground black pepper

1 tablespoon butter or margarine

1 onion, finely chopped

4 large ribs celery

½ cup chopped fresh parsley

1½ cups fat-free, reduced-sodium chicken broth

1. Preheat the oven to 350°F. Coat a 13" × 9" baking dish with nonstick spray. Set aside.

2. In a large bowl, combine the bread, marjoram, sage, and pepper.

3. In a large skillet, melt the butter or margarine over medium heat. Add the onion, celery, and parsley. Cook for 8 to 10 minutes, or until the celery is tender.

4. Combine the celery mixture into the bread mixture. Add the broth. Stir well.

5. Spoon the dressing mixture into the prepared dish. Bake for 45 minutes, or until the top is a deep golden brown.

Makes 6 servings

Per serving: *78 calories* *2 g. fat* *3 mg. cholesterol*
222 mg. sodium *13 g. carbohydrates* *3 g. protein*

Cornbread Stuffing

You can use your own favorite cornbread for this recipe. Or, if you prefer, make 1 package (14½ ounces) fat-free cornbread mix, according to the package directions. Cool before crumbling.

1 package (7 ounces) cooked light sausage links, finely chopped

2 large ribs celery, finely chopped

1 small onion, chopped

2 tablespoons + ½ cup water

1 teaspoon poultry seasoning

¼ teaspoon salt

¼ teaspoon ground black pepper

6 cups crumbled fat-free cornbread

½ cup liquid egg substitute

1. Preheat the oven to 375°F. Coat a 13" × 9" baking pan with nonstick spray. Set aside.

2. In a large skillet, combine the sausage, celery, onion, and 2 tablespoons water. Cook over medium heat for about 20 minutes, or until the onion is translucent. Add the poultry seasoning, salt, and pepper. Stir to mix. Transfer to a large bowl.

3. Add the cornbread to the bowl. Stir to mix well. Add the egg substitute and the remaining ½ cup water. Toss lightly until the mixture is moist. Do not overmix. Spoon into the prepared pan. Bake for 25 minutes, or until golden brown.

Makes 16 servings

Per serving:	124 calories	2 g. fat	9 mg. cholesterol
	459 mg. sodium	22 g. carbohydrates	4 g. protein

Cheesy Grits

Grits are a grain staple in the South that is made from ground hominy, which is hulled dried white or yellow corn kernels. Cooked into a versatile pudding, grits are served from breakfast through dinner, often as an accompaniment for eggs or as a starch with saucy meat, poultry, or seafood dishes.

Homestyle Makeover

Each serving contains

	Before	After
Calories	303	189
Fat g.	17	7

3 cups fat-free, reduced-sodium chicken broth

¾ cup quick grits

1½ cups (6 ounces) shredded reduced-fat sharp Cheddar cheese

2 teaspoons butter or margarine

1 can (4 ounces) diced green chile peppers

1 clove garlic, pressed or minced

Dash of hot-pepper sauce

1 egg

2 egg whites

1. Preheat the oven to 350°F. Coat an 11" × 7" baking dish with nonstick spray. Set aside.

2. In a medium saucepan, bring the broth to a boil over high heat. Gradually add the grits, stirring constantly. Reduce the heat to low. Cook, stirring frequently, for 5 minutes, or until thickened.

3. Remove from the heat. Stir in the Cheddar and butter or margarine. Add the chile peppers (with juice), garlic, and hot-pepper sauce. Stir to mix well. Whisk the egg and egg whites in a small bowl until smooth. Fold into the grits mixture.

4. Spoon into the prepared baking dish. Bake for 45 to 50 minutes, or until lightly browned and a knife inserted in the center comes out clean. Allow to stand for 5 minutes before serving.

Makes 8 servings

Per serving:	189 calories	7 g. fat	54 mg. cholesterol
	535 mg. sodium	17 g. carbohydrates	13 g. protein

Macaroni and Cheese

Photograph on page 38

Homestyle Makeover

Each serving contains

	Before	After
Calories	409	318
Fat g.	23	9

Macaroni and cheese equals creamy spoonfuls of comfort. I have added sour cream to this version to make the sauce even more velvety. If you would like to substitute other reduced-fat cheeses and other bread crumbs, try Swiss with whole-wheat or mild Cheddar with white.

½ pound (2 cups) elbow macaroni, cooked and drained

1½ tablespoons unbleached or all-purpose flour

½ teaspoon salt

½ teaspoon paprika

¼ teaspoon ground black pepper

⅛ teaspoon ground red pepper

2 tablespoons butter or margarine

1 onion, finely chopped

1 clove garlic, pressed or minced

2 cups 2% milk

2 cups (8 ounces) shredded reduced-fat sharp Cheddar cheese

8 ounces fat-free sour cream

1 large slice fresh rye bread, crumbled

1. Preheat the oven to 350°F. Coat a 2-quart baking dish with nonstick spray.

2. In a small bowl, combine the flour, salt, paprika, black pepper, and red pepper. In a medium saucepan over low heat, melt the butter or margarine. Add the onion and garlic. Cook, stirring occasionally, for 8 to 10 minutes, or until the onion is translucent. Add the flour mixture. Cook, stirring constantly, for 3 minutes. Gradually add the milk. Cook, stirring constantly, for 8 to 10 minutes, or until smooth and slightly thickened. Remove from the heat and add the Cheddar. Stir until melted.

3. Place the pasta in a large bowl. Add the sour cream and mix well. Pour the cheese sauce over the macaroni and stir to mix. Spoon into the prepared baking dish. Sprinkle with the bread. Coat lightly with nonstick spray. Bake for 20 to 25 minutes, or until bubbly.

Makes 8 servings

Per serving:	318 calories	9 g. fat	25 mg. cholesterol
	525 mg. sodium	39 g. carbohydrates	18 g. protein

Rice Pilaf

Photograph on page 115

Ever since rice arrived in the port of Charleston in the 1680s, rice pilaf has graced southern tables for nearly three centuries, according to southern culinary expert John Egerton.

Homestyle Makeover

Each serving contains

	Before	After
Calories	140	109
Fat g.	4	2

1 **tablespoon vegetable oil**

1 **cup long-grain white rice**

½ **onion, thinly sliced**

2 **cups fat-free, reduced-sodium chicken broth**

2 **tablespoons reduced-sodium soy sauce**

1 **teaspoon dried thyme**

1. Preheat the oven to 400°F. Coat a 1½-quart baking dish with nonstick spray.

2. Heat the oil in a large skillet over medium heat. Add the rice and onion. Cook, stirring frequently, for 15 to 20 minutes, or until the rice is browned.

3. In a small saucepan, combine the broth, soy sauce, and thyme. Bring to a boil. Transfer the rice mixture to the prepared baking dish. Add the broth mixture. Stir to mix well. Cover with a tight-fitting lid and bake for 40 minutes, or until all of the liquid has been absorbed. Remove from the oven and allow to stand for 10 minutes before removing the lid.

Makes 8 servings

Per serving:	109 calories	2 g. fat	0 g. cholesterol
	311 mg. sodium	19 g. carbohydrates	2 g. protein

Cook's Note

• The flavor of this wonderful side dish is created by careful browning of the rice in butter or oil before the cooking liquid is added.

Wild Rice Dressing

Photograph on page 118

Homestyle Makeover

Each serving contains

	Before	After
Calories	235	165
Fat g.	14	8

Wild rice—with its wonderful nutty flavor and a slightly chewy texture—is not a rice at all. It's a long-grain marsh grass that the Native Americans introduced to the first settlers in the northern Great Lakes region. It is now also grown commercially in several midwestern states and in California.

2 cups fat-free, reduced-sodium chicken broth

¾ cup wild rice

2 tablespoons grated orange peel

1 teaspoon dried thyme

½ cup coarsely chopped almonds

1 tablespoon butter or margarine

1. In a medium saucepan, combine the broth, rice, orange peel, and thyme. Bring to a boil over high heat. Reduce the heat to low. Cover and simmer for 55 to 65 minutes, or until all of the broth is absorbed and the rice is tender. Set aside.

2. Place the almonds in a small skillet. Cook over medium-high heat for 8 to 10 minutes, stirring occasionally, or until golden brown. Watch them carefully because they burn easily. Remove from the skillet. Set aside.

3. When the rice is cooked, add the almonds and butter or margarine. Stir with a fork to mix thoroughly and melt the butter or margarine. Serve immediately.

Makes 6 servings

Per serving: 165 calories | 8 g. fat | 5 mg. cholesterol
229 mg. sodium | 18 g. carbohydrates | 6 g. protein

Cook's Note

• Before cooking wild rice, clean it thoroughly by covering it with cold water and allowing any debris to float to the top, where it can be removed. Be careful not to overcook wild rice or it will become mushy.

Recipes

Sandwiches and Savory Pies

The sandwich is reputed to have been created by an Englishman, the Earl of Sandwich, but it took American ingenuity to elevate this humble meal into a culinary icon.

The mainstay of diners, delis, barbecue pits, and backyard gatherings, classic American sandwiches include Tuna Salad Sandwiches; Club Sandwiches; Bacon, Lettuce, and Tomato Sandwiches; Reuben Sandwiches; Grilled Cheese Sandwiches; Hamburgers; Sloppy Joes; and Corn Dogs as well as cousins like tacos, pizza, and quiche.

The spirit of the American sandwich was captured during the Great Depression by Chic Young in his *Blondie* comic strip. Dagwood Bumstead built edible skyscrapers from cold cuts, lettuce, and condiments placed between as many as five slices of bread, glued together with peanut butter or sewn up with cooked spaghetti. In a case of life imitating art, overstuffed sandwiches have since been known as Dagwood sandwiches.

With some careful substitutions of reduced-fat meats, cheeses, and condiments, sandwiches can continue to be satisfying and convenient as well as healthy.

Chicken Salad Sandwiches

Photograph on page 103

If you have large pieces of leftover cooked chicken, you can slice the chicken rather than chop it. Combine the other ingredients and spread the mixture on the bread, topping it with the chicken slices.

Homestyle Makeover

Each serving contains

	Before	After
Calories	831	500
Fat g.	36	13

¾ **pound boneless, skinless chicken breast, cooked and chopped**

1 **large rib celery, sliced**

1 **small onion, finely chopped**

⅓ **cup reduced-fat mayonnaise**

1 **tablespoon Dijon mustard**

¼ **teaspoon salt**

⅛ **teaspoon ground white pepper**

8 **slices whole-wheat bread, toasted**

4 **large leaves lettuce**

Pickle slices (optional)

1. In a medium bowl, combine the chicken, celery, onion, mayonnaise, mustard, salt, and pepper. Refrigerate, tightly covered, for at least 1 hour.

2. Divide the chicken mixture evenly among 4 of the bread slices. Top with a lettuce leaf and then the remaining bread slices. Cut each sandwich in half diagonally. Garnish with pickles, if using.

Makes 4 servings

Per serving:

500 calories	*13 g. fat*	*110 mg. cholesterol*
784 mg. sodium	*48 g. carbohydrates*	*53 g. protein*

Cook's Note

• If desired, add 1 teaspoon of rinsed, drained capers to the filling.

Egg Salad Sandwiches

Homestyle Makeover

Each serving contains

	Before	After
Calories	649	253
Fat g.	45	5

This recipe came from a reader who had to lower his intake of both fat and cholesterol. By using fat-free mayonnaise-style salad dressing and only two whole eggs, I was able to dramatically reduce both without losing the original taste.

1 large rib celery, finely chopped

1 small onion, finely chopped

¼ cup fat-free mayonnaise-style salad dressing or fat-free mayonnaise

¼ cup Dijon mustard

¼ teaspoon ground black pepper

7 hard-cooked eggs

8 slices rye or white bread

1. In a medium bowl, combine the celery, onion, salad dressing or mayonnaise, mustard, and pepper. Remove the yolks from the eggs. Chop the egg whites and 2 of the yolks. Add to the bowl. Mix well.

2. Spread the egg mixture evenly on 4 bread slices. Top with the remaining slices. Cut each sandwich in half diagonally.

Makes 4 servings

Per serving:	*253 calories*	*5 g. fat*	*106 mg. cholesterol*
	868 mg. sodium	*36 g. carbohydrates*	*14 g. protein*

Cook's Note

• You can use the leftover hard-cooked egg yolks for pet food.

Tuna Salad Sandwiches

This American classic used to be made with tuna packed in oil. It is now almost always made with tuna packed in water for our more calorie-conscious society. It remains among the most frequently ordered sandwiches at lunch counters all across the country.

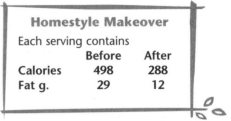

Homestyle Makeover

Each serving contains

	Before	After
Calories	498	288
Fat g.	29	12

½ cup reduced-fat mayonnaise

1 teaspoon lemon juice

¼ teaspoon salt

¼ teaspoon ground black pepper

1 can (6 ounces) water-packed tuna, drained

1 rib celery, finely chopped

1 small onion, finely chopped

½ cup chopped tomato

8 slices whole-grain bread

1. In a medium bowl, combine the mayonnaise, lemon juice, salt, and pepper. Add the tuna, celery, and onion. Mix well. Add the tomato and fold gently into the tuna mixture.

2. Spread the tuna mixture evenly on 4 bread slices. Top with the remaining slices. Cut each sandwich in half diagonally.

Makes 4 servings

Per serving: *288 calories*   *12 g. fat*   *23 mg. cholesterol*
                              777 mg. sodium   *30 g. carbohydrates*   *15 g. protein*

Club Sandwiches

Homestyle Makeover

Each serving contains

	Before	After
Calories	1,270	666
Fat g.	67	26

The origin of this double-decker sandwich differs from one food historian to another, but my favorite version is credited to food writer James Villas. He contends that this sandwich originated on the two-decker railroad club cars, a term first recorded in 1895.

6 **thin slices bread, toasted**

2 **tablespoons mayonnaise**

4 **ounces sliced skinless turkey breast**

4 **leaves lettuce**

1 **tomato, thinly sliced**

4 **slices turkey bacon, cooked and drained**

1. Spread 1 side of each bread slice with 1 teaspoon mayonnaise. Arrange the slices, spread sides up, on a work surface. Place half the turkey and a lettuce leaf on 1 bread slice. Place half the tomato, 2 slices of the bacon, and a lettuce leaf on a second bread slice. Place the bacon-topped slice over the turkey-topped slice. Cover with a third bread slice, mayonnaise side down. Repeat with the remaining ingredients to make another sandwich.

2. To serve, cut each sandwich diagonally into quarters. Secure each quarter with a long toothpick.

Makes 2 servings

Per serving:	666 calories	26 g. fat	76 mg. cholesterol
	978 mg. sodium	78 g. carbohydrates	37 g. protein

Bacon, Lettuce, and Tomato Sandwiches

The bacon, lettuce, and tomato sandwich, or BLT, is an inspired combination. I've revised it using turkey bacon, which is lower in both fat and sodium than pork bacon. I've also cut down on the amount of mayonnaise but insist on the real thing for best flavor.

Homestyle Makeover		
Each serving contains		
	Before	After
Calories	465	267
Fat g.	27	13

2 tablespoons mayonnaise

8 slices whole-wheat bread, toasted

8 slices turkey bacon, cooked and drained

2 large tomatoes, thinly sliced

Ground black pepper

4 large leaves lettuce

1. Spread ¾ teaspoon of the mayonnaise evenly on each bread slice. Arrange 2 bacon slices on each of 4 bread slices. Cover with the tomatoes. Season lightly with the pepper, then top each with a lettuce leaf. Cover each sandwich with the remaining bread slices, mayonnaise side down. Cut each sandwich in half diagonally.

Makes 4 servings

Per serving: *267 calories*   *13 g. fat*   *35 mg. cholesterol*
              674 mg. sodium   *28 g. carbohydrates*   *9 g. protein*

Cook's Note

• For lighter appetites, you can make an open-faced sandwich by eliminating the top bread slice and ending with the tomato on top.

✦ SANDWICHES AND SAVORY PIES ✦

Monte Cristo Sandwich

Homestyle Makeover

Each serving contains

	Before	After
Calories	918	410
Fat g.	44	16

Traditionally fashioned from ham and Swiss cheese, this egg-dipped sandwich is then fried in butter until golden. In this version, I use smoked turkey breast, reduced-fat cheese, liquid egg substitute, and a nonstick skillet to replicate the melting texture and rich flavor without all of the fat.

2 teaspoons butter or margarine, softened

2 slices sourdough bread

2 ounces sliced smoked turkey breast

1 slice (1 ounce) reduced-fat Swiss cheese

¼ cup liquid egg substitute

2 tablespoons fat-free milk

Peach jam (optional)

1. Coat a medium skillet with nonstick spray. Spread the butter or margarine evenly on both sides of the bread. Place the turkey and the Swiss on 1 bread slice. Place the other bread slice on the top.

2. In a shallow bowl or pie pan, combine the egg substitute and milk. Beat the mixture with a fork. Dip the sandwich into the egg mixture, turning until all of the egg mixture is absorbed into the bread. Set aside.

3. Warm the skillet over medium heat until hot enough for drops of water to dance on the surface. Place the sandwich in the skillet and cook for 3 to 5 minutes, or until a rich golden brown. Turn and cook for 3 to 5 minutes, or until a rich golden brown. Cut the sandwich in half diagonally. Serve with a spoonful of peach jam, if using.

Makes 1 serving

Per serving: 410 calories 16 g. fat 51 mg. cholesterol
570 mg. sodium 28 g. carbohydrates 35 g. protein

Muffaletta

The muffaletta was created in 1906 at the Central Grocery in New Orleans, and many devotees of this Louisiana icon think it continues to make the best one in the country. Many of the essential ingredients of this classic sandwich, even the revised version, are quite high in sodium. If you are planning to eat a muffaletta, be sure to drastically reduce your salt intake for the rest of the day.

Photograph on page 104

Homestyle Makeover

Each serving contains

	Before	After
Calories	578	401
Fat g.	34	15

Salad

1 tablespoon extra-virgin olive oil

1 clove garlic, pressed or minced

1 anchovy fillet, mashed, or ½ teaspoon anchovy paste (see note)

9 pimiento-stuffed Spanish olives, chopped

6 kalamata olives, pitted and chopped

½ cup chopped mixed pickled vegetables

1 jar (2 ounces) sliced pimientos

2 tablespoons chopped fresh parsley

1½ teaspoons chopped fresh oregano leaves or ½ teaspoon dried

⅛ teaspoon ground black pepper

Sandwich

1 loaf (1 pound) unsliced round Italian or sourdough bread (8" to 10" diameter)

4 ounces thinly sliced low-fat Italian salami

3 ounces thinly sliced provolone cheese

4 ounces thinly sliced lean smoked ham

1. *To make the salad:* In a medium bowl, combine the oil, garlic, and anchovy. Mix well. Add the Spanish olives, kalamata olives, pickled vegetables, pimientos, parsley, oregano, and pepper. Mix well. Cover tightly and refrigerate for several hours or overnight.

2. *To make the sandwich:* Cut the bread in half horizontally. Remove some of the soft bread from inside of each half, leaving a ½"-thick layer of bread next to the crust.

3. Drain the salad, reserving the marinade. Brush the marinade over the cut sides of the bread. On the bottom half of the bread, layer half of the salad, then the salami, provolone, and ham. Top with the remaining salad. Cover with the top half of the bread.

4. To serve, cut into 6 wedges. Serve immediately.

Makes 6 servings

| *Per serving:* | 401 calories | 15 g. fat | 33 mg. cholesterol |
| | 1,164 mg. sodium | 46 g. carbohydrates | 18 g. protein |

Cook's Notes

• The taste of the anchovy doesn't stand out on its own but is needed to heighten the flavors of the other ingredients.

• You can make fine dried bread crumbs from the leftover bread. Place the bread on a tray. Cover with a cloth and set aside for several days or until dry. Place in a food processor to make fine crumbs. Bread crumbs keep best stored in an airtight container in the freezer.

Reuben Sandwiches

The origin of this sandwich is a matter of debate. Some say it was created by Arthur Reuben, owner of New York's once-famous Reuben's delicatessen. Others credit Reuben Kay, an Omaha grocer, for whipping up the corned beef and sauerkraut special during a poker game.

Homestyle Makeover

Each serving contains

	Before	After
Calories	1,282	343
Fat g.	88	10

⅓ cup fat-free mayonnaise

1 tablespoon chili sauce

8 slices rye bread

1 cup sauerkraut, rinsed and drained

4 slices (1 ounce each) reduced-fat Swiss cheese

4 ounces thinly sliced cooked corned beef, trimmed of all visible fat

1. In a small bowl, combine the mayonnaise and chili sauce. Spread the mixture over 4 bread slices. Top each bread slice with ¼ cup of the sauerkraut, 1 slice of the Swiss, and a quarter of the corned beef. Top with the remaining bread slices.

2. Coat a large nonstick skillet with nonstick spray and place over medium heat. Place sandwiches in the skillet and, away from the heat, coat the tops of each one with the nonstick spray. Cook, uncovered, over low heat for 10 minutes, or until golden brown. Turn and cook for 8 minutes, or until golden brown and the cheese is melted. Cut each sandwich in half diagonally.

Makes 4 servings

Per serving:	343 calories	10 g. fat	39 mg. cholesterol
	1,276 mg. sodium	38 g. carbohydrates	23 g. protein

Grilled Cheese Sandwiches

Photograph on page 30

Photograph on page 30

Homestyle Makeover		
Each serving contains		
	Before	After
Calories	462	274
Fat g.	32	11

For many people, grilled cheese sandwiches conjure up carefree childhood memories because they were among the first foods they learned how to cook for themselves. For variety, you can use Swiss or Monterey Jack and top with a slice of ripe tomato.

4 slices whole-wheat bread

4 ounces thinly sliced reduced-fat Cheddar cheese

1. Coat a large nonstick skillet or griddle with nonstick spray and place over medium heat until hot enough for drops of water to dance on the surface. Place the bread slices on the skillet or griddle and cook until lightly browned on both sides. Add Cheddar slices. Cover and cook for 1 to 2 minutes, or until the cheese melts. Put the slices together to form 2 sandwiches. Cut the sandwiches in half diagonally.

Makes 2 servings

Per serving:	274 calories	11 g. fat	31 mg. cholesterol
	609 mg. sodium	27 g. carbohydrates	20 g. protein

Hamburgers

Photograph on page 105

The classic American hamburger was first served in St. Louis at the Louisiana Purchase Exposition in 1904. Over the years, many variations have become popular, but as far as I'm concerned, lettuce, tomato, and onion are essential.

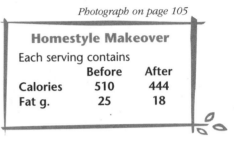

Homestyle Makeover

Each serving contains

	Before	After
Calories	510	444
Fat g.	25	18

1 **pound extra-lean ground beef**	¼ **teaspoon ground black pepper**
½ **small onion, finely chopped**	4 **hamburger buns, toasted**
3 **tablespoons water**	4 **leaves lettuce**
¼ **teaspoon salt**	4 **slices tomato**
	4 **slices onion**

1. Preheat the broiler. Coat the rack of a broiler pan with nonstick spray. Set aside.

2. In a large bowl, combine the beef, chopped onion, water, salt, and pepper. Shape the mixture into 4 patties, each about ¾" thick. Place the patties on the prepared pan.

3. Broil 3" from the heat for 5 to 7 minutes on each side, or until the meat is no longer pink in the center and the juices run clear. Check by inserting a sharp knife into the center of 1 burger.

4. Place the burgers on the buns and top each with the lettuce, tomato, and sliced onion.

Makes 4 servings

Per serving:	444 calories	18 g. fat	52 mg. cholesterol
	989 mg. sodium	51 g. carbohydrates	28 g. protein

Cook's Note

• To make cheeseburgers, 1 minute before the hamburgers are cooked, place a 1-ounce slice of reduced-fat Cheddar cheese on each hamburger. Broil for 1 minute, or until the cheese is melted and the hamburger is cooked.

Sloppy Joes

The name of this popular sandwich, composed of a hamburger bun filled with a cooked ground beef mixture, comes from its sloppy appearance and the fact that it's so messy to eat.

1 large onion, chopped

1 large green bell pepper, chopped

1½ pounds extra-lean ground beef

½ teaspoon ground black pepper

1 cup ketchup

½ cup water

2 tablespoons mustard

1 tablespoon sugar

1 tablespoon cider vinegar

2 teaspoons Worcestershire sauce

8 whole-wheat hamburger buns, toasted

1. In a large nonstick skillet, combine the onion and bell pepper. Cover and cook over low heat for 8 to 10 minutes, or until translucent. Add the beef and black pepper. Stir and cook over medium heat for 5 minutes, or until the meat is no longer pink.

2. Add the ketchup, water, mustard, sugar, vinegar, and Worcestershire sauce to the skillet. Simmer for 10 minutes, or until heated through.

3. Place each bun on a serving plate. Spoon on the mixture and cover.

Makes 8 servings

Per serving:	360 calories	17 g. fat	59 mg. cholesterol
	739 mg. sodium	31 g. carbohydrates	21 g. protein

Barbecued Beef Sandwiches

This recipe, like the recipe for Oven-Barbecued Brisket (page 250), is indeed a pseudo barbecue, but it is a delicious sandwich that can be prepared completely in your kitchen in far less time than traditional barbecue.

3 pounds beef chuck, trimmed of all visible fat

2 cups fat-free, reduced-sodium beef broth

2 onions, sliced

½ teaspoon ground black pepper

1 cup chili sauce

½ cup cider vinegar

½ cup water

1 tablespoon chili powder

⅛–¼ teaspoon hot-pepper sauce

⅛ teaspoon dried thyme

⅛ teaspoon dried basil

1 clove garlic, pressed or minced

2 teaspoons sugar

8 whole-wheat hamburger buns

1. Warm a large pot or a Dutch oven over medium heat until hot enough for drops of water to dance on the surface. Add the beef. Cook for 15 minutes, turning as needed, or until browned on all sides. Add the broth, onions, and pepper. Cover and cook over low heat for 2 to 3 hours, or until the meat is very tender when pierced with a sharp knife.

2. Meanwhile, in a large saucepan, combine the chili sauce, vinegar, water, chili powder, ⅛ teaspoon of the hot-pepper sauce, thyme, basil, garlic, and sugar. Bring to a boil. Reduce the heat to low. Simmer for 10 minutes to blend the flavors.

3. Remove the beef from the pot onto a cutting board and slice it. Transfer the beef slices to the saucepan and heat briefly in the sauce to flavor. Taste and add the remaining ⅛ teaspoon of the hot-pepper sauce, if desired. Toast the buns, if desired. Divide the beef equally on the buns. Spoon the sauce over each and cover.

Makes 8 servings

Per serving: 294 calories   8 g. fat   66 mg. cholesterol
                 566 mg. sodium   24 g. carbohydrates   30 g. protein

Corn Dogs

This remarkable revision turns a deep-fried, high-fat treat into a healthy and satisfying alternative. It takes only 10 minutes to prepare these Corn Dogs, and the kids are usually ready to help. Put out small bowls of mustard and ketchup for dipping.

¾ cup reduced-fat baking mix

¼ cup cornmeal

4 teaspoons sugar

½ cup + 2 tablespoons fat-free milk

2 tablespoons unbleached or all-purpose flour

8 fat-free frankfurters

1. Preheat the oven to 400°F. Coat a baking sheet with nonstick spray. Set aside.

2. In a shallow pan, combine the baking mix, cornmeal, sugar, and milk. Place the flour on a plate.

3. Insert a pointed round wooden skewer into each frankfurter and then roll each frankfurter first in the flour, then in the batter to coat. Place on the prepared baking sheet. Coat each one with nonstick spray.

4. Bake for 5 minutes. Turn the frankfurters over carefully with a spatula. Coat each one with nonstick spray. Bake for 8 minutes, or until golden brown.

Makes 8 servings

Per serving: 206 calories   1 g. fat   0 mg. cholesterol
341 mg. sodium   32 g. carbohydrates   14 g. protein

Cook's Note

• Sturdy, pointed round wooden skewers are sold in many supermarkets. If they are not available, simply bake the frankfurters without them. Serve with a knife and fork, not as finger food.

Bean Burritos

You can serve this wrap sandwich as a vege-tarian entrée or add leftover fish, poultry, or meat to the dish. Using reduced-fat cheese and sour cream lowers the fat greatly but does boost the sodium content. So, when enjoying this sandwich, go easy on your salt intake for the rest of the day.

Homestyle Makeover		
Each serving contains		
	Before	After
Calories	759	482
Fat g.	25	13

2 medium onions, chopped

1 clove garlic, pressed or minced

3 plum tomatoes, chopped

1 can (16 ounces) fat-free refried beans

¼ cup canned diced green chile peppers

½ teaspoon ground cumin

1 teaspoon chili powder

¼ cup chopped fresh cilantro leaves

4 fat-free flour tortillas (10" diameter)

2 cups shredded lettuce

1 cup (4 ounces) shredded reduced-fat Cheddar cheese or Monterey Jack cheese

4 tablespoons reduced-fat sour cream

1. Preheat the oven to 375°F. In a large nonstick skillet, combine the onions and garlic. Cover and cook over low heat for 10 minutes, or until translu-cent. Add the tomatoes and cook for 3 minutes. Add the beans, peppers, cumin, and chili powder. Mix well. Cook, stirring frequently, for 3 min-utes. Remove from the heat and stir in the cilantro.

2. While the bean mixture is cooking, wrap the tortillas in foil. Bake for 10 minutes, or until hot. Carefully unwrap the tortillas. Place on a work surface. Place ½ cup of the bean mixture onto the lower half of each tortilla, folding the bottom of the tortilla up over the beans. Fold both sides of the tortilla into the center and continue to roll up from the bot-tom to the top. Place each burrito, seam side down, on a plate. Con-tinue until all the burritos are filled. Top each burrito with ½ cup of the shredded lettuce, ¼ cup of the Cheddar or Monterey Jack, and 1 table-spoon of the sour cream.

Makes 4 servings

Per serving:	482 calories	13 g. fat	31 mg. cholesterol
	1,453 mg. sodium	67 g. carbohydrates	30 g. protein

Cheddar Cheese Strata

Homestyle Makeover

Each serving contains

	Before	After
Calories	446	314
Fat g.	21	6

I have used Cheddar in this popular brunch dish but feel free to try Monterey Jack, Swiss, or a blend of several cheeses you might have on hand. I've called for liquid egg substitute, rather than whole eggs, to cut the cholesterol and fat. Fat-free milk also reduces calories and fat.

12 slices whole-wheat bread, crusts removed and cut into halves

2 cups (8 ounces) shredded reduced-fat Cheddar cheese

3 cups fat-free milk

1 cup liquid egg substitute

1½ teaspoons dried thyme

¾ teaspoon dried sage

¼ teaspoon ground black pepper

¼ teaspoon salt

1. Coat a 13" × 9" baking dish with nonstick spray. Line the dish with half the bread slices, overlapping to make them fit. Top with half the Cheddar. In a medium bowl, combine the milk, egg substitute, thyme, sage, pepper, and salt. Pour half over the bread and cheese in the dish. Repeat with another layer of bread, cheese, and milk mixture. Cover the dish tightly with plastic wrap. Refrigerate for several hours or overnight. Remove from the refrigerator 2 hours before baking.

2. Preheat the oven to 325°F. Bake for 40 minutes, or until a knife inserted in the center comes out clean. Allow to stand for 5 minutes before cutting.

Makes 6 servings

Per serving:	314 calories	6 g. fat	11 mg. cholesterol
	815 mg. sodium	32 g. carbohydrates	23 g. protein

Cook's Note

• For a heartier strata, scatter 1 cup chopped cooked poultry or meat over the first layer of bread.

Crab Torta

If you're fortunate enough to have leftovers of this wonderful layered sandwich, it makes an exceptional brown-bag lunch. Store portions in resealable plastic bags in the refrigerator or freezer. Pop a serving of frozen Crab Torta into a lunch bag and it will be thawed and ready to eat by midday.

Homestyle Makeover

Each serving contains

	Before	After
Calories	479	218
Fat g.	13	6

1 loaf (1 pound) frozen bread dough, thawed

2 tablespoons fresh thyme leaves or 2 teaspoons dried

1 tablespoon extra-virgin olive oil

½ pound mushrooms, sliced

1 tablespoon chopped onion

1 clove garlic, pressed or minced

¼ teaspoon salt

¼ teaspoon ground black pepper

2 tablespoons chopped fresh dill or 2 teaspoons dried dillweed

4 small zucchini, thinly sliced

1 bag (6 ounces) prewashed baby spinach leaves

¾ cup (3 ounces) shredded reduced-fat mozzarella cheese

½ cup (2 ounces) shredded reduced-fat Monterey Jack cheese

2 cans (6 ounces each) white crabmeat, rinsed and drained

1. Preheat the oven 375°F. Coat a 10" springform pan with nonstick spray. Set aside.

2. Allow the bread dough to rise, until doubled in size. Transfer the dough to a floured surface. Sprinkle with thyme and roll out to a 20" circle. Place the dough in the prepared pan, letting the edges drape over the sides. Set aside.

3. Heat the oil in a large skillet over medium heat. Add the mushrooms, onion, garlic, salt, and pepper. Cook, stirring frequently, for 5 minutes, or until tender. Stir in the dill. Transfer to a bowl. Set aside.

4. Add the zucchini to the skillet and cook, stirring frequently, for 8 minutes, or until tender.

5. Spoon half of the mushroom mixture onto the dough. Top with half the zucchini, half the spinach leaves, half the mozzarella, half the Monterey Jack, and half the crabmeat. Repeat the layers with the remaining ingredients. Bring the dough together over the top; pinch the edges to seal, leaving a small vent for steam to escape. Coat the top with nonstick spray. Bake for 45 to 50 minutes, or until golden brown and crusty.

6. To serve, cut into wedges. Serve warm or at room temperature.

Makes 10 servings

| Per serving: | 218 calories | 6 g. fat | 25 mg. cholesterol |
| | 509 mg. sodium | 29 g. carbohydrates | 14 g. protein |

Quesadillas

Quesadillas are to the Southwest what grilled cheese sandwiches are to the rest of the country. Rather than cooking them in a skillet or on a grill as is usually done, in this recipe I have used the oven so that you can make them all at once, which is easier if you are entertaining.

Homestyle Makeover

Each serving contains

	Before	After
Calories	251	246
Fat g.	14	6

8 fat-free flour tortillas (10" diameter)

2 cups (8 ounces) shredded reduced-fat Monterey Jack cheese

1 can (4 ounces) diced green chile peppers, drained

½ small onion, finely chopped

¼ teaspoon ground cumin

¼ teaspoon salt

1. Preheat the oven to 300°F. Coat the bottom of a broiler pan with nonstick spray. Set aside.

2. Wrap the tortillas in foil. Bake for 15 minutes, or until they are warm and pliable.

3. Remove the tortillas from the oven and increase the temperature to 350°F. Place the tortillas on a work surface. Sprinkle each tortilla with ¼ cup of the Monterey Jack. In a small bowl, combine the peppers, onion, cumin, and salt. Divide the pepper mixture among the tortillas, spreading it evenly over the cheese. Fold the tortillas in half and place them in the prepared pan. Cover tightly and bake for 10 to 12 minutes, or until the cheese melts. Remove the cover and turn on the broiler. Broil 4" from the heat for 1½ minutes per side, or until lightly browned.

Makes 8 servings

Per serving:			
	246 calories	6 g. fat	15 mg. cholesterol
	716 mg. sodium	36 g. carbohydrates	13 g. protein

Quiche Lorraine

During the 1960s and 1970s, this French egg-cheese tart was considered the epitome of gourmet. Recipes for it started to appear, in one form or another, in practically every cook-book. With judicious use of reduced-fat dairy products, I have kept the classic taste but reduced the fat dramatically.

Homestyle Makeover

Each serving contains

	Before	After
Calories	578	292
Fat g.	50	15

1 cup (4 ounces) shredded reduced-fat Swiss cheese

½ onion, finely chopped

8 slices turkey bacon, crisply cooked, drained, and crumbled

1 frozen 9" pie crust, thawed

2 eggs

4 egg whites

1 can (12 ounces) fat-free evaporated milk

¼ teaspoon salt

¼ teaspoon ground black pepper

⅛ teaspoon ground red pepper

1. Preheat the oven to 425°F.

2. Scatter the Swiss, onion, and bacon evenly over the bottom of the pie crust.

3. Add the eggs and egg whites to a medium bowl. Beat lightly. Add the milk, salt, black pepper, and red pepper. Mix well. Pour into the pie crust.

4. Bake for 15 minutes. Reduce the oven temperature to 300°F. Bake for 30 to 35 minutes, or until a knife inserted in the center comes out clean. Remove from the oven. Allow to stand for 10 minutes.

5. To serve, cut into wedges.

Makes 6 servings

Per serving:	292 calories	15 g. fat	103 mg. cholesterol
	671 mg. sodium	19 g. carbohydrates	19 g. protein

Recipes

Salmon, Shrimp, Crab, and More

From sea to shining sea—and all the lakes and rivers in between— the lean protein in fish and shellfish has nourished Americans since colonial times. New England clams and lobsters; Chesapeake Bay blue crabs; Mississippi catfish; Rocky Mountain trout; Gulf of Mexico shrimp, oysters, and crayfish; Northwest Dungeness crabs; and Olympia oysters inspired fine regional dishes such as Cioppino, Crab Cakes, Fried Shrimp, Southern Fried Catfish, Jambalaya, Lobster Thermidor, New England Clambake, and more.

With the advent of commercial canning, fish moved beyond the realm of special occasion dinners to become an important ingredient in daily meals. Salmon and tuna starred in easy, homestyle main dishes like Tuna Noodle Casserole, Salmon Loaf, and Salmon Croquettes.

By modifying some high-fat ingredients and changing to leaner cooking methods, I've made classic fish and shellfish dishes more appealing than ever.

Fish and Fries with Tartar Sauce

Originally this British street fare, called fish and chips, was served on folded newspapers with malt vinegar for dipping. On this side of the Atlantic, the combination of deep-fried fish and potatoes, served with tartar sauce, has become extremely popular. Fitness-conscious folks will appreciate this oven-fried method, which drastically cuts the fat.

Homestyle Makeover

Each serving contains

	Before	After
Calories	417	266
Fat g.	18	1

Fish and Fries

- 1 pound russet potatoes, very thinly sliced
- 2 slices whole-wheat bread, torn into pieces
- ½ teaspoon ground black pepper
- ½ cup unbleached or all-purpose flour
- 2 egg whites
- 4 sole or scrod fillets (4 ounces each)

Sauce

- ¼ cup fat-free mayonnaise
- ¼ cup fat-free sour cream
- 1 tablespoon sweet pickle relish
- 1 tablespoon finely chopped onion
- 1 teaspoon lemon juice
- Pinch of ground red pepper

1. *To make the fish and fries:* Preheat the oven to 450°F. Lightly coat 2 baking sheets with nonstick spray. Arrange the potatoes on 1 sheet in a single layer. Coat lightly with nonstick spray. Bake for 8 minutes.

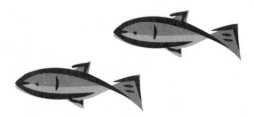

2. Meanwhile, combine the bread and pepper in a blender or food processor. Blend or process to form coarse bread crumbs. Pour the mixture on a plate. Put the flour on another plate. Put the egg whites in a shallow bowl and beat lightly with a fork.

3. One at a time, dip each fillet into the flour to coat both sides. Dip into the egg whites, allowing any excess to drip off. Dip both sides into the bread-and-pepper mixture, pressing gently to coat. Place the fish on the reserved baking sheet.

4. Remove the potatoes from the oven and turn them over. Return the potatoes to the oven, along with the fish. Bake for 8 to 10 minutes, or until the potatoes and fish are browned and the fillets are opaque in the center. Check by inserting a sharp knife into the center of 1 fillet.

5. *To make the sauce:* In a small bowl, combine the mayonnaise, sour cream, relish, onion, lemon juice, and red pepper. Stir to mix well.

6. To serve, place a fish fillet and a quarter of the potatoes on each of 4 plates. Spoon the tartar sauce on top or on the side.

Makes 4 servings

Per serving:	*266 calories*	*1 g. fat*	*0 mg. cholesterol*
	318 mg. sodium	*44 g. carbohydrates*	*20 g. protein*

Southern Fried Catfish

Catfish gets its name from the whiskers that hang down around its mouth. Most catfish available in supermarkets are farm raised. In the South, frying is the most popular cooking method for catfish, but this baked version duplicates the crispy exterior without all the fat.

Homestyle Makeover

Each serving contains

	Before	After
Calories	547	318
Fat g.	33	6

1 cup buttermilk

½ teaspoon hot-pepper sauce

¼ teaspoon salt

4 skinless catfish fillets (6 ounces each)

1 cup white or yellow cornmeal

1 large lemon, quartered

1 tablespoon chopped fresh parsley (optional)

1. In a large glass or ceramic dish, combine the buttermilk, hot-pepper sauce, and salt. Add the fillets and turn to coat evenly. Cover and refrigerate for several hours or overnight.

2. Put the cornmeal on a plate. Remove the catfish from the marinade and dip it in the cornmeal, turning to coat both sides of the fillets. Coat a large skillet with nonstick spray and place over medium heat, until it is hot enough for drops of water to dance on the surface. Place the fillets in the skillet. Cook for 4 to 5 minutes on each side, or until golden brown and opaque in the center. Check by inserting a sharp knife into the center of 1 fillet.

3. To serve, place each fillet and 1 lemon wedge on a plate. Sprinkle with parsley, if using.

Makes 4 servings

Per serving:

318 calories	6 g. fat	101 mg. cholesterol
273 mg. sodium	33 g. carbohydrates	33 g. protein

Pan-Fried Trout

By toasting the almonds instead of sautéing them in butter, and by reducing the butter used to fry the trout, I was able to significantly limit the total fat in this dish. If you do not desire the classic presentation of serving the whole trout, remove both the head and tail before cooking.

¼ cup chopped or slivered almonds

2 whole freshwater trout (8 ounces each), cleaned and trimmed

2 tablespoons snipped fresh sorrel or basil leaves

¼ teaspoon salt

¼ teaspoon ground black pepper

1 tablespoon butter or margarine

2 tablespoons finely chopped fresh parsley

1 lemon, quartered

1. Put the almonds in a large skillet and cook, stirring frequently, over medium heat for about 3 minutes, or until lightly browned. Place nuts in a small bowl and set aside. Reserve the skillet.

2. Stuff the cavity of each trout with 1 tablespoon of sorrel or basil. Sprinkle with the salt and pepper. Melt the butter or margarine in the skillet over medium heat. Add the trout and cook for 8 to 10 minutes, turning once or twice for even cooking, or until golden brown and opaque. Check by inserting a sharp knife into the thickest part of the fish next to the backbone.

3. To serve, sprinkle the fish with the almonds and parsley. Place 2 lemon wedges on the side of each serving.

Makes 2 servings

Per serving: 408 calories   26 g. fat   106 mg. cholesterol
426 mg. sodium   12 g. carbohydrates   38 g. protein

Stuffed Fillet of Sole

This is a great dish for a dinner party because it can be made in the morning or even the night before—up to the point of baking—and refrigerated until you plan to bake and serve it.

Homestyle Makeover

Each serving contains

	Before	After
Calories	230	150
Fat g.	11	3

Sauce

1 tablespoon butter or margarine

2½ tablespoons unbleached or all-purpose flour

2 cups fat-free milk

¼ cup sherry or 2 tablespoons sherry vinegar

Fish

½ onion, finely chopped

½ pound mushrooms, thinly sliced

1 tablespoon finely chopped fresh parsley

8 sole fillets (2 pounds)

1 teaspoon paprika

½ teaspoon salt

½ teaspoon ground white pepper

½ cup (2 ounces) shredded reduced-fat Cheddar cheese

Paprika

1. *To make the sauce:* Melt the butter or margarine in a heavy saucepan over medium heat. Add the flour and cook, stirring constantly, for 3 minutes. Do not brown. Add the milk, whisking constantly, to dissolve the flour mixture. Reduce the heat to low. Cook for about 15 minutes, stirring occasionally, or until thickened. Remove from the heat. Add the sherry or sherry vinegar. Stir to mix. Set aside.

2. *To make the fish:* Preheat the oven to 375°F. Coat a 13" × 9" baking dish with nonstick spray. Set aside.

3. Coat a large nonstick skillet with nonstick spray. Add the onion. Cover and cook over low heat for about 10 minutes, or until the onion is translucent. If needed, add a few teaspoons of water to the skillet to prevent the onion from scorching. Add the mushrooms and parsley. Cook, stirring frequently, for 5 to 7 minutes, or until the mushrooms are tender.

4. Lay the sole fillets on a tray or work surface. Sprinkle both sides evenly with the paprika, salt, and pepper. Spoon the mushroom mixture equally onto the center of each fillet. Fold the end over the filling and fold again to form a little roll. Fasten the end securely with a toothpick. Arrange the stuffed fillets in the prepared baking dish.

5. Spoon the reserved sauce over the stuffed fillets. Sprinkle with the Cheddar. Sprinkle lightly with paprika. Bake for 20 minutes, or until bubbly and the fish is opaque. Check by inserting a sharp knife into the center of 1 fillet.

6. To serve, place each fillet and some of the sauce onto a plate. Carefully remove the toothpicks.

Makes 8 servings

| *Per serving:* | 150 calories | 3 g. fat | 6 mg. cholesterol |
| | 317 mg. sodium | 7 g. carbohydrates | 20 g. protein |

Teriyaki Swordfish Steaks

Mild in flavor and meaty in texture, swordfish has become the surrogate steak for meat lovers who are trying to eat more fish. Its firm texture really takes to broiling or grilling, which reinforces the steak resemblance.

Homestyle Makeover

Each serving contains

	Before	After
Calories	270	210
Fat g.	14	6

1 can (6 ounces) unsweetened pineapple juice

¼ cup dry sherry or 2 tablespoons sherry vinegar

2 tablespoons reduced-sodium soy sauce

1 tablespoon rice wine vinegar or white wine vinegar

2 teaspoons toasted sesame oil

1½ teaspoons sugar

1 clove garlic, pressed or minced

1 pound swordfish steaks

1. In a large glass or ceramic dish, combine the pineapple juice, sherry or sherry vinegar, soy sauce, vinegar, sesame oil, sugar, and garlic. Whisk to mix and to dissolve the sugar. Add the fish. Cover tightly and place in the refrigerator for 2 hours, turning occasionally to evenly marinate.

2. Preheat the broiler. Coat a broiler pan with nonstick spray. Remove the fish from the marinade and place it on the prepared broiler pan. Pour the marinade into a saucepan and set aside. Coat the fish with nonstick spray. Broil 4" from the heat for 4 to 5 minutes per side, or until the fish is opaque. Check by inserting a sharp knife into the center of 1 steak.

3. Meanwhile, bring the reserved marinade to a boil over medium heat. Boil for 3 minutes. Remove from the heat.

4. To serve, pour the sauce over the fish.

Makes 4 servings

Per serving: 210 calories   6 g. fat   44 mg. cholesterol
346 mg. sodium   8 g. carbohydrates   24 g. protein

Poached Salmon

By slightly reducing the portion size and eliminating the butter, I was able to reduce the total fat and let the rich natural flavor of the salmon come through. Thin cucumber slices and fresh sprigs of dill make pretty garnishes for this salmon dish.

Homestyle Makeover

Each serving contains

	Before	After
Calories	322	239
Fat g.	12	6

1½ cups cold water

1 cup dry white wine or nonalcoholic white wine

2 scallions, thinly sliced

8 black peppercorns

4 salmon steaks, ¾" thick (6 ounces each)

1. In a large, deep skillet, combine the water, wine, scallions, and peppercorns. Arrange the salmon steaks in a single layer in the skillet and place over medium-high heat until the liquid starts to simmer. Reduce the heat to low. Cover and cook for 5 to 8 minutes, or until the fish flakes and is opaque in the center. Check by inserting a sharp knife into the center of 1 steak next to the bone. Using a slotted spatula, carefully remove the salmon steaks to a platter. Serve hot or cold (see note).

Makes 4 servings

Per serving: 239 calories | 6 g. fat | 88 mg. cholesterol
121 mg. sodium | 1 g. carbohydrates | 34 g. protein

Cook's Notes

• Use salmon fillets for this dish if you prefer fewer bones.

• To serve the salmon cold, refrigerate, tightly covered, for several hours before serving.

Salmon Mousse

This pretty mousse can be served on low-fat crackers as an appetizer, over greens as a salad, or as a chilled entrée in the summer. I like it over cold pasta, rice, or couscous, surrounded by cut fresh fruits or vegetables.

Homestyle Makeover

Each serving contains

	Before	After
Calories	299	233
Fat g.	22	5

1 envelope (¼ ounce) unflavored gelatin

2 tablespoons cold water

¼ cup boiling water

1 can (12 ounces) fat-free evaporated milk

½ onion, finely chopped

2 teaspoons Worcestershire sauce

1 can (14¾ ounces) salmon, drained and squeezed dry

¼ cup fat-free, reduced-sodium chicken broth or clam juice

2 tablespoons lemon juice

¼ teaspoon ground black pepper

¼ teaspoon liquid smoke

1. In a small bowl, combine the gelatin and cold water. Add the boiling water; stir until the gelatin is completely dissolved. Add the evaporated milk and stir to mix well. Cover tightly and refrigerate for about 1 hour, or until partially set.

2. Coat a 6-cup mold with nonstick spray. Set aside. In a medium nonstick skillet, combine the onion and Worcestershire sauce. Cover and cook over low heat for 8 to 10 minutes, or until the onion is translucent.

3. In a blender or food processor, combine the gelatin mixture, onion, salmon, broth or clam juice, lemon juice, pepper, and liquid smoke. Blend or process until smooth. Spoon into the prepared mold. It should fill the mold to the top. Cover tightly and carefully place the filled mold in the refrigerator for at least 3 hours, or until the mousse is set.

4. To serve, unmold the mousse on a serving platter.

Makes 5 servings

Per serving:	233 calories	5 g. fat	48 mg. cholesterol
	683 mg. sodium	9 g. carbohydrates	37 g. protein

Salmon Croquettes

Photograph on page 108

Homestyle Makeover

Each serving contains

	Before	After
Calories	443	394
Fat g.	19	14

Croquettes are made by combining finely chopped fish, poultry, or meat with a rich white sauce and then forming the mixture into cylinders or patties that are deep-fried. I have cut the fat by using mashed potatoes as a binder. I also cook the croquettes in a small amount of oil in a nonstick skillet.

2 cups mashed potatoes or frozen mashed potatoes, thawed

1 can (14¾ ounces) salmon, drained and flaked

4 scallions, finely chopped

1 tablespoon lemon juice

½ teaspoon ground black pepper

Pinch of ground red pepper

1 egg

2 tablespoons cold water

3 slices fresh whole-wheat bread, crumbled

1 tablespoon vegetable oil

1. In a large bowl, combine the potatoes, salmon, scallions, lemon juice, black pepper, and red pepper. Form into 8 patties, each one 2½" in diameter and 1" thick.

2. To a shallow bowl, add the egg and water. Beat lightly with a fork to blend. Put the bread crumbs on a plate. Dip the patties in the egg mixture, then the bread crumbs, pressing lightly to coat.

3. Warm the oil in a large nonstick skillet over medium heat until hot enough for drops of water to dance on the surface. Put the croquettes into the skillet. Cook, turning frequently, for 6 minutes, or until golden brown.

Makes 4 servings

Per serving:	394 calories	14 g. fat	111 mg. cholesterol
	882 mg. sodium	38 g. carbohydrates	28 g. protein

Salmon Loaf

I'm always torn on whether to serve this loaf hot or cold. It's a satisfying hot main dish served with mashed potatoes and fresh broccoli or asparagus. But it's also a terrific cold sandwich spread on toasted rye bread. The only sensible solution is to make two loaves and enjoy it both ways.

Homestyle Makeover

Each serving contains

	Before	After
Calories	450	330
Fat g.	25	11

1 egg

2 egg whites

1 can (16 ounces) salmon, drained and squeezed dry

1 cup 2% milk

2 tablespoons finely chopped green bell pepper

2 tablespoons lemon juice

1 tablespoon finely chopped onion

1 teaspoon Worcestershire sauce

½ teaspoon salt

¼ teaspoon ground black pepper

1. Preheat the oven to 350°F. Coat a 9" × 5" loaf pan with nonstick spray. Set aside.

2. In a large bowl, beat the egg and egg whites lightly with a fork. Add the salmon, milk, bell pepper, lemon juice, onion, Worcestershire sauce, salt, and pepper. Mix well. Spoon into the loaf pan. Bake for 35 to 40 minutes, or until firm.

3. To serve, cut into 4 pieces.

Makes 4 servings

Per serving:	*330 calories*	*11 g. fat*	*227 mg. cholesterol*
	501 mg. sodium	*4 g. carbohydrates*	*50 g. protein*

Cook's Note

• You can replace the salmon with water-packed tuna.

Halibut Amandine with Dill Sauce

Homestyle Makeover

Each serving contains

	Before	After
Calories	481	199
Fat g.	42	7

If possible, make the dill sauce at least 1 day ahead to develop the flavor. You may even want to double the recipe for the sauce because it is also good served cold with poultry and seafood or as a dip for vegetables.

1 cup fat-free plain yogurt or sour cream

½ cup fat-free mayonnaise

1½ teaspoons dried dillweed

2¾ teaspoons dried tarragon

¼ teaspoon salt

¼ cup almonds, finely chopped

1 pound halibut fillets

¼ cup lemon juice

¼ teaspoon salt

1. In a medium bowl, combine the yogurt or sour cream, mayonnaise, dillweed, ¾ teaspoon tarragon, and salt. Set aside.

2. Preheat the oven to 350°F. Coat an 11" × 7" baking dish with nonstick spray. Set aside.

3. Place the almonds in a small baking dish. Bake for 7 to 8 minutes, or until golden brown, stirring occasionally. Watch them carefully so they don't burn. Set aside.

4. Place the fish in the prepared baking dish. Sprinkle evenly with the lemon juice, the remaining 2 teaspoons tarragon, and salt. Cover and bake for 15 minutes, or until the fish has turned opaque. Check by inserting a sharp knife into the center of 1 fillet.

5. Preheat the broiler. Pour off and discard all excess liquid in the baking dish. Spoon the sauce evenly over the fish. Broil about 4" from the heat for 1 minute, or until the sauce starts to bubble. Do not brown.

6. To serve, carefully place on a serving platter. Cut into 4 portions. Sprinkle with the almonds.

Makes 4 servings

Per serving:

199 calories	*7 g. fat*	*36 mg. cholesterol*
585 mg. sodium	*13 g. carbohydrates*	*21 g. protein*

Tuna Noodle Casserole

Photograph on page 109

Casseroles became popular during the Great Depression because they were economical. Their appeal continued into the 1940s because they were convenient. With more women working outside the home during World War II, a one-dish meal that could be prepared ahead of time and reheated for supper was indeed a blessing.

Homestyle Makeover

Each serving contains

	Before	After
Calories	1,038	622
Fat g.	41	14

8 ounces no-yolk noodles (see note)

1 tablespoon butter or margarine

4 ounces mushrooms, thinly sliced

1 can (10¾ ounces) fat-free, reduced-sodium condensed cream of mushroom soup

1 cup (4 ounces) shredded reduced-fat Monterey Jack cheese

8 ounces fat-free plain yogurt

½ cup sliced scallions

½ teaspoon ground black pepper

¼ teaspoon celery seeds

¼ teaspoon crushed red-pepper flakes

1 package (16 ounces) frozen broccoli florets, thawed (see note)

1 can (12 ounces) water-packed chunk light tuna, rinsed, drained, and flaked

½ cup crushed reduced-fat snack crackers

¼ cup (1 ounce) grated Parmesan cheese

1. Preheat the oven to 350°F. Coat a 2½ quart or 13" × 9" baking dish with nonstick spray. Set aside.

2. In a large covered pot, bring water to a boil over high heat. Add the noodles and cook according to the package directions. Set aside.

3. Meanwhile, melt the butter or margarine in a large skillet over medium heat. Add the mushrooms and cook, stirring frequently, for about 4 minutes, or until tender. Add the soup, Monterey Jack, yogurt, scallions, black pepper, celery seeds, and red-pepper flakes. Mix well. Add the broccoli, tuna, and noodles. Fold to coat with the sauce. Spoon into the prepared baking dish.

4. In a small bowl, combine the crackers and Parmesan. Sprinkle evenly over the noodle mixture. Bake for 30 to 35 minutes, or until bubbly and lightly browned.

Makes 4 servings

Per serving: *622 calories*   *14 g. fat*   *52 mg. cholesterol*
                       947 mg. sodium   *76 g. carbohydrates*   *47 g. protein*

Cook's Notes

• You can replace the noodles with macaroni, shells, corkscrews, wheels, or any other pasta shape you like.

• You can replace the frozen broccoli with 2½ cups of blanched fresh broccoli or other vegetables.

Cioppino

Cioppino was created in San Francisco by a homesick Italian fisherman from Genoa, Italy, who combined a rich tomato sauce with local seafood. I always have bibs for my guests when I serve Cioppino at home because getting the crab out of their shells is a messy, fun task.

Homestyle Makeover		
Each serving contains		
	Before	After
Calories	468	177
Fat g.	8	3

2 teaspoons olive oil

2 cloves garlic, pressed or minced

1 onion, chopped

1 green bell pepper, chopped

8 scallions, chopped

½ cup finely chopped fresh parsley

1 can (14½ ounces) diced tomatoes

1 can (8 ounces) tomato sauce

1 bottle (8 ounces) clam juice

1 cup dry white wine or nonalcoholic white wine

1 bay leaf

¼ teaspoon dried thyme

¼ teaspoon dried oregano

¼ teaspoon ground black pepper

⅛ teaspoon dried rosemary, crushed

4 medium crab legs or 2 cups lump crabmeat

12 clams

¾ pound peeled and deveined medium shrimp

1. Heat the oil in a large pot or Dutch oven over medium heat. Add the garlic and cook until it sizzles. Add the onion, bell pepper, and scallions. Cook, stirring frequently, for 5 minutes, or until the onion is translucent. Add the parsley, tomatoes (with juice), tomato sauce, clam juice, wine, bay leaf, thyme, oregano, black pepper, and rosemary. Mix well. Cover the pot and bring to a boil. Reduce the heat to low and simmer for 1 hour to blend the flavors. Remove and discard the bay leaf.

2. Break the crab legs into pieces. Scrub the clams with a brush, making sure all of the sand is removed.

3. Add the crab legs or crabmeat, clams, and shrimp. Cover and cook for about 5 minutes, or until the shrimp turn pink and the clams are open. If the shrimp turn pink before the clams open, remove them from the pot and set aside until the clams do open. Discard any unopened clams.

4. To serve, ladle the liquid into 6 bowls. Divide the crab, clams, and shrimp equally among the bowls.

Makes 6 servings

Per serving: *177 calories*   *3 g. fat*   *72 mg. cholesterol*
                  1,119 mg. sodium   *10 g. carbohydrates*   *24 g. protein*

Cook's Notes

• This dish is ideal for entertaining because the cooked tomato mixture can be cooled, covered, and refrigerated for up to 1 day before cooking the seafood.

• If you prefer a dish that's easier to eat, use lump crabmeat.

• For a less expensive dish, replace the shellfish with chunks of halibut or snapper.

• For a lower-sodium dish, use low-sodium tomato products.

Seafood Gumbo

Gumbo *is the African word for okra, a vegetable that is often used to thicken this delicious New Orleans stew. There are almost as many versions of this dish as there are cooks who make it. In fact, every old family in New Orleans claims to have the real recipe.*

Homestyle Makeover

Each serving contains

	Before	After
Calories	307	205
Fat g.	8	5

2 tablespoons vegetable oil

⅓ cup unbleached or all-purpose flour

1 onion, chopped

1 green bell pepper, chopped

3 cloves garlic, pressed or minced

¼ cup chopped fresh parsley

4 cups fat-free, reduced-sodium chicken broth

6 tomatoes, chopped

2 cans (8 ounces each) tomato sauce

1 teaspoon ground black pepper

2 bay leaves

1 ounce fresh okra, sliced, or 1 package (16 ounces) frozen okra, thawed

1 cup fresh crabmeat or 2 cans (6 ounces each) lump crabmeat, rinsed and drained

¾ pound cooked, peeled, and deveined shrimp

1. Heat the oil in a large pot over medium-low heat. Add the flour and cook, stirring constantly for 10 to 12 minutes, or until browned. Add the onion, bell pepper, garlic, and parsley. Cook, stirring frequently, for 5 minutes, or until the onion is translucent. Add the broth, stirring to dissolve the flour. Add the tomatoes, tomato sauce, black pepper, and bay leaves. Stir and bring to a boil. Reduce the heat to low. Simmer for 1 hour.

2. Coat a large nonstick skillet with nonstick spray. Place over medium heat until hot enough for drops of water to dance on the surface. Add the okra and cook, stirring frequently, for about 5 minutes, or until tender. Add the okra to the pot. Stir to mix. Add the crab and shrimp. Stir to mix. Cook for 4 to 5 minutes, or until the crabmeat and shrimp are heated through. Remove and discard the bay leaves.

Makes 8 servings

Per serving:	205 calories	5 g. fat	116 mg. cholesterol
	887 mg. sodium	19 g. carbohydrates	21 g. protein

Crab Cakes

Photograph on page 110

Homestyle Makeover

Each serving contains

	Before	After
Calories	497	129
Fat g.	33	1

Old Bay Seasoning is the secret to the flavor of these Chesapeake Bay crab cakes. The 11-spice blend developed by Gustav Brunn in the 1930s consists of celery seeds, mustard seeds, pepper, bay leaves, paprika, allspice, ginger, mace, cloves, cardamom, and cinnamon.

¾ **pound lump crabmeat, cleaned and flaked**

⅔ **cup fat-free mayonnaise**

2 **tablespoons finely chopped onion**

2 **tablespoons finely chopped celery**

2 **tablespoons Dijon mustard**

1 **tablespoon lemon juice**

1 **teaspoon Old Bay Seasoning**

1½ **teaspoons Worcestershire sauce**

¼ **teaspoon salt**

¼ **teaspoon hot-pepper sauce**

4 **slices fresh bread, crumbled**

2 **egg whites**

1. In a large bowl, combine the crabmeat, mayonnaise, onion, celery, mustard, lemon juice, Old Bay Seasoning, Worcestershire sauce, salt, hot-pepper sauce, and half of the bread crumbs. Toss lightly to mix.

2. Beat the egg whites on high in a mixing bowl, for 1 to 2 minutes, or until soft peaks form. Fold into the crabmeat mixture. Form 12 patties (about 2" wide and about ½" thick). Place the remaining bread crumbs on a large plate. Carefully press each patty into the crumbs, coating both sides. Place the breaded patties on a large plate. Cover the plate and refrigerate for 1 hour.

3. Place a large nonstick skillet over medium heat until hot enough for drops of water to dance on the surface. Coat both sides of the crab cakes with nonstick spray. Place the crab cakes in the skillet and cook for 3 minutes on each side, or until browned on the outside and hot in the middle. Check by inserting a sharp knife into the center of 1 cake.

Makes 6 servings

Per serving: 129 calories / 1 g. fat / 51 mg. cholesterol / 605 mg. sodium / 13 g. carbohydrates / 14 g. protein

New England Clambake

Photograph on page 111

Native Americans showed the Pilgrims how to steam seafood and corn in a large pit that was layered with hot stones and seaweed, which to this day is called a New England Clambake. This simplified method uses a pot, instead of the pit, and corn husks, instead of the seaweed, for a clambake in your kitchen.

Homestyle Makeover
Each serving contains

	Before	After
Calories	418	347
Fat g.	4	3

4 **ears corn on the cob**

1 **tablespoon Kosher or canning salt**

2 **dozen littleneck clams**

2 **tablespoons cornmeal**

2 **live lobsters (about 1 pound each)**

4 **red new potatoes, halved**

1. Remove the husks from the ears of corn and discard the silks. Cut the ears in half. Place the husks and the ears of corn in a large bowl. Cover with cold water and sprinkle with the salt. Allow to soak for 1 hour.

2. Meanwhile, scrub the clams with a stiff brush under cold running water to remove all sand. Half fill a large bowl with cold water, stir in the cornmeal, and add the clams. Add more water if needed to cover the clams. Allow them to stand for 30 minutes to disgorge any sand inside. Drain and rinse well.

3. Meanwhile, fill a steamer pot or a large Dutch oven with water. Cover and bring to a boil over high heat. Rinse the lobsters with cold running water and place them in the pot. Cover and return to a boil. Boil for 6 to 7 minutes, or until the lobster shells turn bright red. Remove the lobsters from the pot and set aside. Reserve 6 cups of the cooking liquid. Discard the rest or save for another use.

4. Place a steamer rack or basket in the bottom of the pot. Drain the corn and husks. Cover the rack or basket with half of the corn husks. Place the corn and potatoes on top of the husks. Add the reserved liquid and top with the remaining husks. Bring to a boil over high heat. Reduce the heat to low and simmer, covered, for 20 minutes.

5. While the potatoes and corn are cooking, cut the lobster in half length-wise. Hold the lobster halves under running water to clean and remove the stomach and entrails.

6. During the last 5 minutes of cooking the corn and potatoes, place the cleaned lobster halves and clams in the pot on top of the husks. Cover and simmer for 5 to 8 minutes, or until the clams open. Discard any unopened clams before serving.

7. To serve, place a lobster half in each of 4 large shallow bowls. Arrange 6 of the clams around the lobster half. Remove and discard the corn husks. Add the corn and potatoes to the bowls. Strain the cooking liquid. Pour it into the bowls or into mugs to serve on the side.

Makes 4 servings

Per serving:			
	347 calories	*3 g. fat*	*83 mg. cholesterol*
	354 mg. sodium	*50 g. carbohydrates*	*33 g. protein*

Cook's Note

• To double the recipe, just create another clambake in a separate pot.

Pasta with Clam Sauce

Pasta with clam sauce is an extremely popular seafood dish in this country. It is often served with linguine, but it can be made with any type of pasta you have on hand. In fact, this dish is so quick and easy because all of the ingredients can come from your cupboard.

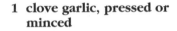

Homestyle Makeover		
Each serving contains		
	Before	After
Calories	471	226
Fat g.	15	2

¾ **pound pasta**

2 **teaspoons extra-virgin olive oil**

2 **cans (6½ ounces each) chopped clams**

1 **clove garlic, pressed or minced**

1. Bring a large covered pot of water to a boil over high heat. Add the pasta and cook according to the package directions. Thoroughly drain the pasta and return to the cooking pot. Add the oil and toss to combine.

2. Meanwhile, drain the clams, pouring the juice into a large saucepan. Set the clams aside. Add the garlic and bring to a boil over medium heat. Add the clams. Cover and remove from the heat for 5 minutes to allow the flavors to blend.

3. To serve, spoon the clam sauce over the cooked pasta.

Makes 4 servings

Per serving:	*226 calories*	*2 g. fat*	*2 mg. cholesterol*
	136 mg. sodium	*43 g. carbohydrates*	*8 g. protein*

Cook's Note

• If desired, toss some leftover cooked vegetables, such as peas or broccoli florets, into the pasta.

Lobster and Broccoli Stir-Fry

Even though this recipe calls for lobster, you can use any seafood you choose or a combination, such as lobster, shrimp, and crab. It is even good made with canned, water-packed tuna.

1 tablespoon sesame seeds

1 cup fat-free, reduced-sodium chicken broth

2 teaspoons cornstarch

2 tablespoons finely chopped fresh ginger

1 tablespoon reduced-sodium soy sauce

1 tablespoon vegetable oil

2 cloves garlic, pressed or minced

¾ pound broccoli florets

2 cups cooked lobster, thinly sliced (½ pound)

1. Place the sesame seeds in a small nonstick skillet. Cook over medium heat, stirring constantly, for about 2 minutes, or until golden brown. Watch carefully, because they burn easily. Set aside.

2. To a small bowl, add the broth and cornstarch. Whisk to dissolve the cornstarch. Add the ginger and soy sauce. Set aside.

3. Heat the oil in a wok or large skillet over medium heat. Add the garlic and cook just until it sizzles. Add the broccoli and cook, stirring constantly, for 2 minutes. Whisk the broth mixture and add to the wok or skillet. Cover and cook for 3 to 4 minutes, or until the broccoli is crisp-tender. Add the lobster. Cover and cook for 1 minute, or until the lobster is heated through. Remove from the heat. Sprinkle with the sesame seeds.

Makes 4 servings

Per serving:	185 calories	6 g. fat	111 mg. cholesterol
	465 mg. sodium	16 g. carbohydrates	20 g. protein

Lobster Thermidor

Lobster Thermidor is an elegant entrée that is surprisingly easy to make. It is perfect for entertaining because the entire dish can be prepared and assembled ahead of time and then placed under the broiler just before serving to reheat it and lightly brown the top.

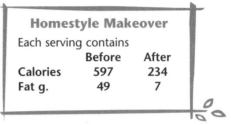

Homestyle Makeover		
Each serving contains		
	Before	After
Calories	597	234
Fat g.	49	7

1 teaspoon + 1 tablespoon butter or margarine

½ pound mushrooms, thinly sliced

2½ tablespoons unbleached or all-purpose flour

2 cups fat-free milk

⅛ teaspoon salt

½ teaspoon dry mustard

2 lobster tails in the shell (about 8 ounces each)

¼ cup (1 ounce) grated Parmesan cheese

1. In a medium skillet, melt 1 teaspoon of the butter or margarine over medium heat. Add the mushrooms. Cook, stirring frequently, for 4 to 5 minutes, or until tender when pierced with a fork. Place the mushrooms on a plate. Set aside.

2. In the skillet, melt the remaining 1 tablespoon of the butter or margarine over low heat. Add the flour and cook, stirring constantly, for 3 minutes. Do not brown. Add the milk slowly, whisking until the flour mixture is dissolved. Add the salt and mustard. Whisk to combine. Cook over low heat for about 15 minutes, whisking occasionally. If you wish to have a thicker sauce, cook for 3 to 4 minutes more. Set aside.

3. Place a steamer over simmering water in a large saucepan. Place the lobster tails on the steamer. Cover and cook for about 5 minutes, or until the shells turn bright red and the meat turns opaque. Check by inserting a sharp knife into the center of the underside of 1 lobster tail. With a large knife or cleaver, split each tail in half lengthwise. Remove the meat from the shells. Set the shells aside. Cut the cooked meat into ½" cubes. Add the lobster and mushrooms to the sauce. Stir to mix well.

4. Preheat the broiler. Coat a baking sheet with nonstick spray. Arrange the empty shells on the prepared sheet and divide the lobster mixture among the shells. Sprinkle each with 1 tablespoon of the Parmesan. Broil 4" from the heat for about 3 minutes, or until lightly browned. To serve, carefully transfer each lobster tail to a dinner plate.

Makes 4 servings

Per serving: *234 calories*   *7 g. fat*   *124 mg. cholesterol*
                         533 mg. sodium   *13 g. carbohydrates*   *29 g. protein*

Cook's Note

• For a more economical dish, you can replace the lobster with 2 cups of cooked shrimp, scallops, or cubed fish, chicken, or turkey. Serve in au gratin dishes.

Jambalaya

This spicy dish is a hallmark of Louisiana cooking. The name is derived from the French word jambon, *meaning ham, which is always a popular southern ingredient. In this recipe, I have used Canadian bacon because it is leaner than ham and, I believe, adds a bit more flavor.*

<table>
<tr><td colspan="3">Homestyle Makeover</td></tr>
<tr><td colspan="3">Each serving contains</td></tr>
<tr><td></td><td>Before</td><td>After</td></tr>
<tr><td>Calories</td><td>512</td><td>407</td></tr>
<tr><td>Fat g.</td><td>17</td><td>7</td></tr>
</table>

1 cup fat-free, reduced-sodium chicken broth

1 bottle (8 ounces) clam juice

1 bay leaf

½ teaspoon dried thyme

1 cup long-grain white rice

4 ounces Canadian bacon, cooked, drained, and chopped

2 large tomatoes, peeled and chopped (see note)

1 onion, finely chopped

1 green bell pepper, finely chopped

1 clove garlic, pressed or minced

½ teaspoon ground black pepper

¼ teaspoon hot-pepper sauce

¾ pound peeled cooked shrimp

1 can (6 ounces) lump crabmeat, rinsed and drained

1. In a large saucepan, combine the broth, clam juice, bay leaf, and thyme. Bring to a boil over high heat. Add the rice and return to a boil. Reduce the heat to low. Cover and cook, for 15 minutes, without removing the lid. Remove from the heat. Allow to stand for 10 minutes before removing the lid.

2. Meanwhile, coat a large deep skillet with nonstick spray. Place over medium heat until hot enough for drops of water to dance on the surface. Add the bacon and cook, stirring frequently, for 4 to 5 minutes, or until lightly browned. Remove the bacon from the skillet. Set aside.

3. To the same skillet, add the tomatoes, onion, bell pepper, and garlic. Place over low heat. Cover and cook for about 15 minutes, or until the onion is translucent. Stir in the black pepper and hot-pepper sauce. Add the shrimp, crabmeat, and bacon. Remove the bay leaf from the rice and discard. Add the rice mixture to the skillet. Stir to mix well. Cook for 4 to 5 minutes, or until the shrimp are heated through.

4. To serve, spoon into 4 shallow serving bowls or large plates.

Makes 4 servings

| Per serving: | 407 calories | 7 g. fat | 234 mg. cholesterol |
| | 881 mg. sodium | 45 g. carbohydrates | 36 g. protein |

Cook's Notes

• The easiest way to peel tomatoes is to submerge them in boiling water for 30 seconds and then plunge them into a bowl or sink full of cold water. This technique loosens the skins and makes them easy to peel.

• Lobster or clams can be substituted for the shrimp and crab, if desired.

• For those who like their jambalaya really hot, pass hot-pepper sauce at the table.

Oysters Rockefeller Casserole

According to legend, this seafood appetizer was created at Antoine's restaurant in New Orleans in the late 1890s and named for John D. Rockefeller because it is so rich. Many versions exist and I have taken further liberties by transforming it from an appetizer into a quick one-dish entrée.

1 tablespoon butter or margarine

2½ tablespoons unbleached or all-purpose flour

2 cups fat-free milk

½ cup clam juice or fish stock

½ cup (2 ounces) shredded Gruyère or Swiss cheese

⅛ teaspoon salt

⅛ teaspoon ground white pepper

⅛ teaspoon ground nutmeg

2 packages (6 ounces each) prewashed baby spinach leaves

1 pound shucked fresh oysters

1 tablespoon grated Parmesan cheese

Paprika

1. Preheat the oven to 350°F. Coat a 13" × 9" baking dish with nonstick spray. Set aside.

2. In a medium saucepan, melt the butter or margarine. Add the flour, stirring constantly. Cook for 3 minutes. Add the milk, whisking to dissolve the flour mixture. Cook over low heat, whisking occasionally, for about 15 minutes, or until thickened.

3. Add the clam juice or stock, Gruyère or Swiss, salt, pepper, and nutmeg. Cook, stirring constantly, for 1 minute, or until the cheese is melted. Set aside.

4. Set a steamer over simmering water in a large saucepan. Place the spinach on the steamer and cover the saucepan. Steam for 1 minute, or until wilted. Remove the spinach and line the bottom of the prepared dish with it. Set aside.

5. Heat a large skillet over medium heat until warm. Add the oysters with 2 tablespoons of the oyster liquid. Discard any remaining liquid. Cook for 2 to 3 minutes, or until the edges curl and the oysters turn white. Place the oysters on the spinach and pour the pan juices over the top. Cover with the cheese mixture. Sprinkle with the Parmesan. Dust lightly with the paprika. Bake for 10 minutes, or until bubbly.

6. Broil 4" from the heat for 1 minute, or until lightly browned.

Makes 4 servings

Per serving:	256 calories	10 g. fat	81 mg. cholesterol
	415 mg. sodium	19 g. carbohydrates	22 g. protein

Cook's Notes

• This recipe can also be prepared and baked on individual oyster shells or in custard cups to serve as an appetizer.

• Bay scallops make an excellent replacement for the oysters in this dish.

Hangtown Fry

During the California Gold Rush, oysters and eggs were expensive. This dish was created for one lucky miner who struck it rich. He demanded the finest meal that gold could buy at a café in Placerville, California, a town unfortunately reputed for its public gallows.

Homestyle Makeover		
Each serving contains		
	Before	After
Calories	347	299
Fat g.	14	10

3 eggs

¼ cup fat-free milk

2 tablespoons finely chopped fresh parsley

¼ teaspoon salt

¼ teaspoon ground black pepper

1 + 2 egg whites

¼ cup unbleached or all-purpose flour

20 saltine crackers, crumbled

1 dozen shucked oysters, rinsed and drained

2 teaspoons vegetable oil

4 slices turkey bacon, cooked, drained, and chopped

1. In a medium bowl, combine the eggs, milk, parsley, salt, pepper, and 1 egg white. Beat lightly with a fork to mix well. Set aside.

2. Place the remaining 2 egg whites in a shallow bowl and beat lightly with a fork. Put the flour on a plate and the crackers on another. One at a time, dip each oyster into the flour, egg whites, and then crackers, pressing firmly to coat. Gently shake off the excess. Reserve the coated oysters on a tray or plate.

3. Heat the oil in a large nonstick skillet over medium heat. Add the oysters and cook for 3 to 4 minutes on each side, or until lightly browned. Pour the reserved egg mixture over the oysters and cook, constantly lifting the eggs with a spatula to allow the uncooked eggs to flow underneath, for 3 to 4 minutes, or until set.

4. To serve, cut into wedges. Sprinkle with the bacon.

Makes 4 servings

Per serving:

299 calories	*10 g. fat*	*169 mg. cholesterol*
849 mg. sodium	*37 g. carbohydrates*	*14 g. protein*

Scampi with Spaghetti

Homestyle Makeover

Each serving contains

	Before	After
Calories	471	376
Fat g.	21	10

On American menus, the term scampi often describes large shrimp that are split and cooked in garlic oil or butter. The original recipe called for 6 tablespoons of butter or margarine and 2 tablespoons of olive oil. I was able to achieve the same taste and almost the same texture with considerably less.

8 ounces spaghetti

2 tablespoons butter or margarine

1 scallion, finely chopped

½ tablespoon extra-virgin olive oil

5 cloves garlic, pressed or minced

1 tablespoon lemon juice

¼ teaspoon salt

1 pound peeled and deveined medium shrimp

2 tablespoons finely chopped fresh parsley

¼ teaspoon grated lemon peel

Dash of hot-pepper sauce

1 zucchini, shredded

Lemon slices or wedges (optional)

1. Bring a large covered pot of water to a boil over high heat. Add the spaghetti and cook according to the package directions.

2. Meanwhile, melt the butter or margarine in a large skillet over medium heat. Add the scallion, oil, garlic, lemon juice, and salt. Cook, stirring constantly, until bubbly.

3. Add the shrimp and cook, stirring constantly, for 2 to 3 minutes, or until they turn opaque. Stir in the parsley, lemon peel, and hot-pepper sauce. Remove the shrimp with a slotted spoon and reserve in a bowl. Add the zucchini and cook over medium-high heat for 2 to 3 minutes, or until tender.

4. To serve, top the spaghetti with the zucchini mixture, shrimp, and the lemon, if using.

Makes 4 servings

Per serving:	376 calories	10 g. fat	130 mg. cholesterol
	318 mg. sodium	47 g. carbohydrates	24 g. protein

Is There Fish in Your Future?

Even if seafood didn't surface often on your childhood dinner plate, it can still make a healthy splash in your kitchen today. It's smart to eat seafood. And here's why.

- Fish varieties that are highest in oil, such as mackerel, salmon, tuna, shrimp, lobster, and scallops, are rich in omega-3 fatty acids, which have a positive impact on heart health.

- The U.S. Department of Agriculture's dietary guidelines recommend two to three servings a day of lean protein. Seafood is among the most healthful of animal proteins because it is so low in saturated fat, which is implicated in the development of heart disease.

- The wide variety of seafood available in supermarkets brings a tremendous range of tastes and textures to the table. And seafood is among the quickest of all protein foods to cook, making it convenient for busy schedules.

Because of advances in fish farming, jet transportation, and refrigeration equipment aboard fishing vessels, high-quality seafood has never been easier for the home cook to buy. Gone are the days when you could smell the fish counter the minute you walked into the supermarket. Fish fresh from the water doesn't smell "fishy" and neither should the fish you buy.

Look for loose-packed flash-frozen fish fillets, shrimp, scallops, and other seafood, packaged in resealable freezer bags. These fish and shellfish often taste fresher than seafood that has been out of the water for days before it is cooked and eaten. And, because the frozen pieces are loose-packed, it's convenient to remove just the amount you need for a recipe and store the rest in the freezer. To thaw, place frozen fish fillets in the refrigerator for at least 24 hours.

When buying fresh fish fillets, look for firm, moist flesh that clings to the bones and springs back when touched. At home, store the fish, tightly covered, in the coldest section of your refrigerator and, if possible, cook it the day you purchase it.

Fried Shrimp

Photograph on page 112

Homestyle Makeover

Each serving contains

	Before	After
Calories	399	167
Fat g.	17	2

In the nineteenth century, most shrimp were eaten by Americans in the coastal regions. Because it is so perishable, it was difficult to transport safely. Today, shrimp is the most popular shellfish in the country. The most frequently ordered shrimp dishes in restaurants are shrimp cocktail and fried shrimp.

1 pound extra-large shrimp	¼ teaspoon salt
⅓ cup unbleached or all-purpose flour	¼ teaspoon ground black pepper
1 teaspoon crab-boil seasoning	1 egg white
	¾ cup crushed corn flakes

1. Preheat the oven to 450°F. Coat a baking sheet with nonstick spray.

2. Peel and devein the shrimp, leaving the tail portions of the shells attached.

3. In a shallow bowl, combine the flour, crab-boil seasoning, salt, and pepper. Place the egg white in another shallow bowl and beat lightly with a fork. Put the crushed corn flakes on a plate.

4. Dip each shrimp into the flour mixture, shaking off the excess flour. Then dip into the egg white and then the corn flakes, pressing firmly to coat. Place the coated shrimp in a single layer on the prepared baking sheet, being careful not to overlap. Coat lightly with nonstick spray. Bake for 5 to 6 minutes, or until golden brown on the outside and opaque in the center. Check by inserting a sharp knife into the center of 1 shrimp.

Makes 4 servings

Per serving:	*167 calories*	*2 g. fat*	*173 mg. cholesterol*
	250 mg. sodium	*10 g. carbohydrates*	*25 g. protein*

Cook's Notes

• If you prefer garlic-flavored shrimp, replace the crab-boil seasoning with garlic powder.

• Serve with Tartar Sauce (page 164) or cocktail sauce for dipping, if desired.

Recipes

Chicken, Turkey, and Duck

Succulent Chicken and Dumplings, savory Roast Turkey, crispy crusted Southern Fried Chicken. Homestyle American cooking would not be the same without poultry.

Prior to World War II, chicken was an expensive special occasion food. Politicians even campaigned with the promise of a chicken in every pot every Sunday. Now that chicken is affordable, each one of us eats about 33 pounds a year in dishes as ethnically diverse as Chicken Enchiladas and Chicken Chop Suey.

As for turkey, Revolutionary War statesman Benjamin Franklin lobbied to make it our national bird. His proposal didn't fly, but turkey is more popular than ever today with the proliferation of easy-to-cook lean turkey parts in our supermarkets.

Poultry, particularly white meat, is nutritious and easy to strip of unwanted fat. By modifying cooking methods and lightening sauces, I promise you a healthy American chicken dish in every pot.

Brunswick Stew

This stew was originally prepared with squir-rel meat and onion in Brunswick County, Vir-ginia, in 1828. However, Brunswick County, North Carolina, also takes credit for the origin of this dish, which later evolved into a stew made with rabbit or chicken as well as okra, lima beans, tomatoes, and corn.

1 broiler-fryer chicken (about 3 pounds), cut into pieces, or 3 pounds chicken parts

5 cups water

1 onion, finely chopped

1 teaspoon salt

1 can (14½ ounces) diced tomatoes, drained

1 can (6 ounces) tomato paste

½ cup sliced okra

1 tablespoon Worcester-shire sauce

1 teaspoon dried thyme

¼ teaspoon ground red pepper

1 cup fresh or frozen baby lima beans

1 cup corn kernels

1 tablespoon cornstarch

¼ cup water

1. In a Dutch oven, combine the chicken, water, onion, and ½ teaspoon of the salt. Cover and simmer for 1½ hours, or until the chicken is tender when pierced with a fork. Remove the chicken from the broth. Set aside to cool. Remove and discard the skin and bones. Cut the chicken into bite-size pieces. Place in a bowl, cover tightly, and refrigerate. Place the broth in another bowl. Refrigerate, uncovered, all day or overnight.

2. Remove and discard the fat. Pour the broth into a Dutch oven. Add the tomatoes, tomato paste, okra, Worcestershire sauce, thyme, red pepper, chicken, and the remaining ½ teaspoon of the salt. Bring to a boil over medium heat. Reduce the heat to low. Simmer for 20 minutes. Add the lima beans and cook for 10 minutes. Add the corn and cook for 10 min-utes. In a small bowl, combine the cornstarch and water. Add to the pot, stirring constantly. Simmer, stirring frequently, for 4 to 5 minutes, or until thickened.

Makes 6 servings

Per serving:

| 349 calories | 6 g. fat | 107 mg. cholesterol |
| 743 mg. sodium | 36 g. carbohydrates | 42 g. protein |

Southern Fried Chicken

Photograph on front cover

Homestyle Makeover

Each serving contains

	Before	After
Calories	419	138
Fat g.	25	2

Southern Fried Chicken is probably the favorite with most families and considered the most all-American of chicken recipes. This easy recipe is for everyone who craves the crispiness of real fried chicken but can do without the outrageous calories and fat.

¾ **cup buttermilk**

3 **pounds cut-up chicken, skinned and trimmed of all visible fat**

¾ **cup corn flakes, crushed**

2 **teaspoons paprika**

1 **teaspoon salt**

½ **teaspoon ground black pepper**

⅛ **teaspoon ground red pepper**

1. Preheat the oven to 400°F. Coat a shallow metal baking or roasting pan with nonstick spray. Set aside.

2. Pour the buttermilk into a shallow bowl. Add the chicken, turning to coat. Refrigerate for at least 15 minutes, turning occasionally.

3. On a plate, combine the corn flakes, paprika, salt, black pepper, and red pepper. One at a time, dip each side of the chicken into the corn flake mixture, pressing firmly to coat. Stir the corn flake mixture occasionally with a fork to keep the seasonings evenly mixed. Place in the prepared pan.

4. Coat the chicken with nonstick spray. Bake, turning the pieces once, for 40 to 45 minutes, or until the chicken is crisp, golden brown, and the juices run clear when pricked with a sharp knife. Check by inserting a sharp knife into the center of 1 piece. An instant-read thermometer inserted into the thickest part of a thigh, not touching the bone, should register 180°F.

Makes 4 servings

Per serving:	*138 calories*	*2 g. fat*	*66 mg. cholesterol*
	230 mg. sodium	*3 g. carbohydrates*	*27 g. protein*

Chicken Potpie

In the lovely Pennsylvania Dutch countryside, potpie refers to a wonderful simmered dish of chicken, vegetables, and broad homemade noodles. The original recipe for this comforting dish came from Alice Ney, the mother of Tom Ney, director of Food Services and the Food Center at Rodale Press.

Homestyle Makeover		
Each serving contains		
	Before	After
Calories	827	411
Fat g.	41	8

Chicken and Vegetables

1 broiler-fryer chicken (about 3 pounds), cut into pieces, or 3 pounds chicken parts

4 ribs celery

1 large onion

4 carrots

2 bay leaves

6 black peppercorns

6 sprigs fresh parsley

¼ teaspoon salt

4 small potatoes, peeled and thinly sliced

Noodles

2 cups baking mix

⅔ cup fat-free milk

1. *To make the chicken and vegetables:* In a large pot or Dutch oven, combine the chicken, 2 ribs of the celery, onion, 2 carrots, bay leaves, peppercorns, parsley, and salt. Cover with cold water. Bring to a boil over medium heat. Reduce the heat to low and simmer, uncovered, for 2 hours. Replenish the water as needed. Set aside to cool.

2. Remove the chicken and set aside. Strain the broth, discarding the remaining solids. Remove and discard the bones and skin from the chicken. Set aside the chicken. After wiping the pot with paper towels, return the broth to the pot. Bring to a boil over high heat.

3. Slice the remaining 2 ribs of the celery and 2 carrots into ¼" slices. Add the celery, carrots, and potatoes to the broth. Reduce the heat to low. Cook for 15 minutes, or until the potatoes and carrots are tender when pierced with a fork.

4. *To make the noodles:* While the vegetables are cooking, combine the baking mix and milk in a mixing bowl by stirring with a fork until moist. Form the dough into a ball, adding a bit more of the baking mix, if necessary, to make a soft dough, or until it is no longer sticky. Turn the dough onto a floured work surface. With a floured rolling pin, roll out the dough to about ¼" thick. With a table knife, cut into large noodles (about 3" × 2").

5. Increase the heat to medium-high and bring the broth and vegetables to a rolling boil. One at a time, drop the noodles into the broth. Return to a boil after each noodle. Reduce the heat to medium and simmer for 10 minutes. Cover and cook for 10 minutes. Add the chicken. Simmer for 1 to 2 minutes to reheat. Serve in shallow bowls.

Makes 8 servings

Per serving:

411 calories	*8 g. fat*	*107 mg. cholesterol*
657 mg. sodium	*46 g. carbohydrates*	*38 g. protein*

Cook's Note

• You can speed the preparation by dropping the dough by spoonfuls into the boiling broth to make dumplings.

Chicken and Dumplings

Dumplings are mounds of dough dropped into a simmering soup or stew to cook. Nothing is more traditional than a Sunday dinner of chicken and dumplings at Grandma's house. Now, even your grandmother can prepare a healthier version by using this recipe.

Photograph on page 113

Homestyle Makeover

Each serving contains

	Before	After
Calories	815	521
Fat g.	35	12

Chicken

8 skinless chicken thighs, trimmed of all visible fat

¼ teaspoon ground black pepper

1 tablespoon vegetable oil

2 large leeks (white part only), chopped

3 carrots, chopped

2 ribs celery, chopped

½ teaspoon dried marjoram

½ teaspoon dried thyme

¼ cup unbleached or all-purpose flour

6 cups low-sodium chicken broth (see note)

1 cup 1% milk

1 teaspoon lemon juice

Dumplings

1⅔ cups reduced-fat baking mix

⅔ cup 1% milk

¼ cup finely chopped fresh parsley

1. *To make the chicken:* Season the chicken with the pepper. Heat the oil in a large deep skillet over medium-high heat. Place the chicken in the skillet and cook for 4 minutes per side, or until browned. Remove to a plate. Cover and set aside.

2. Add the leeks, carrots, celery, marjoram, and thyme to the skillet. Reduce the heat to medium. Cook, stirring occasionally, for 5 minutes, or until the carrots can easily be pierced with a fork. Add the flour and mix well. Cook, stirring constantly, for 3 minutes. Add the broth and milk. Stir to mix well. Increase the heat to high. Cook, stirring constantly, for 5 to 6 minutes, or until the mixture boils and thickens. Add the chicken. Reduce the heat to low.

3. Cover and simmer for 20 minutes, stirring occasionally, until the chicken is cooked. Check by inserting a sharp knife into the center of 1 chicken thigh next to the bone. Remove the chicken. Set aside. Add the lemon juice to the pan. Stir to mix well.

4. *To make the dumplings:* In a medium bowl, combine the baking mix, milk, and parsley. Bring the broth mixture to a boil over high heat. Drop 8 dollops of the dough into the broth mixture. When the mixture returns to a boil, reduce the heat to medium and cook for 10 minutes. Cover and cook for 10 minutes, or until there is no raw dough in the center of the dumplings. Check by inserting a knife into the center of 1 dumpling.

5. For each serving, place 2 dumplings and 2 chicken thighs in a large shallow bowl. Cover with some of the broth and vegetables.

Makes 4 servings

| *Per serving:* | 521 calories | 12 g. fat | 76 mg. cholesterol |
| | 912 mg. sodium | 62 g. carbohydrates | 41 g. protein |

Cook's Note

• Use low-sodium chicken broth (for sodium-restricted diets) in this recipe because the reduced-fat baking mix is also fairly high in sodium.

Chicken Cacciatore

Photograph on page 114

Cacciatore, the Italian word for hunter, refers to any rustic dish prepared with onions, tomatoes, herbs, and wine. The version made with chicken became a popular Italian-American entrée after World War II. It's still found on many Italian restaurant menus.

Homestyle Makeover

Each serving contains

	Before	After
Calories	167	96
Fat g.	6	2

2 large tomatoes, peeled and chopped

1 onion, finely chopped

2 cloves garlic, pressed or minced

1 teaspoon dried rosemary, crushed

1 teaspoon dried oregano

½ teaspoon salt

½ teaspoon ground black pepper

4 boneless, skinless chicken breast halves (about 1 pound)

1½ teaspoons olive oil

1 cup dry Marsala wine or nonalcoholic red wine

1 can (6 ounces) tomato paste

1. Preheat the oven to 350°F. Coat an 11" × 7" baking dish with nonstick spray. Add the tomatoes, onion, garlic, rosemary, and oregano. Toss to mix well. Spread evenly over the bottom of the dish. Set aside.

2. With the salt and pepper, season both sides of the chicken breasts. Heat the oil in a large skillet until hot enough for drops of water to dance on the surface. Place the chicken in the skillet. Cook for 2 to 3 minutes on each side, or until evenly browned.

3. Arrange the chicken breasts on the tomato mixture in the baking dish. Cover and bake for 10 minutes.

4. In a small bowl, combine the wine and tomato paste, stirring to dissolve the paste. Pour over the chicken breasts. Cover and bake for 15 minutes, or until the chicken is cooked. Check by inserting a sharp knife into the center of 1 breast.

Makes 4 servings

Per serving:	96 calories	2 g. fat	20 mg. cholesterol
	243 mg. sodium	7 g. carbohydrates	9 g. protein

Oven-Barbecued Chicken

Homestyle Makeover

Each serving contains

	Before	After
Calories	324	165
Fat g.	14	2

After World War II, the backyard barbecue became the American way to entertain. With Dad manning the grill, the intoxicating aroma of charcoal smoke made the whole neighborhood delirious with hunger. When bad weather made it impossible to be outside, oven barbecuing was the perfect solution.

1 onion, finely chopped	2 tablespoons packed dark brown sugar
1 cup tomato sauce	2 teaspoons dry mustard
½ cup water	½ teaspoon liquid smoke
¼ cup lemon juice	12 boneless, skinless chicken thighs (2 pounds)
3 tablespoons Worcestershire sauce	½ teaspoon garlic powder
2 tablespoons apple cider vinegar	

1. Coat a nonstick saucepan with nonstick spray. Add the onion. Cover and cook over low heat for 8 to 10 minutes, or until translucent. If needed, add a few teaspoons of water to the skillet to prevent the onion from scorching.

2. Combine the tomato sauce, water, lemon juice, Worcestershire sauce, vinegar, brown sugar, and mustard in the saucepan. Increase the heat to high and bring to a boil. Reduce the heat to medium and simmer for 30 minutes to blend the flavors. Remove from the heat and allow to cool slightly. Add the liquid smoke. Set aside.

3. Preheat the oven to 350°F. Coat a 13" × 9" baking dish with nonstick spray. Place the chicken in the baking dish. Sprinkle each thigh with garlic powder. Cover with a lid or foil. Bake for 20 minutes. Remove from the oven and drain off the liquid. Pour the reserved sauce over the chicken thighs. Cover and bake for 20 minutes, or until the chicken is tender and no pink remains. Check by inserting a sharp knife into the center of 1 thigh.

Makes 6 servings

Per serving:	165 calories	2 g. fat	66 mg. cholesterol
	499 mg. sodium	10 g. carbohydrates	27 g. protein

Chicken Divan

Originally this dish, created by the chef at the Divan Parisian Restaurant in New York, was composed of turkey slices served on a rich buttery pastry.

2 cups water

1 onion, quartered

¼ cup chopped celery leaves

½ teaspoon salt

1½ pounds boneless, skinless chicken breast halves

1 pound fresh broccoli florets or 2 packages (10 ounces each) frozen broccoli florets

1 can (10¾ ounces) low-fat cream of chicken soup

½ cup fat-free milk

1 package (0.9 ounce) dry Hollandaise sauce mix

3 tablespoons sherry (optional)

1 teaspoon Worcestershire sauce

1 teaspoon lemon juice

1 cup reduced-fat sour cream

¾ cup grated Parmesan cheese

1. In a large skillet, combine the water, onion, celery leaves, and salt. Add the chicken and bring to a boil. Reduce the heat to low. Cover and simmer for 20 minutes, or until the chicken is cooked. Check by inserting a sharp knife into the center of 1 breast. Remove the chicken to a plate. Allow to cool slightly. Cut into slices diagonally. Set aside.

2. Meanwhile, place a steamer over simmering water in a large saucepan. Place the broccoli on the steamer. Cover and steam for 4 to 5 minutes, or until crisp-tender. Remove the broccoli. Set aside.

3. In a small saucepan, combine the soup and milk. Add the sauce mix and stir until completely blended. Place the pan over medium heat and bring to a boil. Reduce the heat to low and simmer for 1 minute. Stir in the sherry, if using, Worcestershire sauce, and lemon juice. Stir in the sour cream. Set aside.

4. Preheat the oven to 400°F. Coat a 13" × 9" baking dish with nonstick spray. Arrange the broccoli in the baking dish in a single layer and sprinkle with half of the Parmesan. Arrange the chicken slices on top of the broccoli, cover with the sauce, and sprinkle with the remaining Parmesan.

5. Bake for 20 minutes, or until bubbly. If desired, broil 4" from the heat for 1 minute, or until lightly browned. To serve, lift portions with a pancake turner or a large spoon.

Makes 8 servings

| Per serving: | 203 calories | 7 g. fat | 61 mg. cholesterol |
| | 533 mg. sodium | 9 g. carbohydrates | 26 g. protein |

Chicken Paprika

Photograph on page 116

I replaced the highly saturated bacon fat in the original dish with turkey bacon sautéed in a small amount of canola oil. I also cut back on the fat by using reduced-fat sour cream instead of full fat to produce a much lighter Hungarian main dish with all the gusto of the original.

Homestyle Makeover

Each serving contains

	Before	After
Calories	837	354
Fat g.	46	9

½ cup unbleached or all-purpose flour

1 tablespoon paprika (see note)

½ teaspoon ground black pepper

½ teaspoon dried basil

¼ teaspoon ground ginger

¼ teaspoon ground nutmeg

⅛ teaspoon ground red pepper

4 boneless, skinless chicken breast halves (about 1 pound)

2 teaspoons vegetable oil

4 slices turkey bacon, chopped

1¼ cups fat-free, reduced-sodium chicken broth

1 cup reduced-fat sour cream

2 tablespoons Worcestershire sauce

2 tablespoons chili sauce

1 clove garlic, pressed or minced

¼ cup sherry (optional)

1 cup egg noodles

1. Preheat the oven to 325°F. Coat a 1½-quart baking dish with nonstick spray. Set aside.

2. On a plate, combine the flour, paprika, black pepper, basil, ginger, nutmeg, and red pepper. Dip each of the chicken breasts in the flour mixture, pressing gently to coat. Set aside.

3. Heat the oil in a large nonstick skillet over medium heat. Add the bacon and cook, stirring frequently, for 4 to 5 minutes, or until browned. Place the chicken in the skillet. Cook for about 2 minutes per side, or until browned. Transfer the chicken and bacon to the prepared baking dish. Set aside.

4. Add the broth, sour cream, Worcestershire sauce, chili sauce, garlic, and sherry, if using, to the skillet. Cook over medium heat, whisking constantly and scraping the pan to release any browned bits on the bottom, until the mixture comes to a boil. Remove from the heat and pour over the chicken.

5. Bake for 1 hour, or until the chicken is tender and no longer pink. Check by inserting a sharp knife into the center of 1 breast.

6. Meanwhile, bring water to a boil in a medium saucepan. Add the noodles and cook according to the package directions.

7. To serve, top the noodles with a chicken breast and some of the sauce.

Makes 4 servings

Per serving: *354 calories*   *9 g. fat*   *104 mg. cholesterol*
            552 mg. sodium   *31 g. carbohydrates*   *35 g. protein*

Cook's Note

• You can use regular paprika in this recipe, but for a more authentic-tasting dish, use sweet Hungarian paprika, which is available in some supermarkets and specialty food stores.

Chicken Chop Suey

This Chinese-American dish, made of stir-fried vegetables and poultry or meat served over fried noodles, was created by the Chinese immigrants who built the railroads in the American West. It is still a standard dish in many Chinese-American restaurants.

Homestyle Makeover		
Each serving contains		
	Before	After
Calories	724	590
Fat g.	19	9

¾ cup long-grain white rice

2 tablespoons vegetable oil

2 ribs celery with leaves, sliced diagonally in ½" pieces

4 scallions, sliced diagonally in ½" pieces

½ pound boneless, skinless chicken breasts, cut into 2" strips about ¼" wide

½ pound mushrooms, coarsely chopped

2 cups fresh bean sprouts

1 green bell pepper, coarsely chopped

1 can (10½ ounces) chicken consommé

¼ teaspoon ground black pepper

1 tablespoon reduced-sodium soy sauce

3 tablespoons rice wine or nonalcoholic white wine

1. Place the rice in a medium saucepan. Add 1½ cups water and cook according to the package directions.

2. Meanwhile, heat the oil in a wok or large skillet. Add the celery and scallions. Stir-fry for 3 to 4 minutes, or until crisp-tender. Add the chicken, mushrooms, bean sprouts, and bell pepper. Stir-fry for 2 to 3 minutes, or until the chicken is cooked. Check by inserting a sharp knife into the center of 1 breast strip to make sure the juices run clear. Add the consommé, black pepper, soy sauce, and wine. Bring to a boil. Serve over the rice.

Makes 4 servings

Per serving: *590 calories*   *9 g. fat*   *69 mg. cholesterol*
422 mg. sodium   *84 g. carbohydrates*   *39 g. protein*

Chicken Cordon Bleu

Photograph on page 115

Homestyle Makeover

Each serving contains

	Before	After
Calories	790	417
Fat g.	50	17

Cordon bleu is a French term meaning "blue ribbon." It also refers to a dish that has layers of thin scallops of chicken or veal with thin slices of both Swiss cheese and ham. They are breaded and sautéed until golden brown.

4 boneless, skinless chicken breast halves (about 1 pound)

4 thin slices (2 ounces) boiled or baked ham

4 thin slices (2 ounces) reduced-fat Swiss cheese

3 tablespoons unbleached or all-purpose flour

¼ teaspoon ground black pepper

⅛ teaspoon salt

1 egg white

2 slices fresh bread, crumbled

1 tablespoon butter or margarine

1. Place the chicken breasts on a work surface and cover each half with plastic wrap. Using the flat side of a meat mallet, pound each breast until about ¼" thick. Top each breast with a slice of the ham and a slice of the Swiss. Fold each breast in half to make a compact bundle. Secure with a toothpick.

2. On a plate, combine the flour, pepper, and salt. Place the egg white in a shallow bowl. Beat lightly with a fork. Place the bread on a plate. Dip each chicken bundle into the flour mixture, egg white, and bread, pressing gently to coat.

3. Melt the butter or margarine in a large nonstick skillet over medium heat. Place the chicken bundles in the skillet. Cook for 4 to 5 minutes on each side, or until the outside is golden brown and the chicken is cooked with no pink remaining. Check by inserting a sharp knife into the center of 1 breast.

4. Using a spatula, carefully transfer the bundles to individual plates or a serving platter. Remove the toothpicks before serving.

Makes 4 servings

Per serving:	417 calories	17 g. fat	84 mg. cholesterol
	606 mg. sodium	32 g. carbohydrates	35 g. protein

Chicken Kiev

If you cut into classic Chicken Kiev, chances are a gush of melted butter will splash you. Although this lighter version still uses butter, the amount is minimal. It helps bind the seasoning mix and moisten the chicken to achieve superior flavor and texture.

Homestyle Makeover		
Each serving contains		
	Before	After
Calories	423	226
Fat g.	22	8

¼ cup butter or margarine, softened

2 tablespoons finely chopped chives

½ teaspoon salt

½ teaspoon ground black pepper

4 boneless, skinless chicken breast halves (about 1 pound)

4 slices fresh bread, crumbled

1 egg white

1. In a small bowl, combine the butter or margarine with the chives, salt, and pepper. Form into 4 rolls, about 3" long. Place in the freezer for 1 hour, or until solid.

2. Preheat the oven to 400°F. Coat an 11" × 7" baking dish with nonstick spray. Set aside.

3. Meanwhile, place the chicken breasts on a work surface and cover each half with plastic wrap. Using the flat side of a meat mallet, pound each breast until about ¼" thick. Place a butter roll in the center of each chicken breast. Wrap the chicken breast around the butter roll, tucking in the sides. Secure each breast with a 6" bamboo or metal skewer.

4. Place the bread in a shallow bowl. Place the egg white in another shallow bowl and beat lightly with a fork. Roll each chicken bundle in the bread, egg white, and bread again, pressing gently to coat. Place in the prepared baking dish. Coat lightly with nonstick spray. Bake for 10 minutes. Reduce the heat to 350°F. Bake for 25 to 30 minutes, or until well-browned and no pink remains. Check by inserting a sharp knife into the center of 1 chicken bundle. Carefully remove the skewers.

Makes 4 servings

Per serving:

226 calories	8 g. fat	48 mg. cholesterol
433 mg. sodium	20 g. carbohydrates	17 g. protein

Mulligatawny Stew

Inspired by the Tamil cooks of southern India, the name of this dish is derived from a word meaning pepper water. As Indian cuisine becomes increasingly popular in our country, this rich curried chicken stew is frequently served in restaurants and often appears in cookbooks.

Homestyle Makeover

Each serving contains

	Before	After
Calories	610	250
Fat g.	30	3

2 teaspoons vegetable oil

1 clove garlic, pressed or minced

2 teaspoons finely chopped fresh ginger

¾ pound boneless, skinless chicken breast, chopped

⅔ cup basmati or white rice

2 carrots, chopped

1 onion, chopped

4 cups fat-free, reduced-sodium chicken broth

1½ teaspoons curry powder

⅛ teaspoon ground black pepper

¼ cup cornstarch

1 can (12 ounces) fat-free evaporated milk

1. Heat the oil in a large nonstick saucepan over low heat. Add the garlic and ginger and cook until they sizzle and start to brown. Add the chicken. Increase the heat to medium. Cook, stirring frequently, for 5 to 6 minutes, or until lightly browned. Remove the chicken from the saucepan and reserve. Add the rice to the saucepan. Cook, stirring frequently, for 2 to 3 minutes, or until lightly browned. Add the carrots and onion. Cook for 8 to 10 minutes, or until the onion is translucent. Add the broth, curry powder, and pepper. Stir to mix well. Cover and simmer. Cook for 12 to 15 minutes, or until the rice is tender.

2. Place the cornstarch in a small bowl. Gradually add about ½ cup of the milk. Whisk to dissolve the cornstarch. Add to the saucepan. Cook, stirring, for 2 to 3 minutes, or until the mixture thickens. Add the remaining milk and the reserved chicken. Reduce the heat to low. Simmer for 5 to 7 minutes, or until the chicken is hot.

Makes 6 servings

Per serving:	250 calories	3 g. fat	29 mg. cholesterol
	525 mg. sodium	35 g. carbohydrates	19 g. protein

Chicken à la King

Various stories credit the creation of this creamy dish to chefs in New York and London in the late 1800s. It was first mentioned in print in 1912 and went on to become a stylish luncheon item in many restaurants. In this version, toast makes a convenient and low-fat base for the rich topping.

Homestyle Makeover		
Each serving contains		
	Before	After
Calories	400	289
Fat g.	16	6

1 tablespoon butter or margarine

4 ounces mushrooms, chopped

½ green bell pepper, finely chopped

¼ cup unbleached or all-purpose flour

½ teaspoon ground black pepper

2 cups fat-free, reduced-sodium chicken broth

1 can (12 ounces) fat-free evaporated milk

½ pound cooked boneless, skinless chicken breast, chopped

1 jar (4 ounces) chopped pimientos

4 slices whole-wheat bread, toasted

1. Melt the butter or margarine in a large skillet over low heat. Add the mushrooms and bell pepper. Cook, stirring frequently, over medium-low heat for 8 minutes, or until the pepper is just crisp-tender. Add the flour and black pepper. Stir to mix. Cook, stirring constantly, for 3 minutes.

2. Slowly add the broth and evaporated milk, stirring constantly, until the flour mixture dissolves. Increase the heat to medium-high. Bring to a boil, stirring constantly. Boil for 1 minute.

3. Reduce the heat to low. Add the chicken and pimientos. Cook for 2 to 3 minutes, or until the chicken is heated through and no pink remains. To serve, spoon over the toast slices.

Makes 4 servings

Per serving:	289 calories	6 g. fat	61 mg. cholesterol
	571 mg. sodium	29 g. carbohydrates	30 g. protein

Roast Turkey (page 238) and Herbed Bread Dressing (page 134)   215

216   *Chicken Tamale Pie (page 234)*

Turkey Tetrazzini (page 240)

Chicken Enchiladas (page 232)

Oven-Barbecued Brisket (page 250) and Cornbread (page 284)   219

Hungarian Goulash (page 259)

Meat Loaf (page 260) and Scalloped Potatoes (page 126)   221

Lasagna (page 264)

Stuffed Pork Chop (page 270) and Sweet Potato Casserole (page 130) 223

224   *Spaghetti with Meat Sauce (page 266) and Garlic Bread (page 298)*

Shepherd's Pie (page 262)   225

226   *Sweet-and-Sour Pork (page 272)*

Rack of Lamb (page 274)

Peppered Steak (page 251) and Oven French Fries (page 129)

Beef Stew (page 255)

Cheese Bread (page 296)

Chicken Croquettes

Croquettes are a mixture of finely chopped meat or vegetables that are typically deep-fried. These baked croquettes are almost as crunchy as their fried counterparts. They are also easier to make and much lower in dietary fat and calories.

1 tablespoon butter or margarine

3 tablespoons unbleached or all-purpose flour

1 cup fat-free milk

½ pound cooked boneless, skinless chicken breast, finely chopped

½ onion, finely chopped

1 tablespoon chopped fresh parsley

1½ teaspoons dry mustard

½ teaspoon celery salt

3 slices fresh whole-wheat bread, crumbled

2 egg whites

1. Melt the butter or margarine in a large saucepan over medium heat. Add the flour and cook, stirring constantly, for 3 minutes. Add the milk, stirring constantly, to dissolve the flour mixture. Cook, stirring frequently, for 12 to 15 minutes, or until thickened. Remove from the heat.

2. Add the chicken, onion, parsley, mustard, and celery salt. Mix well. Cover and refrigerate for at least 45 minutes, or until well-chilled.

3. Preheat the oven to 450°F. Coat a baking sheet with nonstick spray.

4. Set aside. Place the bread in a shallow bowl. Place the egg whites in another shallow bowl and beat lightly with a fork. Mold the chilled chicken mixture into 6 cones. Roll each one in the bread, egg whites, and bread again, pressing gently to coat. Place the cones on the prepared baking sheet. Coat with nonstick spray. Bake for 15 minutes. Reduce the temperature to 350°F. Bake for about 20 minutes, or until browned.

Makes 6 servings

Per serving:	267 calories	10 g. fat	75 mg. cholesterol
	382 mg. sodium	14 g. carbohydrates	29 g. protein

Chicken Enchiladas

For this dish, I reduce the dietary fat by cooking in a covered nonstick skillet using nonstick spray, instead of frying in lard. Consequently, I am able to significantly improve the nutritional profile of this popular Tex-Mex dish.

Photograph on page 218

Homestyle Makeover		
Each serving contains		
	Before	After
Calories	432	392
Fat g.	17	9

2 onions, finely chopped

2 tablespoons chili powder

1 teaspoon ground cumin

4 large tomatoes, peeled and chopped

1 cup fat-free, reduced-sodium chicken broth

1 can (7 ounces) diced green chile peppers

½ pound cooked boneless, skinless chicken breast, finely chopped

1 cup (4 ounces) shredded reduced-fat Monterey Jack cheese

8 corn tortillas (6" diameter), warmed

1. Preheat the oven to 350°F. Coat a 13" × 9" baking dish with nonstick spray. Set aside.

2. Coat a large nonstick skillet with nonstick spray. Place over low heat. Add the onions. Cover and cook for 8 to 10 minutes, or until translucent. If needed, add a few teaspoons of water to the skillet to prevent the onions from scorching. Add the chili powder and cumin. Stir to coat the onions with the spices. Add the tomatoes, broth, and peppers (with juice). Stir to mix well. Cook for 5 minutes. Remove half the tomato mixture from the skillet. Reserve. Remove the skillet from the heat. To the skillet, add the chicken and ½ cup of the Monterey Jack. Stir to mix.

3. Lay the tortillas on a work surface. Spoon ½ cup of the chicken mixture down the center of each tortilla. Roll the tortilla around it. Place, folded side down, in the prepared baking dish. Spoon the reserved tomato mixture over each enchilada and sprinkle evenly with the remaining ½ cup of Monterey Jack. Bake for 25 to 30 minutes, or until bubbly.

Makes 4 servings

Per serving:	392 calories	9 g. fat	84 mg. cholesterol
	569 mg. sodium	37 g. carbohydrates	41 g. protein

Chicken-Stuffed Bell Peppers

Homestyle Makeover		
Each serving contains		
	Before	After
Calories	415	322
Fat g.	9	2

This is an excellent dish to make when you have leftover cooked rice. Otherwise, cook some rice according to the package directions. Also, you may prefer to use red bell peppers for a more colorful presentation, although green bell peppers are available throughout the year.

4 green or red bell peppers

1 pound ground skinless chicken breast

1 onion, finely chopped

1½ teaspoons Worcestershire sauce

¼ teaspoon salt

¼ teaspoon ground black pepper

1 cup cooked rice

1 can (10¾ ounces) condensed cream of tomato soup

1. Preheat the oven to 375°F. Coat a 1½-quart baking dish with nonstick spray. Set aside. Place a steamer over simmering water in a large saucepan.

2. Cut the tops off the bell peppers and reserve them. Remove and discard the seeds and membranes. Place the peppers and the tops on the steamer. Cover and steam for 3 to 4 minutes, or until the peppers can be pierced with the tip of a knife. Remove to the prepared baking dish.

3. Coat a nonstick skillet with nonstick spray and place over medium heat until hot enough for drops of water to dance on the surface. Add the chicken and cook, stirring frequently, for 4 to 5 minutes, or until crumbly and no pink remains. Add the onion and cook, stirring frequently, for 7 to 8 minutes, or until the onion is translucent.

4. Remove from the heat. Add the Worcestershire sauce, salt, black pepper, rice, and 1 cup of the soup. Stir to mix. Spoon the chicken mixture into the peppers. Cover with the pepper tops. Bake for 25 to 30 minutes, or until the peppers start to brown. Place the remaining soup in a small saucepan or microwaveable bowl. Cook or microwave for 1 to 2 minutes, or until hot. Top each pepper with a spoonful of the heated soup.

Makes 4 serving

Per serving:

322 calories	2 g. fat	49 mg. cholesterol
623 mg. sodium	50 g. carbohydrates	25 g. protein

Chicken Tamale Pie

Tamales are bundles of cornmeal dough stuffed with seasoned poultry or meat. The top chefs in the country, using international ingredients, have turned this simple Mexican dish into haute cuisine.

Photograph on page 216

Homestyle Makeover

Each serving contains

	Before	After
Calories	479	351
Fat g.	17	5

Crust

1½ cups yellow cornmeal

4 cups water

1 tablespoon vegetable oil

½ teaspoon salt

½ teaspoon ground black pepper

Filling

1 onion, finely chopped

1½ pounds ground skinless chicken or turkey breast

2 cups fresh or frozen corn kernels, thawed

1 can (14½ ounces) diced tomatoes

1 can (7 ounces) diced green chile peppers

2 tablespoons chili powder

2 cloves garlic, pressed or minced

2 teaspoons ground cumin

1 teaspoon dried oregano

1 cup (4 ounces) shredded reduced-fat sharp Cheddar cheese

1. *To make the crust:* In a large saucepan, combine the cornmeal with 1 cup of the water. Bring the remaining 3 cups of the water to a boil in another saucepan. Add the boiling water to the cornmeal and mix well. Add the oil, salt, and pepper. Bring to a boil over medium-high heat. Reduce the heat to low. Cover and cook, stirring frequently, for 20 minutes. Set aside.

2. *To make the filling:* Coat a large nonstick skillet with nonstick spray. Add the onion. Cover and cook over low heat for 8 to 10 minutes, or until translucent. If needed, add a few teaspoons of water to the skillet to prevent the onion from scorching. Add the chicken or turkey. Increase the heat to medium. Cook, stirring frequently, for 8 to 10 minutes, or until crumbly and no longer pink. Stir in the corn, tomatoes (with juice), peppers (with juice), chili powder, garlic, cumin, and oregano. Simmer, stirring occasionally, for 15 minutes to blend the flavors.

3. Preheat the oven to 400°F. Coat a 13" × 9" baking dish with nonstick spray. Set aside.

4. Spread half of the cooked cornmeal mixture on the bottom and up the sides of the prepared dish. Spoon the filling evenly over the cornmeal crust. Spread the remaining cornmeal mixture over the top. Sprinkle with the Cheddar.

5. Bake for 30 minutes, or until bubbly and the top is golden brown. Remove from the oven and allow to stand for at least 10 minutes before cutting.

Makes 6 servings

Per serving:	351 calories	5 g. fat	47 mg. cholesterol
	674 mg. sodium	46 g. carbohydrates	29 g. protein

Roast Chicken Tacos

These tacos are a wonderful party meal because the recipe is easy to expand for a group. You can make everything ahead of time and refrigerate it in covered bowls. At serving time, simply heat the tortillas. Include reduced-fat sour cream and Guacamole (page 41) for toppings, if you like.

Homestyle Makeover		
Each serving contains		
	Before	After
Calories	355	249
Fat g.	19	6

1 tablespoon unbleached or all-purpose flour

1 broiler-fryer chicken (3 pounds)

1 tablespoon dry taco seasoning mix

3 scallions, cut into 3" pieces

¼ cup green taco sauce

½ teaspoon ground black pepper

12 corn tortillas (6" diameter)

6 cups shredded iceberg lettuce

2 tomatoes, chopped

1 onion, chopped

1 can (4 ounces) diced green chile peppers

¾ cup (3 ounces) shredded reduced-fat Cheddar cheese

1½ cups bottled salsa

1. Put the flour in a large (20" × 14") oven cooking bag and shake well. Set aside. Wash the chicken and pat dry. Rub the taco seasoning all over the inside cavity of the chicken. Put the scallions inside the chicken.

2. In a small bowl, combine the taco sauce and black pepper. Rub some of the sauce all over the outside of the chicken. Place the chicken in the bag and pour in the remaining sauce. Place the bag in a large baking dish with sides at least 2" high. Close the bag with its nylon tie. Cut 6 slits ½" wide in the top of the bag. Refrigerate for at least 4 hours or as long as 8 hours to allow the chicken to marinate.

3. Preheat the oven to 350°F. Bake the chicken for 1 hour, or until the legs can be easily pulled away from the sides. An instant-read thermometer inserted into the thickest part of a thigh, not touching the bone, should register 180°F. Reduce the oven temperature to 300°F.

4. Remove the chicken from the oven and allow to stand for 10 minutes. With scissors, carefully cut the bag open. Remove the chicken from the bag, and pour the cooking liquid into a bowl. Place the bowl in the freezer for 15 minutes. Remove and discard the fat that accumulates on top. When the chicken is cool enough to handle safely, remove and discard the bones, skin, and all visible fat. Shred the meat and place it in a bowl. Add the defatted liquid to the chicken and mix well. This will make 3 cups of chicken.

5. Meanwhile, wrap the tortillas in foil. While the chicken is cooling, bake for 15 minutes, or until they are warm and pliable.

6. To serve, place the warm tortillas on a buffet or serving table. Place the cooked chicken in a bowl by the tortillas along with bowls of the lettuce, tomatoes, onion, chile peppers (with juice), Cheddar, and salsa.

Makes 12 servings

Per serving:	249 calories	6 g. fat	55 mg. cholesterol
	430 mg. sodium	25 g. carbohydrates	22 g. protein

Cook's Notes

• Oven cooking bags are usually found in the foils and wraps section of the supermarket.

• This roast chicken is so flavorful, tender, and easy to prepare that I often make it just to have the leftovers. Refrigerate, tightly covered, for 2 to 3 days. You can also use it for salads or soups.

Roast Turkey

Photograph on page 215

Some time during the autumn of 1621, settlers from the Plymouth Colony and members of the Wampanoag Tribe shared a feast to commemorate their mutual blessings. It's not known whether turkey was served on that day but at the next recorded Thanksgiving at Plymouth, on July 30, 1623, turkey was served, along with other forerunners of the modern feast—cranberries and pumpkin pie. The celebration gained in popularity throughout the Northeast during the two centuries that followed. By 1863, President Abraham Lincoln declared the last Thursday in November a national holiday of Thanksgiving.

Homestyle Makeover

Each 3-ounce white meat serving contains

	Before	After
Calories	289	207
Fat g.	13	3

Each 3-ounce dark meat serving contains

	Before	After
Calories	289	225
Fat g.	16	8

- 1 turkey (12 to 15 pounds), fresh or frozen and thawed
- 3 onions, peeled and quartered
- ½ cup fresh marjoram or 3 tablespoons dried
- ½ cup chopped fresh parsley
- 2 cups fat-free, reduced-sodium chicken broth

1. Preheat the oven to 325°F. Set a roasting rack in a roasting pan. Coat the rack with nonstick spray. Remove the neck and giblets from the turkey and reserve for another use. Set aside. Wash the turkey, inside and out, and pat dry with paper towels. Stuff the turkey with the onions, marjoram, and parsley. Truss, if desired.

2. Place the turkey, breast side up, on the roasting rack. Pour the broth over the top. Bake for 20 minutes per pound, basting every 15 to 20 minutes with broth from the bottom of the pan. If the turkey starts to get too brown, cover it with a lid or foil.

3. Bake until the turkey is cooked. An instant-read thermometer inserted into the thickest part of the leg, not touching the bone, should register 180°F. Carefully transfer the turkey to a platter, allowing it to rest for 20 minutes before carving.

4. Meanwhile, pour the pan drippings into a bowl and place it in the freezer for 15 minutes. Remove and discard the fat that accumulates on top. Pour the drippings into a saucepan. Bring to a boil over medium heat.

5. Remove and discard the skin before carving. Serve the turkey with the heated drippings.

Makes 26 servings

Per 3-ounce white
meat serving: *207 calories*   *3 g. fat*   *105 mg. cholesterol*
    174 mg. sodium   *1 g. carbohydrates*   *41 g. protein*

Per 3-ounce dark
meat serving: *225 calories*   *8 g. fat*   *120 mg. cholesterol*
    236 mg. sodium   *1 g. carbohydrate*   *35 g. protein*

Cook's Notes

• When buying a turkey, allow about ½ pound per person you plan to serve. If using a cooking bag, eliminate the basting process, which means you won't need the chicken broth.

• Serve the turkey with the pan drippings or add them to the gravy recipe (page 128).

Turkey Tetrazzini

Photograph on page 217

This dish was created in San Francisco and named for the opera singer Luisa Tetrazzini, who was a superstar in the United States in the early 1900s. It is an inexpensive and delicious entrée that is perfect for large parties.

Homestyle Makeover		
Each serving contains		
	Before	After
Calories	438	375
Fat g.	16	8

½ **pound spaghetti**

2 **teaspoons butter or margarine**

1 **pound mushrooms, sliced**

1 **small green bell pepper, cut into thin strips**

3 **tablespoons unbleached or all-purpose flour**

½ **teaspoon ground black pepper**

¾ **cup fat-free dry milk powder**

2 **cups fat-free, reduced-sodium chicken broth**

1 **pound cooked skinless turkey breast, cut into thin strips**

2 **tablespoons sherry or 1 tablespoon sherry vinegar**

1 **jar (4 ounces) sliced pimientos, drained**

1 **cup (4 ounces) grated Parmesan cheese**

1. Preheat the oven to 350°F. Coat a 3-quart baking dish with nonstick spray. Set aside. Bring a large covered pot of water to a boil over high heat. Add the spaghetti and cook according to the package directions. Drain and set aside.

2. Meanwhile, melt the butter or margarine in a large skillet over medium heat. Add the mushrooms and bell pepper. Cook, stirring frequently, for 5 minutes, or until they can easily be pierced with a fork. Add the flour and black pepper. Cook, stirring constantly, for 3 minutes. In a small bowl, whisk the milk powder into the broth until dissolved. Add to the skillet. Reduce the heat to low. Cook, stirring frequently, for about 15 minutes, or until thickened.

3. Add the turkey, sherry or sherry vinegar, and pimientos. Stir to mix well. Remove from the heat and cool slightly.

4. Place the spaghetti in the bottom of the prepared baking dish. Spoon the turkey mixture over the spaghetti and sprinkle with the Parmesan. Bake for 25 minutes, or until the sauce bubbles and the top is lightly browned.

Makes 8 servings

Per serving: 375 calories   8 g. fat   63 mg. cholesterol
                484 mg. sodium   40 g. carbohydrates   34 g. protein

Spicy Turkey Sausage Patties

Photograph on page 117

Because these spicy patties are made with turkey, they contain no preservatives and are much lower in saturated fat than commercial sausage.

Homestyle Makeover

Each serving contains

	Before	After
Calories	153	87
Fat g.	10	1

1 **pound ground turkey breast (see note)**

1½ **teaspoons dried sage**

½ **teaspoon ground mace**

½ **teaspoon garlic powder**

½ **teaspoon ground black pepper**

⅛ **teaspoon ground allspice**

⅛ **teaspoon ground cloves**

¼ **cup fat-free, reduced-sodium chicken broth**

1. In a medium mixing bowl, combine the turkey, sage, mace, garlic powder, pepper, allspice, and cloves. Stir to mix well.

2. Shape the turkey mixture into 12 patties. Place a large skillet over high heat, pour in the broth, and bring to a boil. Add the patties and reduce the heat to medium. Cover and cook for 8 minutes. Uncover and increase the heat to high. Cook for 1 to 2 minutes per side, or until all the broth evaporates and the patties are lightly browned on both sides and no pink remains. Check by inserting a sharp knife into the center of 1 patty. Remove the patties and drain them on paper towels.

Makes 6 servings

Per serving:	87 calories	1 g. fat	44 mg. cholesterol
	75 mg. sodium	0 g. carbohydrates	18 g. protein

Cook's Note

• You can replace the ground turkey breast with ground chicken breast.

Poultry Pointers

Chicken and turkey rank high as sources of lean protein. And with the proliferation of inexpensive chicken and turkey parts sold in supermarkets, cooking poultry has never been easier or faster. Pay attention to a few important details in selection and cooking for rich nutritional rewards from poultry.

- White meat is considerably lower in fat and calories than dark meat, and still lower without the skin. Unlike the fat in red meat, which is spread throughout the muscle, the fat in poultry is concentrated in or just below the skin. By removing the skin and the patches of fat clinging to it, you can remove about half the total amount of fat. This reduction applies even if the skin is removed and discarded after cooking.

- When cooking with ground chicken or turkey, it makes sense to ask the butcher to grind boneless, skinless breast for you. Many supermarkets do offer prepackaged, shrink-wrapped ground boneless, skinless poultry breast in the fresh poultry case. You can also grind it yourself with a food processor. When the skin, and the fat that clings to it, is removed, you're assured of getting the leanest cut possible.

- The U.S. Department of Agriculture's dietary guidelines recommend 2 to 3 servings of lean protein daily. One portion is equal to an average-size boneless chicken breast half, or about 4 ounces.

- Cooking methods that contribute little or no additional dietary fat—such as roasting, broiling, grilling, or poaching—are your best bets for maintaining poultry's lean profile. Whenever you long for the crispy exterior of fried poultry, you can easily duplicate it with a fraction of the fat, by using oven-frying methods (see Southern Fried Chicken on page 199).

Apple and Sage Rock Cornish Hens

Photograph on page 118

Rock Cornish hens are a hybrid of Cornish and White Rock chickens. These miniature chickens are best broiled or roasted because they are so small. I like to place each roasted hen half on top of Rice Pilaf (page 138) before spooning the sauce mixture over the top.

Homestyle Makeover

Each serving contains

	Before	After
Calories	598	308
Fat g.	31	3

---

2 onions, finely chopped

2 Rock Cornish hens, halved (1½ pounds each)

1½ cups apple cider

1½ teaspoons dried sage

½ teaspoon salt

½ teaspoon lemon pepper

---

1. Preheat the oven to 400°F. Coat a 13" × 9" baking dish with nonstick spray. Spread the onions evenly over the bottom of the prepared baking dish. Place the hens, cut side down, on the onions. Bake for 15 minutes, or until the skin starts to crinkle.

2. Meanwhile, in a small saucepan bring the apple cider to a boil. Boil it until reduced to about 1 cup. Stir in the sage, salt, and lemon pepper. Stir to mix well.

3. Remove the hens from the oven and allow to stand until cool enough to handle. Reduce the oven temperature to 350°F.

4. Using a sharp knife or kitchen shears, cut the skin away from each hen and discard it. Pour the cider mixture over the hens. Return to the oven. Bake for about 45 minutes, basting frequently with the pan juices, or until the liquid runs clear when the thigh is pricked with a knife. An instant-read thermometer inserted into the thickest part of the thigh, not touching the bone, should register 180°F.

5. To serve, remove the hens from the pan and arrange on plates, cut side down. Stir the cider mixture thoroughly and spoon over each hen.

Makes 4 servings

Per serving: 308 calories   3 g. fat   132 mg. cholesterol
734 mg. sodium   14 g. carbohydrates   53 g. protein

Duck à l'Orange

Domestication of ducks began in the United States in 1875 when a Yankee clipper ship docked in New York carrying a flock of ducks from Peking, China. This version of classic Duck à l'Orange, made with the breast instead of the whole duck, is considerably easier to prepare as well as lower in dietary fat.

Homestyle Makeover

Each serving contains

	Before	After
Calories	488	238
Fat g.	36	6

1 boneless duck breast, about 1 pound, skinned

1 tablespoon cornstarch

1 cup orange juice

¼ cup currant jelly

2 teaspoons grated orange peel

¼ teaspoon salt

1 tablespoon orange liqueur (optional)

1 navel orange, peeled and thinly sliced

1. Coat a large nonstick skillet with nonstick spray. Place over medium heat until hot enough for drops of water to dance on the surface. Place the duck in the skillet. Cook for 5 minutes per side, or until lightly browned. Reduce the heat to low. Cook for 20 to 25 minutes, turning as needed to cook evenly, or until an instant-read thermometer registers 160°F for medium doneness. For well doneness, cook an additional 5 to 7 minutes, or until an instant-read thermometer registers 180°F. Set aside.

2. Place the cornstarch in a medium saucepan. Gradually add the orange juice, whisking constantly, until dissolved. Add the jelly, orange peel, salt, and orange liqueur, if using. Stir to mix well. Cook over low heat for 4 to 5 minutes, or until clear and slightly thickened. Add the orange. Cook for 2 to 3 minutes, or until the orange is hot. Set aside.

3. To serve, cut the duck breast into 4 equal portions. Spoon the orange mixture over each portion.

Makes 4 servings

Per serving:	238 calories	6 g. fat	71 mg. cholesterol
	209 mg. sodium	27 g. carbohydrates	18 g. protein

Recipes

Steaks, Chops, Stews, and More

Americans have always felt at home on the range. Beef cattle from ranches in the West and Southwest as well as pork from farms in the Midwest and South produced succulent roasts, steaks, and chops for a hungry growing nation. Abundance was applauded as bigger portions were considered better portions.

When hard times hit in the 1930s, meat-and-potato meals gave way to casseroles and other combination dishes that extended meat portions. Ground beef, from tougher inexpensive cuts, starred in everything from Shepherd's Pie to Meat Loaf.

Today, we realize that lean red meat is an important part of a healthy diet, providing readily accessible iron, B vitamins, and zinc for optimal health. But we also know that portion sizes should be kept to about the size of a deck of cards. When we select lean cuts and cooking with lean methods, the meat dishes we love—Pot Roast with Vegetables, Oven-Barbecued Brisket, Beef Stew, and Stuffed Pork Chops—can continue to satisfy.

Pot Roast with Vegetables

Typically, pot roast is made with a tough cut of meat that requires braising—slow cooking in a liquid until tender—to bring out its flavor. This is a slightly fancier version of the traditional Yankee pot roast. A combination of wines gives this savory stew an incredible depth of flavor.

Homestyle Makeover		
Each serving contains		
	Before	After
Calories	425	322
Fat g.	28	7

½ teaspoon salt

3 pounds lean beef pot roast

¼ cup unbleached or all-purpose flour

1 teaspoon vegetable oil

½ cup dry red wine or non-alcoholic red wine

1 cup sherry or apple cider

3 cups fat-free beef broth

2 bay leaves

¼ teaspoon dried basil

¼ teaspoon dried marjoram

¼ teaspoon dried thyme

4 carrots, quartered

4 small red potatoes, halved

3 onions, quartered

2 teaspoons butter or margarine

½ pound mushrooms, sliced

6 tablespoons Madeira (optional)

1 tablespoon finely chopped fresh parsley

1. Sprinkle the salt evenly over the beef. Dust with the flour to coat evenly, shaking off any excess. Heat the oil in a large deep pot or Dutch oven over medium heat until hot enough for drops of water to dance on the surface. Place the beef in the pot. Cook, turning frequently, for 30 minutes, or until browned. Add the wine and sherry or cider. Simmer for 25 to 30 minutes, or until the pan is almost dry. Add the broth, bay leaves, basil, marjoram, and thyme to the pot. Reduce the heat to low. Cover and simmer for 1½ hours.

2. Add the carrots, potatoes, and onions. Cover and cook for 30 to 40 minutes, or until the beef is fork-tender.

3. Meanwhile, warm a large nonstick skillet over medium heat until hot enough for drops of water to dance on the surface. Add the butter or margarine and mushrooms. Cook, stirring frequently, for 5 minutes, or until the mushrooms are tender. When the carrots and potatoes can easily be pierced with a fork, add the mushrooms and 3 tablespoons of the Madeira, if using. Simmer for 10 minutes. Add the remaining 3 tablespoons Madeira, if using. Stir to mix. Remove and discard the bay leaves.

4. To serve, cut the beef into slices. Place on a large deep serving platter. Remove the vegetables from the pot and place around the beef. Pour some of the pan juices over the beef and vegetables. Serve the remainder in a gravy boat. Sprinkle the beef and vegetables with the parsley.

Makes 8 servings

Per serving: 322 calories   7 g. fat   68 mg. cholesterol
                   310 mg. sodium   20 g. carbohydrates   28 g. protein

Cook's Note

• Try an eye round roast for this dish because it's easy to slice. But you can also use a chuck pot roast or a boneless rump roast.

Oven-Barbecued Brisket

Photograph on page 219

Many regional barbecue styles, such as Texas and Kansas City, co-exist in this country. No two are alike, which makes for hours of sampling and debate among barbecue devotees. True barbecue is cooked in a covered pit or covered barbecue, stoked periodically with hot coals or hardwood.

Homestyle Makeover		
Each serving contains		
	Before	After
Calories	469	270
Fat g.	36	14

3 pounds beef brisket, trimmed of all visible fat

1½ cups water

1 tablespoon vegetable oil

½ onion, chopped

3 cloves garlic, pressed or minced

1 cup ketchup

3 tablespoons red wine vinegar

2 tablespoons lemon juice

2 tablespoons packed dark brown sugar

1 tablespoon Worcestershire sauce

2 teaspoons cornstarch

1 teaspoon paprika

1 teaspoon chili powder

¼ teaspoon salt

¼ teaspoon ground black pepper

¼ teaspoon liquid smoke

1. Preheat the oven to 325°F. Place the beef in a Dutch oven and add ½ cup of the water. Cover and bake for 2 hours, or until tender.

2. Meanwhile, heat the oil in a medium saucepan over medium heat. Add the onion and garlic. Cook, stirring frequently, for 5 to 7 minutes, or until the onion is translucent. Add the ketchup, vinegar, lemon juice, brown sugar, Worcestershire sauce, cornstarch, paprika, chili powder, salt, pepper, and the remaining 1 cup water. Simmer, stirring occasionally, for 1 hour over low heat to blend the flavors. Add the liquid smoke. Stir to mix.

3. Remove the beef from the pot. Drain and discard any drippings. Wipe the pot with paper towels. Return the beef to the pot. Pour the ketchup mixture over the beef. Cover and return to the oven. Bake for 1 to 1½ hours, or until the beef is fork-tender.

Makes 8 servings

Per serving:	270 calories	14 g. fat	59 mg. cholesterol
	568 mg. sodium	13 g. carbohydrates	23 g. protein

Peppered Steak

Photograph on page 228

Homestyle Makeover

Each serving contains

	Before	After
Calories	310	182
Fat g.	22	6

This generous recipe serves eight, but if you have fewer diners, the leftovers make marvelous sandwiches the next day. Keep in mind that the steak needs time to absorb the flavor of the crushed peppercorns—from 2 to 8 hours—before cooking.

3 pounds beef top sirloin steak (1¼" thick), trimmed of all visible fat

1–2 tablespoons black peppercorns, crushed

1 teaspoon butter or margarine

½ cup dry white wine or nonalcoholic white wine

1 tablespoon brandy (optional)

1. Wipe the steak with a damp cloth and carefully dry it. Firmly press the peppercorns into both sides of the steak. Place the steak in a large baking dish. Cover and refrigerate for 2 to 8 hours.

2. Warm a large nonstick skillet over medium-high heat until hot enough for drops of water to dance on the surface. Add the butter or margarine to melt. Place the beef in the skillet. Cook for 5 minutes or longer, or until an instant-read thermometer inserted in the center of the beef, not touching the pan, registers 140°F for rare and 160°F for well-done.

3. Remove the steak to a platter. Let stand for 10 minutes. Pour the wine and brandy, if using, into the skillet. Bring to a boil, stirring constantly, and scrape all the browned bits from the bottom. Boil for 2 minutes, or until slightly reduced.

4. Slice the steak into very thin slices. Spoon a little of the wine mixture over each serving.

Makes 8 servings

Per serving:	182 calories	6 g. fat	78 mg. cholesterol
	75 mg. sodium	0 g. carbohydrates	27 g. protein

Swiss Steak

This dish gets its name from the English cooking term Swissing, *which means to smooth and flatten meat before cooking.*

<table>
<tr><td colspan="3">**Homestyle Makeover**</td></tr>
<tr><td colspan="3">Each serving contains</td></tr>
<tr><td></td><td>Before</td><td>After</td></tr>
<tr><td>Calories</td><td>466</td><td>236</td></tr>
<tr><td>Fat g.</td><td>32</td><td>8</td></tr>
</table>

1 tablespoon vegetable oil

3 onions, thinly sliced

3 pounds beef chuck or round steak (1½" thick), trimmed of all visible fat

1 clove garlic, pressed or minced

1 teaspoon seasoned salt

¼ teaspoon ground black pepper

½ cup + 2 tablespoons unbleached or all-purpose flour

3½ cups fat-free, reduced-sodium beef or chicken broth

1 can (14 ounces) diced tomatoes

2 ribs celery, chopped

2 carrots, chopped

¼ cup chopped scallion top

½ teaspoon dried tarragon

½ teaspoon dried thyme

2 tablespoons water

1. Heat the oil in a large nonstick skillet over medium heat. Add the onions and cook, stirring frequently, for 15 to 20 minutes, or until lightly browned. Remove the onions. Set aside.

2. Rub the beef with the garlic, salt, and pepper. Sprinkle with ½ cup of the flour and pound it in on both sides of the meat, using the flat side of a meat mallet or the rim of a heavy skillet. Try to pound in as much of the flour as possible.

3. Add the beef to the skillet. Cook, turning as needed, over medium heat for 10 to 12 minutes, or until browned on all sides. Return the onions to the skillet. Add the broth, tomatoes (with juice), celery, carrots, scallion, tarragon, and thyme. Cover and simmer for 2 to 2½ hours, or until the beef is fork-tender. Remove the beef. Set aside.

4. Place the remaining 2 tablespoons of the flour in a small bowl. Gradually add the water, whisking until smooth. Add to the broth mixture. Cook, stirring constantly, over medium heat for 3 minutes, or until thickened.

5. Slice the meat into 8 pieces. Top each serving with the sauce.

Makes 8 servings

| Per serving: | 236 calories | 8 g. fat | 69 mg. cholesterol |
| | 599 mg. sodium | 13 g. carbohydrates | 27 g. protein |

Cook's Note

• If you have any leftover steak, chop it up, mix it with the leftover broth mixture, and serve over rice, noodles, baked potatoes, or hamburger buns for another meal.

Chicken-Fried Steak with Country Gravy

Chicken-fried steak is said to have been created during the Great Depression. The recipe transforms an inexpensive, tough cut of beef by tenderizing, breading, and frying it like chicken. The genuine article is topped with country gravy, a creamy sauce made from the thickened pan drippings and milk.

Homestyle Makeover		
Each serving contains		
	Before	After
Calories	720	308
Fat g.	45	3

Steak

1 pound beef round steak, trimmed of all visible fat and cut into 4 equal pieces

2 egg whites, lightly beaten

½ cup fat-free milk

1½ cups unbleached or all-purpose flour

1 teaspoon seasoned salt

1 teaspoon ground black pepper

Gravy

3 tablespoons unbleached or all-purpose flour

2 cups fat-free milk

½ teaspoon salt

¼ teaspoon ground black pepper

1. *To make the steak:* Place the beef in a plastic bag. Using the flat side of a meat mallet, pound each piece until ½" thin. In a shallow bowl, combine the egg whites and milk. Divide the flour equally onto 2 plates. Add the salt and pepper to one and mix well. Dip the beef into the unseasoned flour, egg-white mixture, and then the seasoned flour.

2. Coat a large nonstick skillet with nonstick spray. Warm over medium heat. Place the beef in the skillet. Cook for 5 minutes per side, or until golden brown. Remove from the skillet and cover to keep warm.

3. *To make the gravy:* Add the flour to the skillet. Cook, stirring constantly, for 3 minutes. Add the milk, salt, and pepper. Cook, stirring frequently, for 12 to 15 minutes, or until thickened. Spoon over the beef.

Makes 4 servings

Per serving: 308 calories   3 g. fat   26 mg. cholesterol
                    738 mg. sodium   49 g. carbohydrates   21 g. protein

Beef Stew

Photograph on page 229

Homestyle Makeover

Each serving contains

	Before	After
Calories	378	222
Fat g.	20	8

To make this stew even lower in fat, remove it from the heat before adding the vegetables. Cool to room temperature and then refrigerate, uncovered, overnight. The next day, lift all the hardened fat from the top. Reheat the stew to a simmer before adding the pearl onions, turnips, and carrot to simmer for an hour.

1½ pounds lean beef, trimmed of all visible fat and cut into 1" cubes

½ cup unbleached or all-purpose flour

1 tablespoon butter or margarine

1 large onion, chopped

½ pound mushrooms, sliced

1 clove garlic, minced

¼ cup finely chopped fresh parsley

1 bay leaf

½ teaspoon dried dillweed

½ teaspoon dried marjoram

1 teaspoon salt

½ teaspoon ground black pepper

1½ cups water

2 cups dry red wine or nonalcoholic red wine

16 pearl onions, peeled

2 turnips, cut into 2" cubes

1 carrot, sliced

2 cups frozen peas

1. Place the beef and flour in a plastic bag and shake until the meat is thoroughly coated. Set aside. Melt the butter or margarine in a Dutch oven over medium heat. Add the chopped onion, mushrooms, and garlic. Cook, stirring frequently, for 10 minutes, or until the onion is translucent. Remove the onion mixture from the pot. Set aside. Place the beef in the pot. Cook, stirring constantly, for 15 minutes, or until browned. Stir in the parsley, bay leaf, dillweed, marjoram, salt, pepper, and the reserved onion mixture. Stir in ½ cup of the water and 1 cup of the wine. Bring to a boil. Reduce the heat to low. Cover and simmer for 1 hour.

2. Add the remaining 1 cup water and 1 cup wine. Cover and simmer for 30 minutes. Add the pearl onions, turnips, and carrot. Cover and simmer for 1 hour. Add the peas and cook for 10 minutes. Discard the bay leaf.

Makes 8 servings

Per serving:	222 calories	8 g. fat	33 mg. cholesterol
	580 mg. sodium	14 g. carbohydrates	15 g. protein

Beef Stroganoff

Americans have always loved to adopt ethnic dishes and make them their own. This classic—named after the nineteenth-century Russian diplomat Count Paul Stroganov—is a perfect example. Serve over rice, rice pilaf, or noodles.

3 teaspoons butter or margarine

¼ pound mushrooms, sliced

1 onion, sliced

1½ pounds beef sirloin steak, trimmed of all visible fat and cut into 1"-wide strips

2½ tablespoons unbleached or all-purpose flour

2½ cups fat-free, reduced-sodium beef broth

3 tablespoons dry sherry or apple cider

1 tablespoon tomato paste

1 teaspoon paprika

½ teaspoon dried basil

¼ teaspoon ground nutmeg

¾ cup reduced-fat sour cream

1. In a large nonstick skillet, melt 2 teaspoons of the butter or margarine over medium heat. Add the mushrooms and onion. Cook, stirring occasionally, for 10 to 12 minutes, or until the onion is lightly browned. Remove the onion mixture from the skillet. Set aside.

2. Melt the remaining 1 teaspoon butter or margarine in the skillet. Add the beef. Cook, turning as needed, for 15 minutes, or until lightly browned on all sides. Add the beef to the onion mixture.

3. Add the flour to the skillet. Cook, stirring constantly, for 2 to 3 minutes, or until browned. Slowly add the broth, stirring constantly, until smooth.

4. Add the sherry or cider, tomato paste, paprika, basil, and nutmeg. Simmer, stirring occasionally, for 10 minutes, or until the mixture thickens. Add the beef mixture. Simmer for 10 minutes. Add the sour cream. Stir to mix.

Makes 6 servings

Per serving:	222 calories	11 g. fat	47 mg. cholesterol
	343 mg. sodium	10 g. carbohydrates	18 g. protein

Corned Beef and Cabbage

Homestyle Makeover

Each serving contains

	Before	After
Calories	388	327
Fat g.	20	13

I've based this revision on my grandmother's recipe, which includes carrots, celery, and potatoes as well as cabbage. I like it because it provides a complete one-dish meal.

3 pounds lean corned beef, trimmed of all visible fat

1 onion, chopped

2 cloves garlic, halved

2 bay leaves

10 peppercorns

2 tablespoons pickling spices

6 small carrots, halved crosswise

4 ribs celery, quartered crosswise

3 potatoes, quartered

1 medium head cabbage, cut in eighths

1. Place the corned beef in a large pot or Dutch oven. Cover with cold water. Add the onion, garlic, bay leaves, peppercorns, and pickling spices. Bring to a boil over medium heat. Reduce the heat to low. Cover and simmer for 3 hours, or until the corned beef is fork-tender.

2. Remove from the heat and cool to room temperature. Refrigerate, uncovered, overnight.

3. Remove and discard the fat that has hardened on the top. Bring to a boil over medium heat. Reduce the heat to low. Add the carrots, celery, and potatoes. Simmer for 15 minutes. Add the cabbage. Cook for 15 minutes, or until the vegetables are tender. Remove and discard the bay leaves.

4. Cut the corned beef into slices. Serve in shallow bowls with the vegetables and some of the broth.

Makes 8 servings

Per serving:	*327 calories*	*13 g. fat*	*59 mg. cholesterol*
	213 mg. sodium	*28 g. carbohydrates*	*27 g. protein*

Corned Beef Hash

My favorite corned beef hash is made with any leftover corned beef that I have from the Corned Beef and Cabbage on page 257. It has so much more flavor, and is so much lower in fat, than its delicatessen counterpart.

Homestyle Makeover		
Each serving contains		
	Before	After
Calories	297	237
Fat g.	15	8

2 cups finely chopped cooked corned beef

4 small cooked potatoes, chopped

½ onion, chopped

1 tablespoon chopped fresh parsley

¼ teaspoon ground black pepper

1. In a large bowl, combine the corned beef, potatoes, onion, parsley, and pepper.

2. Coat a large nonstick skillet with nonstick spray. Warm it over medium heat until hot enough for drops of water to dance on the surface. Spread the corned beef mixture evenly in the skillet and press it down firmly. Cook, turning frequently, for 10 to 15 minutes, or until brown on both sides.

Makes 4 servings

Per serving:

237 calories
136 mg. sodium

8 g. fat
21 g. carbohydrates

41 mg. cholesterol
18 g. protein

Hungarian Goulash

Photograph on page 220

Homestyle Makeover

Each serving contains

	Before	After
Calories	294	190
Fat g.	22	11

Hungarian immigrants brought this hearty stew with them to America. But don't think the amount of paprika called for in this recipe is a misprint. It actually takes this much paprika to give the authentic taste and color to this hearty goulash, or gulyás as it's called in its native country.

1 tablespoon butter or margarine

6 onions, thinly sliced

2 pounds extra-lean beef, cut into 1" cubes

¼ cup paprika

1 teaspoon salt

1 cup reduced-fat sour cream

1. Warm a large deep pot or Dutch oven over medium-high heat. Add the butter or margarine to melt. Add the onions. Cook, stirring frequently, for 18 to 20 minutes, or until lightly browned. Add the beef, paprika, and salt. Reduce the heat to low. Cover and cook for 1½ to 2 hours, or until the meat is fork-tender.

2. Add the sour cream. Stir to mix. Cook to heat through. Do not allow to boil.

Makes 8 servings

Per serving:

190 calories	11 g. fat	45 mg. cholesterol
755 mg. sodium	7 g. carbohydrates	17 g. protein

Cook's Notes

• A variety of extra-lean cuts of beef will work for this goulash. See page 269 for information about selecting lean cuts.

• Serve over any pasta, rice, or potatoes.

Meat Loaf

Since I have never really decided whether I like meat loaf or leftover meat loaf sandwiches better, my favorite meat loaf has a great tomato topping that can be spread on bread for sandwiches the next day—truly the best of both worlds.

Photograph on page 221

Homestyle Makeover

Each serving contains

	Before	After
Calories	420	296
Fat g.	24	17

- 4 slices whole-wheat bread
- 1 cup fat-free milk
- 1 onion, finely chopped
- 2 cloves garlic, pressed or minced
- 2 pounds extra-lean ground round beef
- 3 egg whites, lightly beaten
- ¼ cup finely chopped fresh parsley
- 1 tablespoon finely chopped fresh marjoram or 1 teaspoon dried
- 1 tablespoon finely chopped fresh thyme leaves or 1 teaspoon dried
- 1 teaspoon salt
- ½ teaspoon ground black pepper
- 1 can (6 ounces) tomato paste

1. Preheat the oven to 375°F. Coat a rack and baking dish with nonstick spray. Set aside.

2. Remove the bread crusts and place in a blender or food processor. Blend or process to form coarse bread crumbs. Set aside. Tear the remaining bread into small pieces and place them in a large bowl. Add the milk. Mix well. Set aside.

3. Warm a large nonstick skillet over medium heat until hot enough for drops of water to dance on the surface. Reduce the heat to low. Add the onion and garlic. Remove from the heat. Coat the onion and garlic with nonstick spray. Return to low heat, cover, and cook for 12 to 15 minutes, or until the onion is translucent. If needed, add a few teaspoons of water to the skillet to prevent the onion from scorching.

4. Add the onion mixture and beef to a large bowl. Mix well. Add the bread mixture, egg whites, parsley, marjoram, thyme, salt, and pepper. Mix well. Form a loaf about 9" × 5" and place on the prepared rack. Bake for 30 minutes.

5. Spread the tomato paste evenly over the loaf. Sprinkle the bread crumbs over the top. Return to the oven. Bake for 40 to 45 minutes, or until cooked. Check by inserting a sharp knife into the center of the loaf to make sure it is no longer pink. An instant-read thermometer inserted in the center of the loaf, not touching the pan, should register 160°F.

6. Remove from the oven and allow to stand for 10 minutes to firm slightly. To serve, cut into 1"-thick slices.

Makes 8 servings

Per serving:			
	296 calories	*17 g. fat*	*57 g. cholesterol*
	557 mg. sodium	*17 g. carbohydrates*	*19 g. protein*

Cook's Note

• Be sure that the sides of the baking dish are at least 2" high so that any fat drippings will not run over the sides.

Shepherd's Pie

Photograph on page 225

This British dish, adopted long ago by Americans, is a meat-and-vegetable stew baked under a tender crust of mashed potatoes.

Homestyle Makeover		
Each serving contains		
	Before	After
Calories	477	427
Fat g.	26	21

1½ pounds potatoes, cubed

½ cup 1% milk

1 tablespoon butter or margarine, melted

¼ cup chopped fresh parsley

½ teaspoon ground black pepper

1½ pounds extra-lean ground round beef or lamb

1 clove garlic, pressed or minced

1 tablespoon vegetable oil

4 large carrots, chopped

6 ounces mushrooms, chopped

1 onion, chopped

1 tablespoon chopped fresh thyme leaves or 1 teaspoon dried

1 tablespoon unbleached or all-purpose flour

1 cup fat-free, reduced-sodium chicken broth

1 package (10 ounces) frozen corn, thawed

1. In a large saucepan, add the potatoes and cover with water. Bring to a boil over high heat. Reduce the heat to low. Cover and cook for 20 to 25 minutes, or until the potatoes can easily be pierced with a fork. Drain and return to the saucepan. Add the milk, butter or margarine, parsley, and ¼ teaspoon of the pepper. Mash with a potato masher or electric mixer. Set aside.

2. Warm a large nonstick skillet over medium-high heat until hot enough for drops of water to dance on the surface. Add the beef or lamb and garlic. Cook, stirring frequently, for 10 minutes, or until the beef or lamb is no longer pink. Remove the beef or lamb mixture to a bowl. Set aside.

3. In the skillet, warm the oil over medium heat. Add the carrots, mushrooms, and onion. Cook, stirring frequently, for 5 minutes, or until the carrots can easily be pierced with a fork. Stir in the thyme and the remaining ¼ teaspoon pepper.

4. Preheat the oven to 375°F. Coat a 2-quart baking dish with nonstick spray.

5. Place the flour in a small bowl. Gradually add the broth, whisking until smooth. Add to the skillet and mix well. Bring to a boil, stirring frequently. Reduce the heat to low. Simmer, stirring occasionally, for 10 minutes, or until slightly thickened. Add the corn and beef or lamb mixture as well as any juices. Stir to mix well. Spread the mixture in the prepared baking dish. Spoon small mounds of the potato mixture on top. Spread to cover the top, if desired. Bake for 30 minutes, or until bubbly and the potatoes are golden.

Makes 6 servings

Per serving: *427 calories*   *21 g. fat*   *63 mg. cholesterol*
                      372 mg. sodium   *42 g. carbohydrates*   *20 g. protein*

Cook's Note

• For a fancier presentation, fit a large pastry bag with a large rosette tip. Spoon the mashed potatoes into the bag. Pipe the mashed potatoes in diagonal strips on top of the stew.

Lasagna

Lasagna has become so Americanized that it's no longer even considered ethnic fare. This truly delicious version is a bit high in fat, so plan on eating low-fat foods for the remaining meals of the day.

Photograph on page 222

Homestyle Makeover

Each serving contains

	Before	After
Calories	355	331
Fat g.	21	15

1½ pounds extra-lean ground round beef

1 onion, chopped

1 can (28 ounces) chopped tomatoes

1 jar (14 ounces) pizza sauce

¼ cup chopped fresh parsley

1 teaspoon dried oregano

1 teaspoon dried basil

1 teaspoon chili powder

1 package (8 ounces) lasagna noodles

2 cups (8 ounces) shredded reduced-fat mozzarella cheese

2 cups (8 ounces) shredded reduced-fat Swiss cheese

2 cups (8 ounces) shredded reduced-fat Cheddar cheese

½ cup (2 ounces) grated Parmesan cheese

1. Preheat the oven to 375°F. Coat a 13" × 9" baking dish with nonstick spray. Set aside.

2. Warm a large nonstick skillet over medium heat until hot enough for drops of water to dance on the surface. Add the beef and onion. Cook, stirring frequently, over medium heat for 10 to 12 minutes, or until the beef is no longer pink and the onion is translucent. Add the tomatoes (with juice), pizza sauce, parsley, oregano, basil, and chili powder. Stir to mix well. Simmer, stirring occasionally, over low heat for 30 minutes, or until thickened.

3. Meanwhile, cook the noodles in a large pot of boiling water according to the package directions. Drain in a colander. Rinse with cold water. Set aside.

4. Spoon about a third of the sauce into the prepared baking dish. Top with half of the lasagna noodles and half of the mozzarella, Swiss, and Cheddar. Top with half of the remaining sauce, all the remaining noodles, and the remaining mozzarella, Swiss, and Cheddar. Top with the remaining sauce. Bake for 35 minutes, or until bubbly. Remove from the oven and sprinkle with the Parmesan. Allow to stand for 15 minutes for the filling to firm slightly.

Makes 12 servings

Per serving:	*331 calories*	*15 g. fat*	*55 mg. cholesterol*
	510 mg. sodium	*22 g. carbohydrates*	*28 g. protein*

Cook's Notes

• For even faster preparation, use no-boil lasagna noodles.

• Cooked lasagna freezes well. Bake in an oven-to-freezer-safe dish. Cool and refrigerate it for several hours until cold before wrapping tightly in foil. Freeze for up to 1 month. Remove the frozen lasagna and bake in a preheated 350°F oven for 1 hour, or until completely heated through.

Spaghetti with Meat Sauce

Photograph on page 224

This savory meat sauce can also be made with extra-lean ground round or ground turkey breast. It is good served over any type of pasta, rice, or baked potatoes or on rolls for hot, open-faced sandwiches. The sauce freezes well and can be made ahead of time for large parties.

Homestyle Makeover		
Each serving contains		
	Before	After
Calories	157	137
Fat g.	11	6

1½ teaspoons vegetable oil
1 carrot, shredded
1 onion, finely chopped
1 rib celery, finely chopped
1 small green bell pepper, finely chopped
1 tablespoon imitation bacon bits
1 pound lean ground veal
1 cup fat-free beef broth
½ cup dry white wine or nonalcoholic white wine

¼ cup tomato sauce
½ teaspoon salt
¼ teaspoon ground black pepper
⅛ teaspoon ground nutmeg
12 ounces spaghetti
1½ teaspoons butter or margarine
¼ pound mushrooms, sliced
½ cup fat-free milk

1. Fill a large deep pot with water. Cover and bring to a boil over high heat.

2. Warm the oil in a large skillet over medium heat. Add the carrot, onion, celery, bell pepper, and bacon bits. Cook, stirring frequently, for 10 to 12 minutes, or until the vegetables are lightly browned. Add the veal. Cook for 5 minutes, or until the veal is no longer pink. Add the broth, wine, tomato sauce, salt, black pepper, and nutmeg. Cover and simmer for 20 minutes. Set aside.

3. Add the spaghetti to the boiling water. Cook, stirring occasionally, according to the package directions.

4. Meanwhile, heat the butter or margarine in a large nonstick skillet. Add the mushrooms. Cook, stirring frequently, for 3 to 5 minutes, or until tender. Add the mushrooms and milk to the veal mixture. Stir to mix. Keep warm over low heat.

5. Serve 1 cup of spaghetti on each of 6 plates and top with about ½ cup of the sauce.

Makes 6 servings

Per serving:			
	137 calories	*6 g. fat*	*42 mg. cholesterol*
	413 mg. sodium	*6 g. carbohydrates*	*12 g. protein*

Diamond Jim's Special

<table>
<tr><td colspan="3">Homestyle Makeover</td></tr>
<tr><td colspan="3">Each serving contains</td></tr>
<tr><td></td><td>Before</td><td>After</td></tr>
<tr><td>Calories</td><td>354</td><td>246</td></tr>
<tr><td>Fat g.</td><td>29</td><td>16</td></tr>
</table>

This dish is named for the legendary California Gold Rush baron Diamond Jim Brady. This tasty concoction is said to have been his favorite breakfast that, historians tell us, he topped with ketchup. It is an easy dish for brunch or dinner.

1 **pound extra-lean ground round beef**

1 **onion, finely chopped**

1 **package (10 ounces) frozen chopped spinach, thawed and squeezed dry**

2 **eggs, lightly beaten**

½ **teaspoon salt**

1. Warm a large nonstick skillet over medium heat. Add the beef and onion. Cook, stirring frequently, for 8 to 10 minutes, or until the beef is no longer pink. Add the spinach. Stir to mix well. Add the eggs and salt. Cook, stirring constantly, for 3 to 4 minutes, or until the eggs are cooked.

Makes 4 servings

Per serving:			
	246 calories	*16 g. fat*	*158 mg. cholesterol*
	575 mg. sodium	*6 g. carbohydrates*	*21 g. protein*

Frankfurters with Baked Beans

I have moderated the fat in this comforting childhood favorite just enough to make it acceptable as a once-in-a-while indulgence for grown-ups. If you have a brand of reduced-fat frankfurters that you enjoy, feel free to substitute them in this recipe.

Homestyle Makeover		
Each serving contains		
	Before	After
Calories	345	264
Fat g.	23	15

1 lemon, halved
1 tablespoon butter or margarine
1 onion, finely chopped
2 cans (16 ounces each) baked beans

3 tablespoons molasses
½ teaspoon dry mustard
¼ teaspoon ground nutmeg
   Pinch of baking soda
6 all-beef frankfurters

1. Preheat the oven to 375°F. Coat a 3-quart baking dish with nonstick spray. Set aside.

2. Squeeze 1 tablespoon of juice from one of the lemon halves. Set aside. Cut the remaining half into thin slices and reserve.

3. Melt the butter or margarine in a large nonstick skillet over medium heat. Add the onion and cook, stirring frequently, for 7 to 8 minutes, or until translucent. Add the lemon juice, beans, molasses, mustard, nutmeg, and baking soda. Stir to mix well. Spoon the mixture into the prepared baking dish.

4. Score the frankfurters on one side in a crisscross fashion and arrange them on top of the bean mixture. Coat lightly with nonstick spray. Place the lemon slices on top. Bake for 1 hour, or until the frankfurters are browned.

Makes 6 servings

Per serving:	*264 calories*	*15 g. fat*	*33 mg. cholesterol*
	882 mg. sodium	*26 g. carbohydrates*	*9 g. protein*

Meaty Matters

Beef, pork, and lamb are packed with B vitamins and abundant in minerals such as iron and zinc. The biggest drawback, and the main reason to moderate intake of red meat, is that it can contain high amounts of saturated fat.

The U.S. Department of Agriculture's dietary guidelines recommend two to three portions of protein per day choosing from a variety of sources: dried beans, poultry, fish, eggs, and nuts. With care in selecting the trimmest cuts and leanest cooking methods, meat can be a satisfying component of your healthy eating style several times a week. Follow these guidelines.

- Beef is divided into three grades: select, choice, and prime. The grade is determined by the amount of marbling, or fat running through the muscle of the meat. Select contains the least amount of fat and prime, the most.

- When buying beef, pork, and lamb, look for cuts that have "loin" or "round" in the name. Good choices are eye of round, top steak, tip round, top sirloin, top loin, and tenderloin.

- Always trim all visible fat from the meat before cooking it. Use cooking methods such as roasting, braising, broiling, or grilling to allow excess fat to melt off in cooking. Setting meat on a rack in a baking dish, or cooking it in a ridged-surface grill pan on the stove top, allows the fat to run off more easily.

- When making stews or soups with meat, prepare them a day ahead and refrigerate overnight. The saturated fat will rise to the top and harden so that you can easily remove it before reheating and serving. Not only will you have a healthier dish, it won't look or taste greasy.

Stuffed Pork Chops

I love to serve these hearty chops in the fall and winter, accompanied by sweet potatoes and brussels sprouts. Even though these stuffed chops are much lower in fat than the original version, the portions are still outstanding.

Photograph on page 223

Photograph on page 223

Homestyle Makeover

Each serving contains

	Before	After
Calories	469	264
Fat g.	22	12

3 slices whole-wheat bread, torn into small pieces

6 bone-in pork chops (2" thick), trimmed of all visible fat and butterflied (see note)

¼ teaspoon ground black pepper

1 teaspoon salt

1 tablespoon butter or margarine

½ onion, chopped

¾ teaspoon ground cinnamon

¼ teaspoon ground allspice

1 large green apple, quartered and thinly sliced

⅓ cup raisins

2–3 tablespoons water

1. Place the bread in a food processor or blender. Process or blend to form coarse bread crumbs. Set aside.

2. Open the 2 flaps of each chop like a book with the bone as the spine. With the flat side of a meat mallet or rim of a heavy skillet, pound the flaps thin. Sprinkle the chops with the pepper and ½ teaspoon of the salt. Set aside.

3. Preheat the oven to 350°F. Coat a large shallow baking dish with non-stick spray. Set aside.

4. Melt the butter or margarine in a large skillet over medium heat. Add the onion and bread crumbs. Cook, stirring frequently, for 6 minutes, or until the onion is translucent. Stir in the cinnamon, allspice, and the remaining ½ teaspoon salt. Add the apple, raisins, and 2 tablespoons water. Stir to mix. Add up to 1 tablespoon more of water, if needed, to moisten. Spoon ⅓ cup of the stuffing onto one flap of each of the chops. Fold the other flap over the stuffing. Fasten with toothpicks. Place the chops in a single layer in the prepared baking dish. Bake for 1 to 1¼ hours, or until the chops are tender and an instant-read thermometer inserted in the center of the chop, not touching the bone, registers 155°F. Turn once during baking. If needed, remove the pan from the oven and spoon off and discard any excess fat accumulated in the baking pan.

Makes 6 servings

Per serving: *264 calories*   *12 g. fat*   *54 mg. cholesterol*
                 573 mg. sodium   *20 g. carbohydrates*   *20 g. protein*

Cook's Note

• To butterfly a pork chop, place it on a large cutting board. With a sharp knife parallel to the cutting board, cut through the middle of the chop from the outer edge toward the bone. Leave the meat attached to the bone. If possible, ask your butcher to butterfly the pork chops for you.

Sweet-and-Sour Pork

Photograph on page 226

This is an update of one of my mother's favorite party dishes from the 1950s. I like to serve it with cooked rice or Asian noodles, accompanied by stir-fried pea pods.

Homestyle Makeover

Each serving contains

	Before	After
Calories	397	273
Fat g.	23	12

2 pounds pork tenderloin, trimmed of all visible fat

1 can (20 ounces) pineapple chunks

2 tablespoons cornstarch

½ teaspoon salt

⅓ cup cider vinegar

3 tablespoons sugar

1 tablespoon soy sauce

½ pound mushrooms, sliced

1 can (8 ounces) sliced water chestnuts, drained

1 green bell pepper, thinly sliced

1 onion, thinly sliced

1. Preheat the oven to 350°F. Coat a 13" × 9" baking dish with nonstick spray. Place the pork in the prepared baking dish. Roast for 45 minutes, or until an instant-read thermometer inserted in the thickest part of the pork, not touching the baking dish, registers 155°F. Remove from the oven and allow to cool enough to handle. Cut into 1" cubes. Set aside.

2. Set a fine mesh strainer over a large saucepan. Drain the pineapple so that the juice goes into the saucepan. Reserve the pineapple. Place the cornstarch and salt in a small bowl. Gradually add the vinegar, whisking constantly, until smooth. Add it to the saucepan. Cook, stirring constantly, over medium heat for 4 minutes, or until thickened. Add the pork, pineapple, sugar, and soy sauce. Stir to mix well. Refrigerate for at least 30 minutes to blend the flavors.

3. Heat the pork mixture over medium heat. Add the mushrooms, water chestnuts, pepper, and onion. Stir to mix. Cook for 4 to 5 minutes, or until the vegetables are crisp-tender.

Makes 8 servings

Per serving:	273 calories	12 g. fat	63 mg. cholesterol
	365 mg. sodium	21 g. carbohydrates	20 g. protein

Baked Ham with Pineapple Rings

This rendition of baked ham is infinitely easier to prepare and carve than a whole ham scored in a lattice pattern, studded with cloves, and covered with pineapple rings. Plan to serve this savory ham main dish when you can reduce your sodium intake during the other meals of the day.

1 center-cut extra-lean, fully cooked ham slice, about 3 pounds (3" thick), trimmed of all visible fat

1 can (20 ounces) pineapple slices

1 cup cider vinegar

¾ cup packed light brown sugar

1 tablespoon Worcestershire sauce

½ teaspoon ground ginger

1. Coat a large baking dish with nonstick spray. Place the ham in the prepared dish.

2. Drain the juice from the pineapple into a large bowl. Reserve the pineapple in a bowl, tightly covered, in the refrigerator.

3. Add the vinegar, brown sugar, Worcestershire sauce, and ginger to the pineapple juice. Mix well. Pour over the ham. Cover tightly and refrigerate for 4 hours or overnight.

4. Preheat the oven to 300°F. Remove the ham from the refrigerator and uncover. Bake, basting occasionally with the pan juices, for 2 hours. Arrange the reserved pineapple rings on top of the ham. Bake, basting frequently, for 1 hour, or until well-glazed.

5. Remove from the oven and allow to rest for 10 minutes before slicing.

Makes 8 servings

Per serving:	248 calories	5 g. fat	53 mg. cholesterol
	1,524 mg. sodium	28 g. carbohydrates	22 g. protein

Rack of Lamb

This is a quite elegant old family recipe. I particularly like the crumb topping served on it but it certainly isn't essential. It makes a lovely dinner in spring served with new potatoes and sugar snap peas.

Photograph on page 227

Homestyle Makeover

Each serving contains

	Before	After
Calories	424	327
Fat g.	33	21

1 lamb rib roast (about 2½ pounds), trimmed of all visible fat

2 tablespoons Dijon mustard

½ teaspoon salt

½ teaspoon ground black pepper

2 tablespoons butter or margarine

⅔ cup dried bread crumbs

2 tablespoons finely chopped fresh parsley

½ teaspoon chopped fresh rosemary or dried rosemary, crushed

1. Preheat the oven to 400°F.

2. Coat a roasting rack with nonstick spray. Place in a shallow roasting pan. Place the lamb, bone side down, on the prepared rack. Spread the mustard over the meat's surface. Sprinkle with the salt and pepper. Roast the lamb for 20 to 25 minutes, or until an instant-read thermometer inserted in the center of the roast, not touching the pan, registers 145°F.

3. Meanwhile, in a small nonstick skillet, melt the butter or margarine over medium heat. Add the bread crumbs. Cook, stirring frequently, for 3 to 5 minutes, or until golden brown. Stir in the parsley and rosemary. Set aside.

4. Remove the lamb from the oven. Allow to stand for 10 minutes before carving into individual chops. Sprinkle each chop with the crumb mixture before serving.

Makes 4 servings

Per serving:	327 calories	21 g. fat	74 mg. cholesterol
	622 mg. sodium	15 g. carbohydrates	19 g. protein

Spicy Braised Lamb Shanks

A long, slow-cooking method, such as braising, is always required to tenderize lamb shanks. I like to serve these spicy lamb shanks with the Cornbread on page 284.

2 teaspoons cumin seeds, crushed	¼ cup raisins
4 cloves garlic, quartered	1 tablespoon lemon pepper
4 medium lamb shanks (3 pounds), trimmed of all visible fat	1 tablespoon Worcestershire sauce
1 can (28 ounces) chopped tomatoes	1 teaspoon sugar
¾ cup dry red wine or non-alcoholic red wine	1 teaspoon dried oregano
1 onion, thinly sliced	½ teaspoon ground allspice
	½ teaspoon paprika
	2 bay leaves

1. Preheat the oven to 325°F. Coat a large deep pot or Dutch oven with nonstick spray. Warm it over medium heat until hot enough for drops of water to dance on the surface. Add the cumin seeds and garlic. Cook until browned. Add the lamb. Cook, turning frequently, for 15 minutes, or until well-browned on all sides.

2. In a medium bowl, combine the tomatoes (with juice), wine, onion, raisins, lemon pepper, Worcestershire sauce, sugar, oregano, allspice, paprika, and bay leaves. Stir to mix well. Pour over the lamb. Cover with a lid or foil. Bake for 2 to 2½ hours, or until the lamb is fork-tender. Remove and discard the bay leaves.

3. To serve, place each shank in a large soup bowl and spoon the tomato mixture over the top.

Makes 4 servings

Per serving: 393 calories   21 g. fat   101 mg. cholesterol
                    391 mg. sodium   16 g. carbohydrates   30 g. protein

Lamb Curry

David Nelson, a good friend and highly respected food critic living in San Diego, is renowned for his curry parties. I am happy to report that I have his blessing in streamlining his recipe for contemporary taste.

1 teaspoon vegetable oil

1 teaspoon mustard seeds

2 large onions, chopped

3 tablespoons finely chopped fresh ginger

4 tablespoons Madras-style curry powder (see note)

3 cloves garlic, peeled and crushed

2 bay leaves

3 pounds extra-lean lamb, trimmed of all visible fat and cut into 1½" cubes

½ cup water

1 tablespoon cider vinegar

1 large apple, cored, peeled, and cubed

1 banana, sliced

2 tablespoons mango chutney

1 can (12 ounces) fat-free evaporated milk

Juice from 1 lime

1 teaspoon coconut extract

1. Heat the oil in a large deep pot or Dutch oven over medium heat. Add the mustard seeds. Cover and cook. The seeds will pop like popcorn. When the seeds are done popping, remove the cover. Add the onions. Cook, stirring frequently, for 10 to 12 minutes, or until translucent. Increase the heat to high. Add the ginger. Stir-fry for 1 to 2 minutes. Add the curry powder. Cook, stirring constantly, for 5 minutes, or until browned. Stir in the garlic and bay leaves.

2. Add the lamb, water, and vinegar. Bring to a boil. Stir in the apple, banana, and chutney. Reduce the heat to low. Cover and simmer, stirring occasionally, for 1½ to 2 hours, or until the lamb is fork-tender.

3. Stir in the milk. Simmer, stirring constantly, for 5 minutes. Remove from the heat. Add the lime juice and coconut extract. Stir to mix. Remove and discard the bay leaves.

Makes 8 servings

Per serving: *309 calories*   *14 g. fat*   *61 mg. cholesterol*
                  367 mg. sodium   *20 g. carbohydrates*   *27 g. protein*

Cook's Notes

• Madras-style curry powder is slightly hotter than regular. If you'd like more curry punch after you've tried this recipe, add an extra tablespoon the next time you make the recipe.

• You can make the dish a day or two in advance. Completely cook the lamb as directed, then cool and refrigerate, uncovered. Remove and discard any congealed fat. To serve, warm the lamb mixture over medium heat and finish the recipe.

• The curry can be served with cooked rice and an array of condiments, such as mango chutney, slivered almonds, shredded coconut, raisins, or sliced bananas tossed with lemon juice. Pass the condiments for guests to help themselves.

Veal Parmesan with Tomato Sauce

Alla Parmigiana *is the classic Italian term describing a dish that is cooked with Parmesan cheese. Veal Parmesan is the most popular dish in this category.*

Tomato Sauce

1 tablespoon extra-virgin olive oil	½ teaspoon salt
1 onion, finely chopped	¼ teaspoon ground black pepper
3 cloves garlic, pressed or minced	1 can (8 ounces) tomato sauce
6 plum tomatoes, peeled and chopped (see note)	1½ teaspoons Italian seasoning

Veal

1 pound veal round steak, trimmed of all visible fat	2 egg whites, lightly beaten
¼ cup (1 ounce) grated Parmesan cheese	1½ cups (6 ounces) shredded reduced-fat mozzarella cheese
½ slice whole-wheat bread, crumbled	

1. *To make the tomato sauce:* Heat the oil in a large nonstick skillet over medium heat. Add the onion and garlic. Cook, stirring frequently, for 10 to 12 minutes, or until browned. Stir in the tomatoes, salt, and pepper. Bring to a boil, then reduce the heat to low. Simmer for 15 minutes, or until softened. Add the tomato sauce and Italian seasoning. Cover and simmer for 30 minutes to blend the flavors. Set aside.

2. *To make the veal:* While the tomato sauce is cooking, preheat the oven to 350°F. Coat an 11" × 7" baking dish with nonstick spray. Set aside.

3. Place the veal on a work surface. Cover it with plastic wrap. Using the flat side of a meat mallet, pound the veal until it is about ⅛" thick. Slice the veal into 6 equal pieces. Set aside.

4. In a shallow bowl, combine the Parmesan and bread. Dip the veal first into the egg whites and then the Parmesan mixture.

5. Coat a large nonstick skillet with nonstick spray. Warm over medium-high heat until hot enough for drops of water to dance on the surface. Place the veal in the skillet. Cook for 1 to 1½ minutes per side, or until golden brown. Place the veal in the prepared baking dish. Pour the tomato sauce over it. Sprinkle evenly with the mozzarella. Bake for 20 minutes, or until the cheese is bubbly.

Makes 6 servings

Per serving:			
249 calories	*12 g. fat*	*59 mg. cholesterol*
812 mg. sodium	*14 g. carbohydrates*	*23 g. protein*

Cook's Notes

• If desired, substitute chicken breast for the veal.

• To make Eggplant Parmesan, see page 132.

• The easiest way to peel tomatoes is to submerge them in boiling water for 30 seconds and then plunge them into a bowl or sink full of cold water. This technique loosens the skins and makes them easy to peel.

Recipes

Breads, Biscuits, and Pancakes

From Caramel-Pecan Sticky Buns for breakfast to Banana Bread at snack time to steaming Baking Powder Biscuits for dinner, who doesn't have a warm spot for fresh baked goods?

Because quick breads and muffins rely on baking soda or baking powder, they can be whipped up in minutes to add good aromas, fine flavors, and comforting textures to your everyday table. If you've gotten out of the habit of baking, try your hand at Blueberry Muffins, Cornbread, or Cinnamon–Sour Cream Coffee Cake.

Baked goods leavened with yeast need a bit more time to develop but don't require much hands-on attention. They are best to make on a stay-at-home day when you're busy with other tasks.

To boost the vitamin E and fiber in these recipes, you can replace up to half the amount of flour with regular whole-wheat flour or whole-wheat pastry flour, which is sold in some supermarkets, natural food stores, and mail-order food catalogs.

Banana Bread

Banana bread is a great way to use overripe bananas. In fact, when I have a lot on hand, I peel and freeze them in resealable plastic bags. Then I can make the bread in a wink whenever I have time.

Photograph on page 312

Homestyle Makeover

Each serving contains

	Before	After
Calories	281	132
Fat g.	16	4

¼ cup butter or margarine, softened

½ cup sugar

1½ cups mashed very ripe bananas (about 3 bananas)

2 eggs, lightly beaten

1 egg white, lightly beaten

½ cup buttermilk

1 teaspoon vanilla extract

1¾ cups unbleached or all-purpose flour

1½ teaspoons baking soda

½ teaspoon salt

¼ cup chopped walnuts, toasted (optional)

1. Preheat the oven to 350°F. Coat a 9" × 5" loaf pan with nonstick spray.

2. In a large bowl, combine the butter or margarine and sugar. Add the bananas, eggs, and egg white. Mix until well-blended. Add the buttermilk and vanilla. Stir until well-blended. In a small bowl, combine the flour, baking soda, and salt. Add to the banana mixture. Stir just until the flour mixture is moistened. Stir in the nuts, if using.

3. Spread the batter in the prepared pan. Bake for 50 to 55 minutes, or until a toothpick inserted in the center of the bread comes out clean. Cool in the pan on a rack for 10 minutes. Set the bread on the rack and allow to cool completely before cutting.

Makes 16 servings

Per serving:	132 calories	4 g. fat	34 mg. cholesterol
	233 mg. sodium	22 g. carbohydrates	3 g. protein

Zucchini Bread

Homestyle Makeover

Each serving contains

	Before	After
Calories	148	89
Fat g.	8	3

Every zucchini gardener panics during high season when the zucchini is plentiful. Well, here is the solution. This quick bread is so good that I urge you to try it even if you don't grow zucchini.

1½ cups unbleached or all-purpose flour

½ cup sugar

1 teaspoon baking powder

½ teaspoon baking soda

¼ teaspoon salt

¼ teaspoon ground allspice

¼ teaspoon ground cinnamon

¼ teaspoon ground nutmeg

⅛ teaspoon ground cloves

1 egg

1 egg white

1¼ cups tightly packed shredded zucchini

½ cup crushed pineapple, drained

3 tablespoons vegetable oil

1 teaspoon vanilla extract

1. Preheat the oven to 350°F. Coat a 9" × 5" loaf pan with nonstick spray.

2. In a large bowl, combine the flour, sugar, baking powder, baking soda, salt, allspice, cinnamon, nutmeg, and cloves.

3. In a medium bowl, lightly beat the egg and egg white with a fork. Add the zucchini, pineapple, oil, and vanilla. Stir to mix. Add to the flour mixture. Stir just until blended.

4. Pour into the prepared pan. Bake for 50 to 60 minutes, or until a toothpick inserted in the center of the bread comes out clean. Cool in the pan on a rack for 10 minutes. Set the bread on the rack and allow to cool completely before cutting.

Makes 16 servings

Per serving:

89 calories	*3 g. fat*	*13 mg. cholesterol*
71 mg. sodium	*14 g. carbohydrates*	*2 g. protein*

Cornbread

This popular quick bread originated in the South, but it is now a national favorite. Cornbread can be baked either Southern-style in a skillet or Yankee-style in a baking pan.

Photograph on page 219

Homestyle Makeover		
Each serving contains		
	Before	After
Calories	368	280
Fat g.	20	6

1 cup buttermilk

2 eggs, lightly beaten

1 tablespoon sugar

1 cup yellow cornmeal

1 cup unbleached or all-purpose flour

1 teaspoon baking powder

¾ teaspoon salt

½ teaspoon baking soda

2 tablespoons butter or margarine, melted

1. Preheat the oven to 400°F. Coat a 9" round cake pan with nonstick spray. Set aside.

2. In a medium bowl, combine the buttermilk, eggs, and sugar. In another medium bowl, combine the cornmeal, flour, baking powder, salt, and baking soda. Add to the buttermilk mixture. Mix well. Stir in the butter or margarine just until blended.

3. Pour into the prepared pan. Bake for 25 to 30 minutes, or until a toothpick inserted in the center of the bread comes out clean. Cool in the pan on a rack for 10 minutes. Set the bread onto the rack and allow to cool completely before cutting.

Makes 6 servings

Per serving: 280 calories   6 g. fat   84 mg. cholesterol
603 mg. sodium   45 g. carbohydrates   10 g. protein

Cook's Note

• Leftovers can be used in your favorite bread pudding recipe to serve in place of rice, pasta, or potatoes.

Baking Powder Biscuits

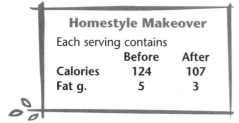
In the classic cookbook James Beard's American Cookery, *the author describes the historic importance of the humble quick breads called biscuits. According to Beard, "In former times, biscuits were the bread of many people. Breakfast, lunch, and dinner brought them to the table hot, light, and fresh."*

2 cups unbleached or all-purpose flour

¾ teaspoon salt

1 tablespoon baking powder

3 tablespoons cold butter or margarine, cut into small chunks

¾ cup fat-free milk

1. Preheat the oven to 450°F.

2. Sift the flour, salt, and baking powder into a medium bowl. Scatter the butter or margarine slices over the flour mixture. Using a pastry blender or a fork, cut the butter or margarine into the flour mixture until it resembles the texture of cornmeal. Add the milk. Stir quickly just to bind into a light, soft dough.

3. Turn the dough onto a lightly floured work surface. Knead it gently for no more than 30 seconds. Pat to a ½" thickness. With a floured 2" cookie cutter or rim of a juice glass, cut out 12 biscuits. Place them several inches apart on an ungreased baking sheet.

4. Bake for 10 to 12 minutes, or until lightly browned. Serve warm.

Makes 12

Per biscuit:	107 calories	3 g. fat	8 mg. cholesterol
	261 mg. sodium	17 g. carbohydrates	3 g. protein

Popovers

A popover is a muffin-shaped bread with a crispy brown crust and a nearly hollow interior. The thin batter—a combination of milk, eggs, flour, and butter—creates so much steam during baking that the popovers literally pop over the sides of the pan as they bake.

Homestyle Makeover

Each serving contains

	Before	After
Calories	107	99
Fat g.	4	3

2 eggs
1 cup fat-free milk
1 tablespoon butter or margarine, melted

1 cup unbleached or all-purpose flour
¼ teaspoon salt

1. Preheat the oven to 450°F. Coat 8 custard cups (8 ounces each) with nonstick spray. Set aside.

2. In a medium bowl, beat the eggs with a fork. Add the milk and butter or margarine. Stir to mix. Add the flour and salt. With an electric mixer, beat on high speed for 2 minutes.

3. Pour the batter into the custard cups, filling each half-full. Bake for 15 minutes. Reduce the heat to 350°F. Bake for 15 minutes. Pierce the side of each popover with a sharp knife. Bake for 5 minutes to dry out the interiors. Serve warm.

Makes 8

Per popover:	99 calories	3 g. fat	58 mg. cholesterol
	113 mg. sodium	14 g. carbohydrates	4 g. protein

Cook's Notes

• Popovers also can be baked in muffin pans or popover pans, which have extra-deep cups.

• To freeze, cool the popovers to room temperature and wrap them in airtight plastic wrap followed by foil. To reheat, completely unwrap them and place on a baking sheet. Bake at 350°F for 15 minutes, or until thoroughly heated.

Blueberry Muffins

Blueberry muffins are quick to whip together. Frozen berries, which plump up during baking, taste and look better than either thawed or fresh. In fact, I always freeze fresh blueberries before using them in baked goods.

¼ cup sugar

2 tablespoons butter or margarine, softened

2 tablespoons unsweetened applesauce

1 egg, lightly beaten

2 cups unbleached or all-purpose flour

1 tablespoon baking powder

¼ teaspoon salt

1 cup fat-free milk

1½ cups frozen blueberries

1. Preheat the oven to 400°F. Coat a 12-cup muffin pan with nonstick spray.

2. In a medium bowl, combine the sugar, butter or margarine, and applesauce. Stir in the egg.

3. In a small bowl, combine the flour, baking powder, and salt. Add to the sugar mixture, alternating with the milk, stirring just until blended. Do not overmix.

4. Add the blueberries and fold into the batter. Fill the muffin cups two-thirds full. Bake for 25 to 30 minutes, or until a toothpick inserted in the center of a muffin comes out clean. Cool in the pan on a rack for 5 minutes. Set the muffins onto the rack and allow to cool completely.

Makes 12

Per muffin:

135 calories	3 g. fat	23 mg. cholesterol
172 mg. sodium	23 g. carbohydrates	3 g. protein

Bran Muffins

These marvelous muffins are very high in fiber because they contain both whole-wheat flour and unprocessed wheat bran, the outer layer of the wheat kernel. Sometimes called millers' bran, it is available in the cereal section of most supermarkets and in all natural food stores.

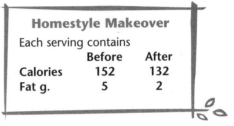

Homestyle Makeover

Each serving contains

	Before	After
Calories	152	132
Fat g.	5	2

1 cup unprocessed wheat bran	1 egg
¾ cup buttermilk	1 cup whole-wheat flour
⅓ cup raisins	2½ teaspoons baking powder
¼ cup molasses	½ teaspoon baking soda
1 tablespoon butter or margarine, melted	

1. Preheat the oven to 400°F. Coat 10 cups in a muffin pan with nonstick spray. Set aside.

2. In a small bowl, combine the bran and buttermilk. Stir and allow to stand for 5 minutes. In another small bowl, add the raisins. Pour in enough hot water to cover them. Set aside.

3. In a large bowl, combine the molasses and butter or margarine. Add the egg and beat to mix well. Stir in the bran mixture.

4. In a small bowl, combine the flour, baking powder, and baking soda. Add to the bran mixture. Stir until just combined. Drain the raisins. Add to the batter and fold to combine.

5. Spoon the batter into the prepared muffin cups, filling each two-thirds full. Fill the 2 empty cups with water. Bake for 20 minutes, or until a toothpick inserted in the center of a muffin comes out clean. Cool in the pan on a rack for 5 minutes. Set the muffins onto the rack and allow to cool completely.

Makes 10

Per muffin:	132 calories	2 g. fat	26 mg. cholesterol
	226 mg. sodium	26 g. carbohydrates	5 g. protein

Light-as-a-Cloud Pancakes

Surprise your family and friends with these pancakes. They are just as delicious as they are fragile and light. I like them best served with light sour cream and fresh strawberries or an all-fruit strawberry jam.

4 egg whites
⅓ cup liquid egg substitute
1 cup 1% cottage cheese

¼ cup unbleached or all-purpose flour
¼ teaspoon salt

1. In a large bowl, beat the egg whites with an electric mixer on high speed until stiff peaks form. Set aside. In a medium bowl, combine the egg substitute, cottage cheese, flour, and salt. Fold in the egg whites.

2. Warm a large nonstick skillet or griddle over high heat until hot enough for drops of water to dance on the surface. Coat with nonstick spray. Pour or ladle batter for 3 pancakes (5" wide) onto the skillet or griddle. Cook for 3 to 4 minutes, or until bubbles form on the top and the bottoms are golden brown. Turn the pancakes over. Reduce the heat to medium. Cook for 1 to 2 minutes, or until lightly browned and cooked through. Repeat by coating the skillet or griddle with nonstick spray and cooking the remaining batter, until all the pancakes are cooked.

Makes 8

Per pancake:

56 calories	1 g. fat	3 mg. cholesterol
232 mg. sodium	4 g. carbohydrates	7 g. protein

Cook's Note

• Leftover pancakes freeze very well. To freeze the cooled pancakes, place them in a single layer on a tray. Freeze until solid. Stack, separated by pieces of waxed paper, and pack in a plastic bag or wrap in foil. Before serving, thaw the pancakes, remove the pieces of waxed paper, wrap in foil, and bake at 300°F for 15 minutes, or until thoroughly heated.

Buttermilk Pancakes

This is my grandmother's original recipe for pancakes. I have always liked these pancakes better than any I have ever tasted—and they were always fat-free. Chalk it up to childhood memory if you like, but do try them—you'll agree.

Homestyle Healthy Classic		
Each serving contains		
	Before	After
Calories	37	37
Fat g.	0	0

2 eggs
2½ teaspoons baking powder
¼ teaspoon baking soda
¼ teaspoon salt

1 cup buttermilk
1 cup unbleached or all-purpose flour

1. In a large bowl, combine the eggs, baking powder, baking soda, and salt. With a whisk, beat until frothy. Add the buttermilk and flour. Stir until the flour is completely moistened. The mixture will be lumpy.

2. Place a large skillet or griddle over medium-low heat until hot enough for drops of water to dance on the surface. Coat the surface with non-stick spray. Pour or ladle batter for 4 pancakes (3" wide) onto the skillet or griddle. Cook for 2 minutes over medium heat, or until bubbles form on the surface and start to break. Turn the pancakes over. Cook for 1 to 2 minutes, or until browned. Set aside. Repeat by coating the skillet or griddle with nonstick spray and cooking the remaining batter, until all the pancakes are cooked.

Makes 20

Per pancake: 37 calories   0 g. fat   22 mg. cholesterol
                 109 mg. sodium   6 g. carbohydrates   2 g. protein

Crunchy Grain Waffles

Photograph on page 311

Homestyle Makeover

Each serving contains

	Before	After
Calories	429	248
Fat g.	17	7

Adding an uncooked four-grain cereal to the batter gives these tasty waffles a wonderfully crunchy texture. The waffles can be made ahead of time and reheated in a toaster, toaster oven, conventional oven, or microwave oven. Leftover waffles can be served as a snack with dips and also make great sandwiches.

½ cup uncooked four-grain cereal (see note)

1¾ cups whole-wheat flour

2 tablespoons sugar

2 teaspoons baking powder

½ teaspoon salt

1½ cups fat-free milk

2 tablespoons vegetable oil

2 eggs, separated

1. Put the cereal in a small bowl. Add enough warm water to cover it by at least 2". Set aside. Coat the griddle of a nonstick waffle iron with nonstick spray. Preheat according to the manufacturer's directions.

2. In a medium bowl, combine the flour, sugar, baking powder, and salt. Set aside. In a large bowl, combine the milk, oil, and egg yolks. Drain the cereal. Combine the cereal and flour mixture with the milk mixture. Set aside. Place the egg whites in a large bowl. Beat the whites with an electric mixer on high speed until stiff peaks form. Fold into the batter.

3. Spoon ½ cup of the batter into the center of the waffle iron and cook for 5 to 6 minutes, or until it stops steaming. (Cooking time will vary greatly, depending on the waffle iron you are using.) Repeat with the remaining batter, until all the waffles are cooked. Coat the waffle iron with nonstick spray, as needed.

Makes 6

Per waffle:

248 calories	*7 g. fat*	*72 mg. cholesterol*
353 mg. sodium	*38 g. carbohydrates*	*10 g. protein*

Cook's Note

• Stone-Buhr cereal, a mixture of cracked wheat, cracked rye, cracked barley, and steel-cut oats, is sold at natural foods stores.

Spoon Bread

Southern to its core, this delicate casserole dish is more like a soufflé than a bread. Best eaten warm, it's often served as a side dish. In the South, spoon bread is traditionally made with white cornmeal; however, the taste and texture are just the same when made with yellow cornmeal.

Homestyle Makeover

Each serving contains

	Before	After
Calories	376	132
Fat g.	21	4

⅔ cup cornmeal

1 teaspoon salt

1 teaspoon baking powder

1 teaspoon sugar

2 cups fat-free milk

1 tablespoon butter or margarine

3 eggs, separated

1. Preheat the oven to 350°F. Coat a 2-quart baking dish with nonstick spray. Set aside.

2. In a small bowl, combine the cornmeal, salt, baking powder, and sugar. In a medium saucepan over high heat, bring the milk almost to a boil. Gradually add the cornmeal mixture, stirring constantly. Cook, stirring constantly, for 3 minutes, or until the mixture just comes to a boil. Remove from the heat. Stir in the butter or margarine. Set aside.

3. In another small bowl, add the egg yolks and beat with a whisk for 1 minute, or until creamy. Add a quarter of the cornmeal mixture. Mix well. Pour the yolk mixture back into the saucepan and mix well again.

4. In a large bowl, beat the egg whites with an electric mixer on high speed until stiff peaks form. Fold into the cornmeal mixture. Spoon into the prepared baking dish. Bake for 25 to 30 minutes, or until puffed and lightly browned. Serve immediately.

Makes 6 servings

Per serving: *132 calories*   *4 g. fat*   *62 mg. cholesterol*
224 mg. sodium   *17 g. carbohydrates*   *6 g. protein*

English Muffins

Homemade English muffins are always a pleasure to serve to brunch guests. People who have seen only supermarket muffins are surprised to see how easy (and tasty) they are to make at home.

1 cup water

½ cup 2% milk

2 teaspoons sugar

1 package active dry yeast

4 cups + 1 tablespoon unbleached or all-purpose flour

3 tablespoons butter or margarine, softened

1 teaspoon salt

1 tablespoon yellow cornmeal

1. In a large saucepan, combine the water, milk, and sugar. Cook until very warm to the touch, 105°–115°F. Add the yeast. Stir and let stand for 5 minutes, or until bubbly. Beat 2 cups of the flour gradually into the yeast mixture. Cover with a cloth. Let rise in a warm place for 1¼ to 1½ hours, or until it collapses into the saucepan.

2. Add the butter or margarine; beat to mix. Gradually add 2 cups of the flour and the salt. Beat or knead to incorporate. Coat a large baking sheet with nonstick spray. Sprinkle a work surface with the remaining 1 tablespoon flour and the cornmeal. Pat or press the dough to a thickness of about ½". With a floured 3" round cookie cutter, cut out 20 muffins. With a metal spatula, transfer to the baking sheet. Cover and allow to rise for 30 minutes, or until doubled in size.

3. Coat a large nonstick skillet or griddle with nonstick spray. Place over high heat until hot. With a pancake turner, transfer the muffins to the skillet or griddle. Reduce the heat to medium and cook for 4 to 5 minutes, or until light brown. Turn and cook for 4 to 5 minutes, or until light brown. Remove to cool slightly on a rack. Continue until all the muffins are cooked.

Makes 20

Per muffin:

113 calories	2 g. fat	5 mg. cholesterol
128 mg. sodium	20 g. carbohydrates	3 g. protein

Cinnamon–Sour Cream Coffee Cake

Photograph on page 314

This scrumptious breakfast treat is based on my grandmother's favorite coffee cake. As a tribute to her love of baking, I've retained the easy preparation but trimmed the fat considerably.

Homestyle Makeover

Each serving contains

	Before	After
Calories	426	299
Fat g.	21	3

3 cups unbleached or all-purpose flour

2 teaspoons baking powder

1 teaspoon baking soda

1 teaspoon salt

1 cup fruit-based fat replacement

2½ cups sugar

2 teaspoons vanilla extract

1 cup liquid egg substitute

2 cups fat-free sour cream

½ cup chopped walnuts, toasted (see note)

2 tablespoons ground cinnamon

1. Preheat the oven to 350°F. Coat a 10" tube or Bundt pan with nonstick spray. In a medium bowl, combine the flour, baking powder, baking soda, and salt. Set aside.

2. In a large bowl, combine the fat replacement and 2 cups of the sugar. Using an electric mixer, beat on high speed until fluffy. Add the vanilla. Add the egg substitute, ¼ cup at a time, beating well after each addition. Add the flour mixture alternately with the sour cream, beating just enough after each addition to keep the batter smooth. Spoon one-third of the batter into the prepared pan.

3. In a small bowl, combine the nuts, cinnamon, and the remaining ½ cup sugar. Sprinkle one-third over the batter in the pan. Repeat layering the batter and nut mixture two more times, ending with the nut mixture.

4. Bake for 1 to 1¼ hours, or until a toothpick inserted in the center of the cake comes out clean. Cool in the pan on a rack for 10 minutes. Set the cake onto the rack and allow to cool completely before cutting.

Makes 16 servings

Per serving:

| 299 calories | 3 g. fat | 0 mg. cholesterol |
| 341 mg. sodium | 62 g. carbohydrates | 8 g. protein |

Beer Bread

Homestyle Makeover

Each serving contains

	Before	After
Calories	114	101
Fat g.	2	0

This old-time recipe dates back to the early German immigrants. In the original recipe, the loaf was brushed with 2 tablespoons of melted butter as soon as it was removed from the oven—an unnecessary extravagance considering how full-flavored this bread is on its own.

3 cups self-rising flour

3 tablespoons sugar

1 can (12 ounces) beer or nonalcoholic beer

1. Preheat the oven to 350°F. Coat a 9" × 5" loaf pan with nonstick spray. Set aside.

2. In a large bowl, combine the flour and sugar. Add the beer. Stir just until blended. Spoon the batter into the pan. Allow to rise for 10 minutes.

3. Bake for 40 to 50 minutes, or until a toothpick inserted in the center of the bread comes out clean. Cool in the pan on a rack for 10 minutes. Set the bread onto the rack and allow to cool completely before cutting.

Makes 16 servings

Per serving: 101 calories   0 g. fat   0 mg. cholesterol
299 mg. sodium   21 g. carbohydrates   2 g. protein

Cheese Bread

Photograph on page 230

This yeast bread is great toasted and is wonderful for sandwiches. For additional fiber, substitute whole-wheat flour for half of the flour called for. Also, you can use other types of cheese to vary the flavor.

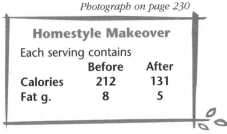

Homestyle Makeover

Each serving contains

	Before	After
Calories	212	131
Fat g.	8	5

½ cup fat-free milk

¼ cup water

1 tablespoon sugar

1 package active dry yeast

1 cup (4 ounces) shredded sharp Cheddar cheese

2⅓ cups unbleached or all-purpose flour

½ teaspoon salt

1. In a large saucepan, combine the milk, water, and sugar. Cook over medium heat for 2 to 3 minutes, or until very warm. Remove from the heat and allow to cool until warm (105°–115°F). Sprinkle with the yeast. Allow the yeast to soften.

2. Add the Cheddar and beat with a spoon until smooth. Add 1⅓ cups of the flour and the salt. Beat until well-blended. Add the remaining 1 cup flour. Stir until blended. Turn out onto a lightly floured work surface. Knead for 10 minutes, or until the dough is smooth.

3. Coat a large bowl with nonstick spray. Put the dough in the bowl, turning to coat all sides. Cover with plastic wrap. Allow to rise in a warm place for about 45 minutes, or until doubled.

4. Coat an 8" × 4" loaf pan with nonstick spray. Punch down the dough and shape into a loaf. Place in the pan. Coat lightly with nonstick spray. Allow to rise in a warm place for 20 to 25 minutes, or until doubled.

5. Preheat the oven to 375°F. Bake for 25 minutes, or until golden brown. Cool in the pan on a rack for 10 minutes. Set the bread on the rack and allow to cool completely before cutting.

Makes 16 servings

Per serving:	*131 calories*	*5 g. fat*	*15 mg. cholesterol*
	159 mg. sodium	*16 g. carbohydrates*	*6 g. protein*

Cottage Cheese–Dill Bread

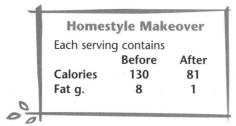

Homestyle Makeover

Each serving contains

	Before	After
Calories	130	81
Fat g.	8	1

This batter bread is delicious right from the oven; however, it is much easier to slice when cool. Keep it, tightly wrapped, in the refrigerator until ready to use, then warm it in the oven before serving.

1 **package active dry yeast**

¼ **cup warm water (105°–115°F)**

1 **cup small-curd cottage cheese**

4 **teaspoons sugar**

½ **small onion, finely chopped**

1 **egg, lightly beaten**

2 **tablespoons dill seeds**

1 **teaspoon salt**

¼ **teaspoon baking soda**

2 **cups unbleached or all-purpose flour**

1. Preheat the oven to 350°F. Coat a 9" × 5" loaf pan with nonstick spray.

2. In a large bowl, combine the yeast and water. Allow to stand for 5 minutes, or until softened. Add the cottage cheese, sugar, onion, egg, dill seeds, salt, and baking soda. Stir to mix well.

3. Add the flour, a little at a time, stirring to mix well. Cover with plastic wrap and allow to stand at room temperature for at least 1½ hours, or until doubled in size. Stir batter to deflate to original size. Pour it in the prepared pan. Cover the pan and allow the dough to rise for at least 60 minutes, or until doubled in size.

4. Bake for 40 minutes, or until a toothpick inserted in the center of the bread comes out clean. Cool in the pan on a rack for 10 minutes. Invert the bread onto the rack and allow to cool completely before cutting.

Makes 16 servings

Per serving: *81 calories*   *1 g. fat*   *14 mg. cholesterol*
        225 mg. sodium   *14 g. carbohydrates*   *4 g. protein*

Garlic Bread

Garlic bread is too often so saturated with melted butter that you can't even taste the bread. The flavor of this lighter version is just as garlicky as its traditional counterpart but lower in both calories and fat.

Photograph on page 224

Homestyle Makeover

Each serving contains

	Before	After
Calories	154	122
Fat g.	7	3

¼ cup fat-free cream cheese

2 tablespoons butter or margarine, softened

2 cloves garlic, pressed or minced

1 loaf (16 ounces) Italian or French bread, sliced in half lengthwise

1. In a small bowl, combine the cream cheese, butter or margarine, and garlic. Allow to stand at room temperature for 1 hour to blend the flavors.

2. Preheat the oven to 350°F. Spread the cut surfaces of the bread evenly with the garlic mixture. Put the two halves together and wrap in foil.

3. Bake for 18 to 20 minutes, or until heated through. Cut into diagonal slices.

Makes 12 servings

Per serving: 122 calories 3 g. fat 5 mg. cholesterol
253 mg. sodium 20 g. carbohydrates 3 g. protein

Cook's Note

• If you like a crispy browned garlic bread, after baking, unwrap the bread halves and place on a broiler pan. Broil 6" from the heat for 3 to 4 minutes, or until golden.

French Toast

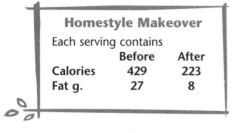

Homestyle Makeover

Each serving contains

	Before	After
Calories	429	223
Fat g.	27	8

In New Orleans, following the French tradition, this dish is called pain perdu, *or lost bread, because it makes appetizing use of an ingredient that's now old.*

¼ cup fat-free milk	4 slices dry whole-wheat bread
1 egg, lightly beaten	Confectioners' sugar (optional)
1 egg white, lightly beaten	
⅛ teaspoon salt	
2 teaspoons butter or margarine	

1. In a shallow bowl, combine the milk, egg, egg white, and salt.

2. Melt 1 teaspoon of the butter in a large nonstick skillet or griddle over medium heat. Using pot holders, tilt the pan to coat the bottom evenly. Dip 2 bread slices in the egg mixture. Place in the skillet or griddle. Cook for 3 to 4 minutes per side, turning to brown both sides. Place on a plate. Repeat cooking with the remaining 1 teaspoon butter, 2 bread slices, and egg mixture.

3. To serve, dust lightly with confectioners' sugar, if using.

Makes 2 servings

Per serving:	*223 calories*	*8 g. fat*	*118 mg. cholesterol*
	515 mg. sodium	*27 g. carbohydrates*	*10 g. protein*

Cook's Note

• This recipe can be doubled. Cook in shifts or use two skillets.

Caramel-Pecan Sticky Buns

Photograph on page 313

Gooey, sweet, warm, and yeasty. Few of us can resist caramel-pecan sticky buns fresh from the oven. And with this revised nutritional profile, why should we even try?

Homestyle Makeover

Each serving contains

	Before	After
Calories	403	236
Fat g.	21	6

Sticky Buns

3½–4 cups unbleached or all-purpose flour

¼ cup sugar

½ teaspoon salt

2 packages active dry yeast

1 cup fat-free milk, warmed to 120°–130°F

1 egg

1 tablespoon butter or margarine, softened

½ cup raisins

¼ cup packed dark brown sugar

2 teaspoons ground cinnamon

Topping

½ cup packed dark brown sugar

¼ cup butter or margarine

2 tablespoons dark corn syrup

½ cup finely chopped pecans, toasted (see note)

1. *To make the sticky buns:* In a large bowl, combine 2 cups of the flour, the sugar, salt, and yeast. Stir to mix well. Add the milk, egg, and butter or margarine. Beat with an electric mixer on low speed for 2 to 3 minutes, scraping the sides of the bowl frequently. Stir in enough of the remaining flour to make a dough.

2. Turn the dough out onto a lightly floured surface. Knead for about 5 minutes, or until the dough is smooth and elastic. Coat a clean large bowl with nonstick spray. Place the dough in the bowl, turning until all sides are coated with the spray. Cover with plastic wrap and allow to rise in a warm place for about 1 hour, or until doubled in size. The dough is ready if an indentation remains when touched.

3. *To make the topping:* While the dough is rising, in a medium saucepan, combine the brown sugar and butter or margarine. Cook over medium heat, stirring constantly, for 1 to 2 minutes, or until the mixture boils. Remove from the heat. Stir in the corn syrup. Pour into an ungreased 13" × 9" baking dish. Sprinkle with the pecans. Set aside.

4. *To assemble:* Punch down the dough. On a lightly floured surface, use your hands to flatten the dough into a 16" × 10" rectangle. Scatter the raisins, brown sugar, and cinnamon evenly over the surface. Starting with the 16" side, roll the rectangle into a tight tube. Pinch the edges to seal. Cut the tube into 16 slices. Lay the slices, evenly spaced, on the caramel topping in the pan with some space between. Cover with plastic wrap and let rise in a warm place about 30 minutes, or until doubled in size.

5. Preheat the oven to 350°F. Bake for 25 to 30 minutes, or until golden brown. Remove from the oven and carefully turn upside down onto a heatproof tray or serving plate. Allow to stand for 1 minute so that the caramel-pecan topping drizzles down over the rolls. Remove the pan and scrape any remaining topping out of the pan and onto the buns. Serve warm.

Makes 16

| Per bun: | 236 calories | 6 g. fat | 23 mg. cholesterol |
| | 115 mg. sodium | 41 g. carbohydrates | 5 g. protein |

Cook's Notes

• To toast the pecans, place them in a medium skillet. Cook over medium-high heat, stirring occasionally, for 8 to 10 minutes, or until golden. Watch them carefully because they burn easily. Set aside to cool.

• You can also make cinnamon rolls with this basic dough. Eliminate the caramel-pecan topping and increase the filling. Scatter 1 cup raisins, ¾ cup packed dark brown sugar, and 2 tablespoons ground cinnamon over the rolled dough. Bake for about 20 minutes, or until lightly browned. Cool for 5 minutes. Mix 1½ cups confectioners' sugar with 3 or 4 tablespoons milk. Drizzle the glaze over the rolls.

Recipes

Cakes, Pies, Cobblers, and Cookies

More than half of all the readers' mail I receive requests makeovers of family heirloom desserts. So, you can imagine how difficult it was to restrain myself from filling half of this book with desserts.

I have done my best to include the most popular and traditional specialties: Strawberry Shortcake, Cherry Pie, Apple Crisp, Devil's Food Cake with Fudge Frosting, Boston Cream Pie, Black-Bottom Pie, Pecan Pie, Carrot Cake with Cream Cheese Frosting, Cheesecake, Pumpkin Pie, and more.

I have lightened these treasured confections enough for us to enjoy them more often. But I haven't sacrificed one bit of the down-home flavor or texture. With reduced amounts of both sugar and fat whenever possible, these keepsakes will have a sweet future in the kitchens of generations to come.

Boston Cream Pie

I have never been able to figure out why this delicious dessert is called a pie when it is really a cake. Classically, it consists of two layers of sponge cake filled with a vanilla pudding and topped with a chocolate glaze. This lighter version seems every bit as rich as the original.

Cake

1 package (18.25 ounces) light yellow cake mix

¼ teaspoon baking soda

1⅓ cups water

4 egg whites

2 teaspoons vanilla extract

Filling

1 package (3.4 ounces) fat-free instant vanilla pudding mix

1⅓ cups fat-free milk

½ teaspoon vanilla extract

Chocolate Glaze

1 cup confectioners' sugar

1½ tablespoons cocoa powder

1½ tablespoons water

¾ teaspoon vanilla extract

1. *To make the cake:* Preheat the oven to 350°F. Coat two round 9" cake pans with nonstick spray. Coat lightly with flour, shaking out any excess. Set aside.

2. In a large bowl, combine the cake mix and baking soda. Add the water, egg whites, and vanilla. With an electric mixer, beat on low speed for 30 seconds. Increase the speed to medium and beat for 2 minutes.

3. Pour the batter into the prepared pans. Bake for 30 minutes, or until the cakes pull away from the sides of the pans and spring back when touched lightly in the center. Cool in the pan on a rack for 10 minutes. Invert the cakes onto the rack and allow to cool completely.

4. *To make the filling:* In a medium bowl, combine the pudding mix, milk, and vanilla. With an electric mixer, beat on low speed for 2 minutes, or until slightly thickened. Set aside for 5 minutes to thicken.

5. *To make the chocolate glaze:* Sift the confectioners' sugar and cocoa into a medium bowl. Add the water and vanilla. Stir to mix well. Add a few drops more water, if necessary, for the desired spreading consistency.

6. Place 1 cake layer on a serving dish. Spread evenly with the pudding mixture. Top with the remaining cake layer. Spread the glaze evenly over the top. Allow to stand for 10 to 15 minutes, or until the glaze sets.

Makes 12 servings

| Per serving: | 234 calories | 2 g. fat | 1 mg. cholesterol |
| | 445 mg. sodium | 56 g. carbohydrates | 3 g. protein |

Carrot Cake with Cream Cheese Frosting

Photograph on page 316

Because this is a moist cake, I was able to eliminate all of the fat and use a fruit-based fat replacement. I reduced the number of eggs and supplemented them with egg whites, which lowers the fat, calories, and cholesterol. I halved the amount of pecans and toasted them to intensify their flavor. Reduced-fat cream cheese replaces regular cream cheese in the frosting.

Homestyle Makeover

Each serving contains

	Before	After
Calories	611	291
Fat g.	25	14

Cake

- 2 cups unbleached or all-purpose flour
- 1½ cups sugar
- 2 teaspoons baking soda
- 2 teaspoons ground cinnamon
- 1 teaspoon salt
- 2 eggs
- 3 egg whites
- ¾ cup fruit-based fat replacement

- ⅓ cup frozen orange juice concentrate, thawed
- 1 teaspoon vanilla extract
- 2 cups shredded carrots
- ½ cup chopped pitted dates
- 1 small red apple, shredded
- ½ cup chopped pecans, toasted (see note)

Frosting

- 6 ounces reduced-fat cream cheese, softened
- 1½ teaspoons vanilla extract

- ⅛ teaspoon salt
- 1 package (16 ounces) confectioners' sugar

1. *To make the cake:* Preheat the oven to 350°F. Coat a 10" Bundt pan with nonstick spray, dust with flour, and shake out the excess. Set aside.

2. In a large bowl, combine the flour, sugar, baking soda, cinnamon, and salt.

3. In a small bowl, combine the eggs and egg whites. Beat lightly with a fork. Stir in the fat replacement, orange juice concentrate, and vanilla. Add the carrots, dates, apple, and pecans. Stir to mix well. Pour into the flour mixture, stirring until just moistened.

4. Pour the batter into the prepared pan. Bake for 55 to 60 minutes, or until a toothpick inserted in the center of the cake comes out clean. Cool in the pan on a rack for 10 minutes. Invert the cake onto the rack and allow to cool completely before frosting.

5. *To make the frosting:* In a medium bowl, combine the cream cheese, vanilla, and salt. With an electric mixer, beat on low speed until creamy. Gradually add the confectioners' sugar. Beat until smooth. Spread the frosting on the top and sides of the cake.

Makes 16 servings

Per serving:

291 calories	*14 g. fat*	*30 mg. cholesterol*
376 mg. sodium	*60 g. carbohydrates*	*5 g. protein*

Cook's Notes

• To toast the nuts, place them in a medium skillet. Cook over medium-high heat, stirring occasionally, for 8 to 10 minutes, or until golden. Watch them carefully because they burn easily. Set aside to cool.

• This cake can be refrigerated, covered tightly, for up to 1 week.

Devil's Food Cake with Fudge Frosting

Photograph on page 323

Although it will never pass for spa food, this cake is scrumptious though considerably lighter than the original version. The decadent frosting alone will earn raves from chocoholic friends. Save it for special occasions.

Homestyle Makeover

Each serving contains

	Before	After
Calories	586	400
Fat g.	35	13

Cake

1½ cups unbleached or all-purpose flour	½ cup butter or margarine, softened
½ cup cocoa powder	1 cup sugar
1 teaspoon baking soda	1 egg
½ cup 1% milk	2 teaspoons vanilla extract
2 teaspoons white or cider vinegar	½ cup hot water

Frosting

1 package (16 ounces) confectioners' sugar	⅔ cup cocoa powder
½ cup water	¼ cup butter or margarine
1 teaspoon instant coffee granules	⅛ teaspoon salt
	1½ teaspoons vanilla extract

1. *To make the cake:* Preheat the oven to 350°F. Coat two 8" round cake pans with nonstick spray.

2. In a medium bowl, combine the flour, cocoa, and baking soda. Stir with a fork or whisk. Set aside.

3. In a measuring cup, combine the milk and vinegar. Set aside.

4. In a large bowl, beat the butter or margarine on medium speed for 3 to 4 minutes, or until very creamy. Gradually add the sugar, continuing to beat, until smooth and creamy. Add the egg and vanilla. With an electric mixer, beat on low speed until creamy. Gradually add the flour mixture, alternating with the milk mixture and water.

5. Pour the batter into the prepared pans. Bake for 20 to 25 minutes, or until the tops of the cakes spring back when lightly touched.

6. Cool in the pan on a rack for 5 minutes. Invert the cakes onto the rack and allow to cool completely before frosting.

7. *To make the frosting:* Sift the confectioners' sugar into a large bowl. Set aside.

8. In a small saucepan, bring the water and coffee to a boil over medium heat. Stir to dissolve the coffee. Add the cocoa and butter or margarine. Reduce the heat to low. Cook, stirring constantly, for 3 to 4 minutes, or until the mixture bubbles and thickens slightly. Add the salt and vanilla. Remove from the heat. Pour into the bowl with the confectioners' sugar. With an electric mixer, beat on high speed for 2 to 3 minutes, or until a spreadable consistency. If the frosting is too thick, add 1 to 2 tablespoons hot water and beat until smooth.

9. To assemble, place 1 cake layer on a serving plate. Spread the top with frosting. Top with the remaining cake layer. Spread the top with frosting. Spread the remaining frosting over the sides.

Makes 12 servings

| *Per serving:* | *400 calories* | *13 g. fat* | *49 mg. cholesterol* |
| | *256 mg. sodium* | *72 g. carbohydrates* | *5 g. protein* |

Cook's Note

• If you want to make this cake even lower in fat, frost it with Seven-Minute Frosting on page 328.

Pound Cake

This finely textured cake was originally made with 1 pound each of flour, butter, sugar, and eggs. Hence the name pound cake. For today's more health-conscious folks, this recipe produces a lighter, lower-fat cake that retains the delicate texture and flavor of its prototype.

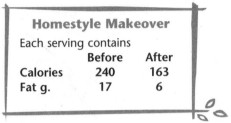

Homestyle Makeover		
Each serving contains		
	Before	After
Calories	240	163
Fat g.	17	6

2¼ cups cake flour (see note)	3 egg whites
¾ teaspoon baking powder	1½ teaspoons vanilla extract
¼ teaspoon baking soda	1 cup sugar
¼ teaspoon salt	½ cup butter or margarine, softened
¼ teaspoon ground nutmeg	
¾ cup buttermilk	

1. Preheat the oven to 350°F. Coat a 9" × 5" loaf pan with nonstick spray. Set aside.

2. In a medium bowl, combine the flour, baking powder, baking soda, salt, and nutmeg. In a medium bowl, combine the buttermilk, egg whites, and vanilla. Beat lightly with a fork.

3. In a large bowl, combine the sugar and butter or margarine. With an electric mixer, beat on medium speed until smooth. Alternately add the flour mixture and buttermilk mixture, in two additions each, beating on low speed to mix after each addition. Spoon into the prepared pan.

4. Bake for 50 to 60 minutes, or until lightly browned, and a toothpick inserted in the center of the cake comes out clean. Cool on a rack for 5 minutes. Invert the cake onto the rack and allow to cool completely.

Makes 16 servings

Per serving:	163 calories	6 g. fat	16 mg. cholesterol
	151 mg. sodium	25 g. carbohydrates	2 g. protein

Cook's Note

• You can approximate 1 cup cake flour by using a cup of all-purpose flour minus 1 tablespoon and adding 1 tablespoon cornstarch.

Crunchy Grain Waffles (page 291)   311

Banana Bread (page 282)

Caramel-Pecan Sticky Buns (page 300)

314   *Cinnamon–Sour Cream Coffee Cake (page 294)*

Cheesecake (page 327)

316   *Carrot Cake with Cream Cheese Frosting (page 306)*

Blueberry Buckle (page 346)

Black-Bottom Pie (page 336)

Oatmeal Raisin Cookies (page 352), Peanut Butter Cookies (page 353), and Chocolate Chip Cookies (page 351)

Strawberry Shortcake (page 348)

Pecan Pie (page 339)

Butterscotch Pudding (page 355)

Devil's Food Cake with Fudge Frosting (page 308)

Apple Crisp (page 345)

Cherry Pie (page 338)

Chocolate Fondue (page 359)

Cheesecake

Photograph on page 315

Homestyle Makeover

Each serving contains

	Before	After
Calories	593	252
Fat g.	41	8

Cheesecakes can be light and airy or dense, smooth, and creamy. Tastes vary dramatically as to which texture is preferable. This recipe is decidedly in the smooth and creamy category, but a great deal less dense in both calories and fat than the original.

1 cup graham cracker crumbs

¼ cup sugar

¼ cup butter or margarine, melted

16 ounces fat-free cream cheese, softened

2 eggs

⅔ cup + 2 tablespoons sugar

2 teaspoons vanilla extract

8 ounces fat-free sour cream

1. Preheat the oven to 375°F. Coat a 9" springform pan or round cake pan with nonstick spray.

2. In a medium bowl, combine the graham cracker crumbs, sugar, and butter or margarine. Press into the bottom of the pan. Set aside.

3. In a medium bowl, beat the cream cheese with an electric mixer on medium speed until smooth. Add the eggs, ⅔ cup of the sugar, and 1 teaspoon of the vanilla. Beat on low speed to mix well. Pour the filling into the crust.

4. Bake for 25 minutes. Place on a rack and allow to stand for 15 minutes. Increase the heat to 425°F.

5. Meanwhile, in a medium bowl, combine the sour cream with the remaining 2 tablespoons sugar and 1 teaspoon vanilla. Carefully spread the mixture over the cheesecake. Return the cheesecake to the oven and bake for 10 minutes, or until the sour cream sets.

6. Place on the rack to cool completely. Cover tightly and refrigerate for up to a day before serving to allow the cake to set.

Makes 8 servings

Per serving:	252 calories	8 g. fat	70 mg. cholesterol
	223 mg. sodium	40 g. carbohydrates	5 g. protein

Velvet Cake with Seven-Minute Frosting

Photograph on back cover

I revised this cake for Heloise several years ago for her column, "Hints from Heloise." We both still get many letters from readers asking for the recipe.

Homestyle Makeover		
Each serving contains		
	Before	After
Calories	913	425
Fat g.	61	20

Cake

2½ cups unbleached or all-purpose flour

1 cup sugar

1 tablespoon cocoa powder

1 teaspoon baking powder

1 teaspoon baking soda

½ teaspoon salt

1 cup buttermilk

1 cup vegetable oil

1 egg

2 egg whites

1½ teaspoons vanilla extract

1 teaspoon white or cider vinegar

Frosting

1½ cups sugar

3 large egg whites

¼ cup water

1 teaspoon cream of tartar

2 teaspoons vanilla extract

3 tablespoons chopped walnuts, toasted (see note)

1. *To make the cake:* Preheat the oven to 350°F. Coat three 8" round cake pans with nonstick spray. Set aside.

2. In a large bowl, combine the flour, sugar, cocoa, baking powder, baking soda, and salt. Set aside.

3. In a medium bowl, combine the buttermilk, oil, egg, egg whites, vanilla, and vinegar. Stir to mix well. Pour into the flour mixture. Stir to mix well. Pour into the prepared pans.

4. Bake for 22 to 25 minutes, or until the cakes spring back when lightly touched. Cool on racks for 5 minutes. Invert the cakes onto racks and allow to cool completely before frosting.

5. *To make the frosting:* In the top of a double boiler, combine the sugar, egg whites, water, and cream of tartar. Place over the top of the pan of simmering water. With an electric mixer, beat on high speed for about 5 minutes, or until the mixture holds soft peaks. Add the vanilla and beat for 4 to 5 minutes, or until the mixture is thick and glossy and registers a temperature of 160°F on an instant-read thermometer. Allow to cool completely before frosting the cakes.

6. Place 1 cake layer on a serving plate. Spread the top with frosting. Stack the remaining 2 layers on top of the first, frosting the tops of each layer. Spread the remaining frosting over the sides. Sprinkle with the walnuts.

Makes 12 servings

| Per serving: | 425 calories | 20 g. fat | 18 mg. cholesterol |
| | 282 mg. sodium | 56 g. carbohydrates | 6 g. protein |

Cook's Notes

• If you desire a red velvet cake, simply add 2 ounces of liquid red food coloring to the batter.

• To toast the nuts, place them in a medium skillet. Cook over medium-high heat, stirring occasionally, for 8 to 10 minutes, or until golden. Watch them carefully because they burn easily. Set aside to cool.

• When cooking the frosting, the egg whites must reach 160°F to destroy any potentially harmful bacteria.

Pineapple Upside-Down Cake

The original recipe for this cake called for an enormous amount of butter to produce a moist topping. To lower the fat, I have used fresh pineapple, which contains an enzyme called bromelain that actually moistens the cake top.

Homestyle Makeover

Each serving contains

	Before	After
Calories	216	129
Fat g.	15	6

2 tablespoons butter or margarine

3 tablespoons packed dark brown sugar

1 can (12 ounces) frozen unsweetened pineapple juice concentrate, thawed

1 pineapple (4½ pounds), peel and core removed, sliced into ¼" rings (see note)

1½ cups unbleached or all-purpose flour

1 tablespoon baking powder

1 tablespoon ground cinnamon

½ teaspoon salt

3 egg whites

¼ cup vegetable oil

1 tablespoon vanilla extract

¼ cup chopped walnuts, toasted (see note)

1. Preheat the oven to 350°F.

2. Melt the butter or margarine in a 12" ovenproof skillet over low heat. Add the brown sugar and ¼ cup of the pineapple juice concentrate. Bring to a boil and simmer, stirring constantly, over low heat for 2 minutes.

3. Place 1 pineapple ring in the center of the skillet. Cut the remaining rings into halves and arrange them around the central ring in a spoke pattern. Set aside.

4. In a medium bowl, combine the flour, baking powder, cinnamon, and salt. Set aside.

5. In a large bowl, add the egg whites and beat on high speed with an electric mixer until soft peaks form. Continue beating while adding the remaining pineapple juice concentrate, oil, and vanilla. Reduce the mixer speed to low. Continue beating while adding in the flour mixture. Add the walnuts and fold into the batter. Spoon over the pineapple in the skillet.

6. Bake for 50 minutes, or until golden brown and a toothpick inserted in the center of the cake comes out clean. Cool in the pan on a rack for 15 minutes. Invert the cake onto a serving plate. Remove any pineapple that sticks to the skillet and place on top of the cake.

Makes 16 servings

Per serving:	*129 calories*	*6 g. fat*	*0 mg. cholesterol*
	166 mg. sodium	*17 g. carbohydrates*	*3 g. protein*

Cook's Notes

• For convenience, use a peeled and cored pineapple, sold in the produce section of many supermarkets.

• To toast the nuts, place them in a medium skillet. Cook over medium-high heat, stirring occasionally, for 8 to 10 minutes, or until golden. Watch them carefully because they burn easily. Set aside to cool.

Gingerbread

For the gingerbread purist, this is the real thing. It is a moist, rich-tasting cake that satisfies from morning to night. For breakfast, serve it with fat-free lemon yogurt or ricotta cheese. For dessert, pair it with low-fat whipped topping, or fat-free frozen vanilla yogurt.

Homestyle Makeover		
Each serving contains		
	Before	After
Calories	293	259
Fat g.	14	7

⅓ cup packed dark brown sugar

¼ cup butter or margarine, melted and cooled

¼ cup buttermilk

2 eggs, lightly beaten

1 cup unbleached or all-purpose flour

1 cup whole-wheat flour

1½ teaspoons baking soda

1 teaspoon ground cinnamon

1 teaspoon ground ginger

½ teaspoon salt

1 cup hot water

½ cup molasses

¼ cup honey

1. Preheat the oven to 350°F. Coat a 9" × 9" or an 11" × 7" baking pan with nonstick spray. Set aside.

2. In a large bowl, stir together the brown sugar, butter or margarine, buttermilk, and eggs. Set aside.

3. In a medium bowl, stir together the unbleached or all-purpose flour, whole-wheat flour, baking soda, cinnamon, ginger, and salt. Set aside.

4. In a small bowl, combine the water, molasses, and honey. Add the flour mixture and molasses mixture alternately to the egg mixture. Stir just until most lumps are gone. Do not overmix.

5. Spoon into the prepared pan. Bake for 35 to 40 minutes, or until a toothpick inserted in the center of the cake comes out clean. Place on a rack to cool.

Makes 8 servings

Per serving:	259 calories	7 g. fat	53 mg. cholesterol
	482 mg. sodium	44 g. carbohydrates	5 g. protein

Buttermilk Pie

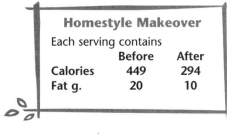

Homestyle Makeover

Each serving contains

	Before	After
Calories	449	294
Fat g.	20	10

This creamy and delicious pie is a real favorite all over the South. It is similar to a chess pie but a bit tangier in taste. Some people like to add a little nutmeg to the custard.

1¼ cups sugar	2 tablespoons butter or margarine, melted
1 cup buttermilk	1½ teaspoons vanilla extract
¼ cup unbleached or all-purpose flour	1 frozen and thawed deep-dish pie crust (9" diameter)
3 egg whites	
1 egg	

1. Preheat the oven to 350°F.

2. In a medium bowl, combine the sugar, buttermilk, flour, egg whites, egg, butter or margarine, and vanilla. Beat with a fork until smooth. Pour into the pie crust.

3. Bake for 50 minutes, or until lightly browned and a toothpick inserted in the center of the pie comes out clean. Allow to cool completely on a rack.

Makes 8 servings

Per serving:	294 calories	10 g. fat	28 mg. cholesterol
	207 mg. sodium	46 g. carbohydrates	4 g. protein

Apple Pie

Apple pie aficionados seem to fall into two categories: those who like it served with a slice of Cheddar cheese and those who prefer it à la mode. Whatever your preference, this pie is sure to please—whether served warm or cold.

Homestyle Makeover		
Each serving contains		
	Before	After
Calories	465	363
Fat g.	24	14

Crust

2 cups whole-wheat flour

2 cups unbleached or all-purpose flour

1 teaspoon salt

¾ cup vegetable oil

¾ cup low-fat liquid nondairy creamer

Filling

¾ cup packed light brown sugar

1 tablespoon lemon juice

1 teaspoon grated lemon peel

¼ teaspoon ground cinnamon

¼ teaspoon ground nutmeg

¼ teaspoon salt

8 Golden Delicious apples, cored and thinly sliced

1. *To make the crust:* In a medium bowl, stir together the whole-wheat flour, unbleached or all-purpose flour, and salt. Set aside.

2. In a small bowl, combine the oil and creamer. Pour into the flour mixture. Mix with a fork until it forms a ball. Divide the mixture into 2 equal balls. Place 1 ball between 2 pieces of waxed paper, flattening it slightly with your hands. With a rolling pin, roll into a 14" circle, ⅛" thick. Repeat with the second ball.

3. Remove 1 layer of the paper from 1 crust and place the crust in a 10" deep-dish pie pan. Peel away the top layer of paper. Trim any excess dough, leaving a ½" border around the edge of the pan. Set aside.

4. *To make the filling:* Preheat the oven to 450°F. In a small bowl, combine the brown sugar, lemon juice, lemon peel, cinnamon, nutmeg, and salt. Arrange one-third of the apple slices in the pie pan. Sprinkle with one-third of the sugar mixture. Repeat two more times to use all the apples and sugar. Coat with nonstick spray.

5. Peel away the waxed paper from the remaining crust. Place over the apples. Fold the edges under and crimp to seal. Make several small slits in the top of the crust for the steam to escape.

6. Bake for 20 minutes. Reduce the heat to 350°F. Bake for 25 to 30 minutes, or until the crust is golden brown. Allow to cool on a rack for 15 minutes before slicing.

Makes 12 servings

| Per serving: | 363 calories | 14 g. fat | 0 mg. cholesterol |
| | 227 mg. sodium | 53 g. carbohydrates | 5 g. protein |

Cook's Note

• The pie can safely sit at room temperature for up to 12 hours. To store, cover tightly and refrigerate.

Black-Bottom Pie

This classic layered wonder—chocolate cookie crust, dark chocolate custard, rum custard, sweet whipped cream, and pecans—would seem impossible to lighten. However, it's nearly impossible to tell the difference between this version and the original—until you look at the nutritional analysis.

Photograph on page 318

Homestyle Makeover

Each serving contains

	Before	After
Calories	685	450
Fat g.	42	10

¾ cup sugar

1 tablespoon + 1 teaspoon cornstarch

½ teaspoon salt

1¾ cups fat-free milk

⅓ cup liquid egg substitute

1¼ cups cocoa powder

1½ tablespoons butter or margarine

1½ teaspoons vanilla extract

1 chocolate cookie crumb pie crust (9" diameter)

1 envelope (¼ ounce) unflavored gelatin

2 tablespoons cool water

¼ cup boiling water

2 tablespoons dark rum or 2 teaspoons rum extract

1 container (8 ounces) frozen light whipped topping

¼ cup chopped pecans, toasted (see note)

1. In a medium saucepan, combine the sugar, cornstarch, and salt. Gradually add the milk, stirring until smooth. Add the egg substitute. Stir to mix well. Cook, stirring constantly, over medium heat for 6 to 8 minutes, or until the mixture thickens to a custard. Do not let it boil.

2. Spoon ⅓ cup of the custard into a small bowl. Set aside. To the saucepan, add the cocoa, butter or margarine, and vanilla. Whisk until the cocoa is completely dissolved. Spread in the pie crust and place in the refrigerator.

3. In a medium bowl, combine the gelatin and the cool water. Allow to soften. Add the boiling water. Stir until completely dissolved. Add the rum or rum extract and the reserved ⅓ cup custard. Stir to mix well. Place the bowl in the refrigerator for 10 minutes, or until cold.

4. Meanwhile, remove the whipped topping from the freezer and allow to stand at room temperature for 5 minutes to slightly soften. Remove the rum custard from the refrigerator. Fold half of the whipped topping into the rum custard. Spoon it over the chocolate custard in the pie shell; spread evenly. Spoon on the remaining whipped topping, swirling into peaks. Refrigerate for at least 3 hours, or until set. Sprinkle with the pecans.

Makes 8 servings

Per serving:			
	450 calories	*10 g. fat*	*7 mg. cholesterol*
	417 mg. sodium	*58 g. carbohydrates*	*14 g. protein*

Cook's Note

• To toast the nuts, place them in a medium skillet. Cook over medium-high heat, stirring occasionally, for 8 to 10 minutes, or until golden. Watch them carefully because they burn easily. Set aside to cool.

Cherry Pie

Using the refrigerated ready-to-bake pie crusts in this recipe is an enormous time-saver. Of course, if you have a favorite pie crust recipe, by all means use that.

Photograph on page 325

Homestyle Makeover

Each serving contains

	Before	After
Calories	523	333
Fat g.	18	12

2½ **tablespoons cornstarch**

1 **cup sugar**

   Pinch of salt

1 **can (16 ounces) sour cherries, packed in water**

2 **teaspoons lemon juice**

¼ **teaspoon almond extract**

1 **package (15 ounces) refrigerated ready-to-bake pie crusts (two 9" diameter crusts)**

1. Preheat the oven to 425°F.

2. In a medium saucepan, combine the cornstarch, sugar, and salt. Drain the cherries and pour the liquid into the saucepan. Whisk to partially dissolve the sugar. Cook, whisking or stirring constantly, over medium-high heat for 4 to 5 minutes, or until the mixture is thickened and clear. Add the cherries, lemon juice, and almond extract. Allow to cool slightly.

3. Fit one of the pie crusts into a 9" pie pan. Spoon the cherry mixture into the pan. Cover with the other pie crust. Tuck the edge of the top crust under the edge of the bottom crust. Pinch the edges to seal. Make a few cuts in the top with a knife to allow steam to escape.

4. Bake for 10 minutes. Reduce the oven temperature to 350°F and bake for 30 minutes, or until lightly browned. Allow to cool completely on a rack.

Makes 8 servings

Per serving: *333 calories*   *12 g. fat*   *0 mg. cholesterol*

                    309 mg. sodium   *54 g. carbohydrates*   *3 g. protein*

Pecan Pie

Photograph on page 321

Homestyle Makeover

Each serving contains

	Before	After
Calories	596	399
Fat g.	25	18

No dessert seems more opulent than southern pecan pie, generously topped with whipped cream. The good news is that you can now make this pecan pie, covered with light whipped topping, for a fraction of the calories and fat.

1 **cup pecan halves**

1 **frozen and thawed pie crust (9" diameter)**

2 **eggs, lightly beaten**

1 **cup sugar**

⅔ **cup light corn syrup**

1 **tablespoon butter or margarine, melted**

1 **tablespoon unbleached or all-purpose flour**

½ **teaspoon vanilla extract**

1. Preheat the oven to 350°F. Place the pecans in the bottom of the crust. Set aside.

2. In a medium bowl, add the eggs, sugar, corn syrup, butter or margarine, flour, and vanilla. Stir to mix well. Pour over the pecans in the pie crust.

3. Bake for 45 minutes, or until the pecans are glazed. Allow to cool completely on a rack.

Makes 8 servings

Per serving:	399 calories	18 g. fat	57 mg. cholesterol
	209 mg. sodium	59 g. carbohydrates	4 g. protein

Lemon Meringue Pie

Fresh as an April morning, this sunny pie makes a refreshing dessert for a seafood dinner. To achieve an absolutely smooth meringue, beat the sugar into the egg whites 1 tablespoon at a time.

Homestyle Makeover		
Each serving contains		
	Before	After
Calories	499	327
Fat g.	19	9

1¾ cups sugar

6 tablespoons cornstarch

2 pinches of salt

2 cups boiling water

1 teaspoon grated lemon peel

1 tablespoon butter or margarine

2 eggs, separated

½ cup lemon juice

1 baked deep-dish pie crust (9" diameter)

1 egg white

1. Preheat the oven to 400°F. In a large saucepan, combine 1¼ cups of the sugar, the cornstarch, and 1 pinch of salt. Stir in the water and lemon peel. Cook, stirring constantly, over medium heat until the mixture comes to a boil and starts to thicken. Boil, stirring constantly, for 2 minutes. Remove from the heat. Stir in the butter or margarine.

2. In a large bowl, combine the egg yolks and lemon juice. Beat lightly to mix. Add the sugar mixture. Beat into the yolk mixture until smooth. Pour back into the saucepan. Place the saucepan over medium-high heat. Cook, stirring constantly, until steaming hot. Pour into the crust. Bake for 5 minutes. Reduce the oven temperature to 350°F.

3. Meanwhile, in a large bowl, add the egg whites and the remaining 1 pinch of salt. With an electric mixer, beat on high speed until soft peaks form. Continue beating, while adding the remaining ½ cup sugar, 1 tablespoon at a time, until the stiff peaks of the meringue form. Spoon over the lemon layer, spreading it evenly to the edge of the crust. Bake for 10 to 12 minutes, or until the meringue is lightly browned. Allow to cool completely on a rack. The pie will set as it cools.

Makes 8 servings

Per serving:			
	327 calories	9 g. fat	57 mg. cholesterol
	212 mg. sodium	61 g. carbohydrates	3 g. protein

Have Your Dessert and Your Health, Too

By cutting the fat and sugar in your homemade desserts, you can occasionally indulge. They are healthier and taste far better than commercial fat-free baked goods, which tend to be very high in sugar and calories.

- In almost all baked desserts, you can reduce the sugar by at least one-fourth without missing it. If you want to reduce it further, try cutting back ¼ cup at a time until you find an acceptable low level.

- In some recipes, you can substitute undiluted frozen fruit juice concentrates for some of the sugar, as I have done in the Apple Brown Betty (page 343).

- Adding slightly more vanilla extract and ground cinnamon in a recipe will enhance the level of perceived sweetness and allow you to use less sugar.

- Replace up to one-fourth of the fat in many recipes with either drained applesauce or baby food prunes. The cellulose in apples and the pectin in prunes trap moisture in much the same way fat does and can therefore be used to replace it. Convenient fruit-based fat replacements combine prunes or plums with apples. Look for them in the cooking oil section of the supermarket. In some recipes, like Carrot Cake (page 306), these products can take the place of fat completely.

- Phyllo dough makes wonderful flaky pastry that's extremely low in fat. Spray the phyllo sheets with nonstick spray, rather than brushing them with melted butter, as I have done in Apple and Raisin Turnovers (page 344).

- Replace solid baking chocolate—which is high in saturated fat—with virtually fat-free cocoa powder as in Black-Bottom Pie (page 336) and Brownies (page 350).

- For unbaked desserts, fat-free and reduced-fat products can help shave fat, while contributing volume and moistness. Try canned fat-free sweetened condensed milk, low-fat ice creams, fat-free whipped toppings, reduced-fat baking mixes, reduced-fat cake mixes, and fat-free pudding mixes as substitutes for their full-fat counterparts.

Pumpkin Pie

We can all give thanks for a lighter version of this popular holiday pie that tastes every bit as good as the original. For an even lighter dessert, bake the pumpkin mixture in a baking dish and call it pumpkin pudding.

1 frozen and thawed deep-dish pie crust (9" diameter)

1 can (15 ounces) solid-pack pumpkin

⅔ cup packed light brown sugar

1 teaspoon ground cinnamon

½ teaspoon ground ginger

⅛ teaspoon ground nutmeg

⅛ teaspoon salt

1 can (12 ounces) fat-free evaporated milk

2 eggs, lightly beaten

2 egg whites, lightly beaten

1. Preheat the oven to 450°F. Set the pie crust on a baking sheet. Set aside.

2. In a large bowl, combine the pumpkin, brown sugar, cinnamon, ginger, nutmeg, and salt. Stir in the milk, eggs, and egg whites. Pour into the pie crust.

3. Bake for 15 minutes. Reduce the heat to 350°F. Bake for 20 to 25 minutes, or until a toothpick inserted into the edge of the filling comes out clean. The center of the pie will firm up as it cools. Allow to cool completely on a rack.

Makes 8 servings

Per serving: 221 calories   7 g. fat   55 mg. cholesterol
                 265 mg. sodium   32 g. carbohydrates   8 g. protein

Apple Brown Betty

This baked spicy fruit pudding dates back to colonial times in America. It is made with layers of sliced fresh and dried fruits, sprinkled with sugar and spices, and topped with buttered crumbs. I prefer to use Golden Delicious apples in this recipe because they are so sweet that you can use less sugar.

6 **Golden Delicious apples, cored and thinly sliced**

¾ **cup (6 ounces) frozen apple juice concentrate, thawed**

½ **cup golden raisins**

1 **teaspoon ground cinnamon**

3 **tablespoons + ⅓ cup whole-wheat flour**

⅓ **cup quick oats**

3 **tablespoons packed dark brown sugar**

3 **tablespoons butter or margarine, melted**

1. Preheat the oven to 375°F. Coat an 11" × 7" baking dish with nonstick spray. Set aside.

2. In a large bowl, combine the apples, apple juice concentrate, raisins, cinnamon, and 3 tablespoons of the flour. Spoon into the prepared dish.

3. In a medium bowl, combine the oats, brown sugar, butter or margarine, and the remaining ⅓ cup of the flour. Stir to mix until crumbly. Sprinkle evenly over the apple mixture. Bake for 1 hour, or until bubbly and golden brown. Serve warm.

Makes 12 servings

Per serving:	*151 calories*	*3 g. fat*	*8 mg. cholesterol*
	34 mg. sodium	*30 g. carbohydrates*	*2 g. protein*

Cook's Note

• If desired, replace the apples with pears.

Apple and Raisin Turnovers

These yummy turnovers are wonderful served warm with a dollop of either low-fat vanilla ice cream or fat-free frozen yogurt. They are also good cold and make a great dessert for a brown bag lunch.

Homestyle Makeover

Each serving contains

	Before	After
Calories	245	136
Fat g.	13	1

2 tablespoons packed dark brown sugar

2 teaspoons ground cinnamon

¼ teaspoon ground nutmeg

4 large Golden Delicious apples, cored and sliced

½ cup raisins

2 teaspoons vanilla extract

8 sheets (17" × 11") frozen phyllo dough, thawed

1. Preheat the oven to 375°F. Coat a baking sheet with nonstick spray.

2. In a large saucepan, combine the brown sugar, cinnamon, and nutmeg. Add the apples and raisins. Toss to mix. Cook over low heat for about 5 minutes, or until the sugar has melted and the apples can easily be pierced with a fork. Stir in the vanilla. Allow to cool.

3. Lay 1 sheet of the phyllo dough on a work surface with the narrow end toward you. Cover the remaining sheets. Coat lightly with nonstick spray. Fold into thirds lengthwise. Coat lightly with nonstick spray.

4. Spoon ¼ cup of the apple–raisin mixture about 2" from the bottom of the strip. Fold up a 2" flap from the bottom of the strip to cover the filling. Fold the lower left-hand corner of the phyllo diagonally to the right side, just as if you were starting to fold a flag. Then continue folding diagonally until you reach the end of the sheet. Set the turnover, seam side down, onto the prepared baking sheet. Coat lightly with nonstick spray. Make the other 7 turnovers.

5. Bake for 8 to 10 minutes, or until golden brown. Allow to cool slightly on a rack. Serve warm.

Makes 8 servings

Per serving:	136 calories	1 g. fat	0 mg. cholesterol
	94 mg. sodium	30 g. carbohydrates	2 g. protein

Apple Crisp

Photograph on page 324

Homestyle Makeover

Each serving contains

	Before	After
Calories	391	209
Fat g.	16	5

This wonderful, old-fashioned baked fruit dessert can also be made with peaches or pears. I like to serve it warm, topped with a dollop of low-fat vanilla ice cream or frozen yogurt.

6 **Golden Delicious apples, peeled, cored, and sliced**	¼ **cup light butter**
½ **teaspoon ground cinnamon**	⅓ **cup unbleached or all-purpose flour**
¼ **cup hot water**	⅓ **cup sugar**

1. Preheat the oven to 400°F. Coat an 11" × 7" baking dish with nonstick spray.

2. Arrange the apple slices in the prepared dish and sprinkle evenly with the cinnamon. Pour the water evenly over the top. Bake for 15 minutes.

3. Meanwhile, in a medium bowl, combine the butter, flour, and sugar. Blend with a fork to form crumbs. Sprinkle the apples evenly with the crumb mixture. Bake for 25 minutes, or until the topping starts to turn golden brown. Serve warm.

Makes 6 servings

Per serving: *209 calories*   *5 g. fat*   *10 mg. cholesterol*
                   54 mg. sodium   *43 g. carbohydrates*   *2 g. protein*

Blueberry Buckle

Photograph on page 317

This scrumptious dessert got its silly name in colonial times because it buckles during baking. I call this revision buckle tightening because I was able to cinch in the calories and fat without losing the taste or moist texture.

Homestyle Makeover		
Each serving contains		
	Before	After
Calories	308	185
Fat g.	14	3

¾ **cup sugar**

3 **tablespoons butter or margarine, softened**

½ **cup fat-free milk**

½ **cup unsweetened applesauce**

2 **egg whites, lightly beaten**

2¼ **cups unbleached or all-purpose flour**

2½ **teaspoons baking powder**

¼ **teaspoon salt**

2 **cups frozen or fresh blueberries (see note)**

½ **teaspoon ground cinnamon**

1. Preheat the oven to 350°F. Coat an 11" × 7" baking dish with nonstick spray. Set aside.

2. In a medium bowl, combine ½ cup of the sugar and 2 tablespoons of the butter or margarine. Mix until smooth. Stir in the milk, applesauce, and egg whites.

3. In a medium bowl, combine 2 cups of the flour and the baking powder and salt. Mix well, then add to the milk mixture. Stir only until the flour mixture is moistened. Do not overmix. Spoon into the prepared dish. Scatter the blueberries over the top.

4. In a small bowl, combine the cinnamon and the remaining ¼ cup sugar and ¼ cup flour. Add the remaining 1 tablespoon butter or margarine. Cut until the mixture is crumbly. Sprinkle over the berries. Bake for 45 minutes, or until lightly browned and bubbly. Cut into pieces and serve warm.

Makes 12 servings

Per serving: *185 calories*   *3 g. fat*   *5 mg. cholesterol*
                              155 mg. sodium   *36 g. carbohydrates*   *4 g. protein*

Cook's Note

• You can replace the blueberries with a variety of fresh or frozen fruits. Try raspberries, sliced strawberries, sliced peaches, sliced apples, or sliced pears

Strawberry Shortcake

Photograph on page 320

Classic American shortcake calls for a sweet biscuit—tender but firm enough to soak up plenty of glistening ruby-red strawberry juice. I've created a lower-fat biscuit with traditional taste and texture. To lighten the dessert further, you can use fat-free whipped topping.

Homestyle Makeover

Each serving contains

	Before	After
Calories	368	246
Fat g.	21	7

2 pints strawberries, sliced

3 tablespoons sugar

2¼ cups reduced-fat baking mix

⅔ cup fat-free milk

3 tablespoons sugar

3 tablespoons butter or margarine, melted

1 cup reduced-fat whipped topping

1. In a medium bowl, combine the strawberries and sugar. Allow to stand at room temperature, stirring occasionally, for 25 to 30 minutes.

2. Preheat the oven to 450°F.

3. In a medium bowl, combine the baking mix, milk, sugar, and butter or margarine. Stir until a soft dough forms. Place the dough on a lightly floured work surface. Pat to ½" thickness. With a floured 2½" round cookie cutter or rim of a juice glass, cut out 8 biscuits.

4. Place 1" apart on an ungreased baking sheet. Bake for 8 to 10 minutes, or until puffed and golden brown. Allow to cool completely on a rack.

5. With a fork, split the biscuits in half. Place the biscuit bottoms on serving plates. Cover each with ¼ cup of the strawberries. Place the tops over the berries. Spoon 2 tablespoons of the berries over each. Top each with 2 tablespoons of the whipped topping.

Makes 8 servings

Per serving:	*246 g. calories*	*7 g. fat*	*12 mg. cholesterol*
	453 mg. sodium	*41 g. carbohydrates*	*4 g. protein*

Almond Macaroons

These wonderfully chewy cookies look so professional, yet they are remarkably easy to make. For variety, you can add a couple teaspoons of grated lemon, lime, or orange peel.

½ cup granulated sugar

½ cup confectioners' sugar

¼ teaspoon salt

1 cup almond paste, crumbled (see note)

2 egg whites

1 teaspoon vanilla extract

1. Preheat the oven to 325°F. Line a baking sheet with parchment paper or foil. Set aside.

2. In a large bowl, combine the granulated sugar, confectioners' sugar, and salt. Add the almond paste and 1 egg white. With an electric mixer, beat on low speed until well-blended. Add the vanilla and the remaining egg white. With an electric mixer, beat on high speed until smooth.

3. Drop the batter by teaspoonfuls onto the prepared sheet. Allow enough room between for the cookies to double in size. Bake for 12 to 15 minutes, or until a light beige.

4. Cool on the baking sheet on a rack for 5 minutes. Slide the paper off the pan and onto the rack. Allow to cool completely before peeling the cookies off the paper. Continue until all the macaroons are baked. Store the cooled macaroons in a tightly sealed container to keep them chewy.

Makes 60

Per cookie:	29 calories	0.5 g. fat	0 mg. cholesterol
	12 mg. sodium	4.5 g. carbohydrates	0.5 g. protein

Cook's Note

• Almond paste, a mixture of ground almonds and sugar, is sold in the baking section of most supermarkets.

Brownies

Using cocoa powder in place of solid baking chocolate reduces the fat significantly. Enjoy these easy-to-make cake brownies with a tall glass of frosty fat-free milk.

Homestyle Makeover		
Each serving contains		
	Before	After
Calories	174	128
Fat g.	10	4

1 cup unbleached or all-purpose flour	3 tablespoons butter or margarine, melted
½ cup cocoa powder	1 egg
¾ teaspoon baking powder	3 egg whites
¼ teaspoon salt	1 teaspoon vanilla extract
1⅓ cups sugar	¼ cup coarsely chopped pecans, toasted
¼ cup fruit-based fat replacement	

1. Preheat the oven to 350°F. Coat a 9" × 9" baking pan with nonstick spray. Set aside.

2. In a large bowl, combine the flour, cocoa, baking powder, and salt. Add the sugar. Stir to mix well.

3. In a medium bowl, combine the fat replacement, butter or margarine, egg, egg whites, and vanilla. Add to the flour mixture. Mix just until moistened. Stir in the pecans.

4. Spoon into the prepared pan. Bake for 25 to 30 minutes, or until the top springs back when lightly touched. Do not overbake. Allow to cool completely in the pan on a rack before cutting into squares.

Makes 18

Per brownie:

128 calories	*4 g. fat*	*16 mg. cholesterol*
78 mg. sodium	*24 g. carbohydrates*	*2 g. protein*

Chocolate Chip Cookies

Photograph on page 319

Fans of tender chocolate chip cookies will love this lighter version of everyone's favorite after-school snack.

2¼ cups unbleached or all-purpose flour

1 teaspoon baking soda

½ teaspoon salt

½ cup sugar

½ cup packed light brown sugar

¼ cup butter or margarine, softened

2 tablespoons buttermilk

1 teaspoon vanilla extract

3 egg whites

½ cup (3 ounces) semi-sweet chocolate chips

½ cup chopped walnuts, toasted (optional)

1. Preheat the oven to 375°F.

2. In a medium bowl, combine the flour, baking soda, and salt. Set aside.

3. In another medium bowl, combine the sugar, brown sugar, butter or margarine, buttermilk, and vanilla. With an electric mixer, beat on medium speed until creamy. Add the egg whites. Beat until creamy. Slowly add the flour mixture, stirring to mix. Add the chocolate chips and walnuts, if using. Stir to mix.

4. Drop the dough by rounded tablespoonfuls onto an ungreased baking sheet. Bake for 10 to 12 minutes, or until golden brown. Allow to cool completely on a rack. Continue until all the cookies are baked.

Makes 30

Per cookie:

71 calories	*2 g. fat*	*0 mg. cholesterol*
89 mg. sodium	*12.5 g. carbohydrates*	*3 g. protein*

Oatmeal-Raisin Cookies

Photograph on page 319

These tasty, old-fashioned cookies are not only lower in calories and fat than the original version but also higher in fiber because they are made with whole-wheat flour. Leftover cookies are good crumbled over cooked fruit, yogurt, or ice cream.

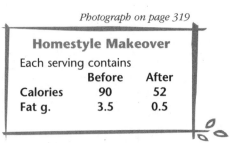

Homestyle Makeover

Each serving contains

	Before	After
Calories	90	52
Fat g.	3.5	0.5

½ cup raisins

1½ cups quick oats

½ cup whole-wheat flour

¾ teaspoon baking soda

½ teaspoon ground cinnamon

¼ teaspoon salt

1 egg, lightly beaten

2 tablespoons fruit-based fat replacement

1 tablespoon honey

1 tablespoon vanilla extract

¼ cup sugar

¼ cup packed light brown sugar

1. Preheat the oven to 350°F. Coat a large baking sheet with nonstick spray.

2. Place the raisins in a small bowl. Cover with hot water. Allow to soak for 10 minutes.

3. In a large bowl, combine the oats, flour, baking soda, cinnamon, and salt.

4. In a medium bowl, combine the egg, fat replacement, honey, vanilla, sugar, and brown sugar.

5. Add to the oats. Stir to mix well. Drain the raisins and stir into the bowl.

6. Drop the dough by rounded tablespoonfuls onto the prepared baking sheet. Allow a 2" space between them. Bake for 8 minutes, or until lightly browned. Cool on the pan on a rack for 10 minutes. Remove the cookies from the pan and allow to cool completely. Continue until all the cookies are baked.

Makes 24

Per cookie:	52 calories	0.5 g. fat	9 mg. cholesterol
	66 mg. sodium	11 g. carbohydrates	1 g. protein

Peanut Butter Cookies

Photograph on page 319

Homestyle Makeover

Each serving contains

	Before	After
Calories	145	65
Fat g.	9.5	3.5

I love these cookies! While they are not exactly low-fat, the entire nutritional analysis is a great deal better than that of the original recipe. They still retain their mouthwatering goodness and crunchiness like the higher-fat version.

⅔ cup + 1 tablespoon sugar

¼ cup butter or margarine

¼ cup buttermilk

¾ cup natural peanut butter (see note)

1 egg

1 teaspoon vanilla extract

1¼ cups unbleached or all-purpose flour

1 teaspoon baking powder

1 teaspoon baking soda

½ teaspoon salt

1. Preheat the oven to 375°F.

2. In a medium bowl, combine ⅔ cup of the sugar, the butter or margarine, and buttermilk. With an electric mixer, beat on medium speed until creamy. Add the peanut butter, egg, and vanilla. Beat on low speed to mix well. In a medium bowl, combine the flour, baking powder, baking soda, and salt. Stir into the peanut butter mixture.

3. Drop the dough by teaspoonfuls onto an ungreased baking sheet. Flatten the dough with a fork dipped in the remaining tablespoon of sugar.

4. Bake for 10 to 12 minutes, or until lightly browned. Cool cookies on a rack for 10 minutes before removing them from the pan. Allow to cool completely on the rack. Continue until all the cookies are baked.

Makes 40

Per cookie: 65 calories 3.5 g. fat 6 mg. cholesterol 86 mg. sodium 7.5 g. carbohydrates 2 g. protein

Cook's Note

• Natural peanut butter can be found in any supermarket. If the peanut butter and oil separate, stir until smooth.

Bread and Butter Pudding

By using fat-free evaporated milk instead of whipping cream and by reducing the amount of egg yolks and butter, I have duplicated the richness and comfort of this homestyle dessert, but with less fat than the original.

Homestyle Makeover

Each serving contains

	Before	After
Calories	277	211
Fat g.	13	5

2 tablespoons butter or margarine, softened

12 slices firm white or whole-wheat bread, crusts removed

¾ teaspoon ground cinnamon

2 cans (12 ounces each) fat-free evaporated milk

⅓ cup sugar

1½ teaspoons vanilla extract

2 eggs

3 egg whites

¼ teaspoon salt

Fat-free whipped topping (optional)

1. Preheat the oven to 325°F. Coat an 8" × 8" baking dish with nonstick spray.

2. Spread ½ teaspoon of the butter or margarine on each bread slice and cut into 1" squares. Arrange one-third of the bread squares in the prepared dish and sprinkle with ¼ teaspoon of the cinnamon. Make 2 more layers.

3. In a medium bowl, combine the evaporated milk, sugar, vanilla, eggs, egg whites, and salt. Whisk until well-blended. Pour over the bread.

4. Bake for 1 hour and 10 minutes, or until a toothpick inserted in the center of the pudding comes out clean. Serve warm or cold. Top each serving with fat-free whipped topping, if using.

Makes 8 servings

Per serving: 211 calories   5 g. fat   62 mg. cholesterol
374 mg. sodium   32 g. carbohydrates   9 g. protein

Butterscotch Pudding

Photograph on page 322

Homestyle Makeover

Each serving contains

	Before	After
Calories	319	233
Fat g.	21	0

For an even more foolproof way of making this recipe, cook it in the top of a double boiler over simmering water rather than in a saucepan. This yummy pudding can double as a sweet sauce for angel food cake.

½ cup packed dark brown sugar

1 tablespoon + 2 teaspoons cornstarch

1 can (12 ounces) fat-free evaporated milk

½ cup butterscotch chips

1½ teaspoons vanilla extract

Fat-free whipped topping (optional)

1. In a medium saucepan, combine the brown sugar and cornstarch. Gradually add the evaporated milk, stirring constantly, until the brown sugar is dissolved. Stir in the chips.

2. Place over medium heat and cook, stirring constantly, for 10 minutes, or until the mixture comes to a slow boil. Stir for 2 to 3 minutes, or until thickened.

3. Stir in the vanilla. Cover with plastic wrap. Allow to cool to room temperature, or refrigerate for several hours to chill. Serve with a dollop of whipped topping, if using.

Makes 4 servings

Per serving: 233 calories   0 g. fat   5 mg. cholesterol
114 mg. sodium   51 g. carbohydrates   6 g. protein

Cherry Tapioca Pudding

Tapioca pudding is an old-fashioned dessert that is making a major comeback. Top with a dollop of fat-free whipped topping or pour on a bit of milk to serve as a great alternative dish for breakfast.

Homestyle Makeover

Each serving contains

	Before	After
Calories	133	121
Fat g.	1	0

½ cup sugar

¼ cup quick tapioca

¼ teaspoon salt

1 can (16 ounces) sour cherries, packed in water

½ teaspoon almond extract

½ teaspoon lemon juice

1. In a medium saucepan, combine the sugar, tapioca, and salt. Stir until well-blended.

2. Drain the cherries over a measuring cup. Add enough water to the cherry juice to measure 2½ cups of liquid. Add to the tapioca mixture. Cook over medium heat, stirring frequently, for 4 minutes, or until the mixture comes to a full boil. Allow to cool, stirring occasionally, for 20 minutes.

3. Stir in the cherries, almond extract, and lemon juice. Spoon into bowls and refrigerate for at least 3 hours, or until set.

Makes 6 servings

Per serving: 121 calories   0 g. fat   0 mg. cholesterol
                 90 mg. sodium   31 g. carbohydrates   0 g. protein

Sticky Date Pudding with Caramel Sauce

The revised version of this holiday pudding is every bit as delicious and satisfying as the original. My family actually preferred the makeover.

¾ cup self-rising flour

¾ cup sugar

2 eggs

1 teaspoon baking soda

1 package (8 ounces) chopped pitted dates

1 cup water

⅓ cup fruit-based fat replacement

1½ teaspoons vanilla extract

1 tablespoon cornstarch

1¼ cups 2% milk

½ cup packed dark brown sugar

2 tablespoons butter or margarine

1. Preheat the oven to 375°F. Coat a 9" × 5" loaf pan with nonstick spray. Set aside. In a medium bowl, combine the flour, sugar, eggs, and baking soda. In a medium saucepan, combine the dates, water, and fat replacement. Cook over medium heat for 3 to 4 minutes, or until it comes to a boil. Stir in ½ teaspoon of the vanilla. Pour into the flour mixture, stirring to mix well. Spoon into the prepared pan.

2. Bake for 25 to 30 minutes, or until a toothpick inserted in the center of the pudding comes out clean. Be careful not to overcook the pudding.

3. Place the cornstarch in a small saucepan. Gradually whisk in the milk until the cornstarch is completely dissolved. Add the brown sugar and butter or margarine. Cook over medium heat, whisking constantly, for 4 minutes, or until the mixture boils and thickens. Boil for 1 minute. Stir in the remaining 1 teaspoon vanilla. Pour the sauce over the pudding just out of the oven. Cool for about 30 minutes.

Makes 8 servings

Per serving:			
	301 calories	5 g. fat	56 mg. cholesterol
	238 mg. sodium	62 g. carbohydrates	5 g. protein

Rice Pudding

Because rice pudding is an edible American icon, I have purposely made this a very basic recipe. It's a wonderful way to use up leftover plain cooked rice. Add your own favorite spices or ½ teaspoon almond, coconut, maple, or rum extract, along with the vanilla extract.

Homestyle Makeover		
Each serving contains		
	Before	After
Calories	426	189
Fat g.	16	1

3 egg whites

1 egg

1 can (12 ounces) fat-free evaporated milk

⅓ cup sugar

1 teaspoon vanilla extract

1 cup cooked rice

½ cup raisins

1. Preheat the oven to 325°F. Coat a 1½-quart baking dish with nonstick spray. Set aside.

2. In a medium bowl, combine the egg whites, egg, milk, sugar, and vanilla. Whisk until well-combined. Stir in the rice and raisins. Pour into the prepared dish.

3. Bake for 30 minutes. Stir the pudding. Bake for 20 to 25 minutes, or until the liquid is absorbed.

Makes 6 servings

Per serving:

189 calories	*1 g. fat*	*37 mg. cholesterol*
105 mg. sodium	*37 g. carbohydrates*	*8 g. protein*

Chocolate Fondue

Photograph on page 326

Homestyle Makeover

Each serving contains

	Before	After
Calories	433	196
Fat g.	33	0

The original version of this fondue was made with cream, unsweetened chocolate, sugar, and cornstarch. Not only was it appreciably higher in fat, it took longer to make.

1 can (14 ounces) fat-free sweetened condensed milk

6 tablespoons cocoa powder

1 teaspoon vanilla extract

1. In a medium saucepan, combine the milk and cocoa. Cook, stirring frequently, over low heat for 5 minutes, or until the mixture is smooth and hot. Stir in the vanilla.

Makes 6 servings

Per serving: 196 calories   0 g. fat   0 mg. cholesterol
68 mg. sodium   43 g. carbohydrates   6 g. protein

Cook's Note

• Try this combination of fruit to serve 6: 4 small bananas, 2 small pears, and 1 pint strawberries. To serve, arrange the peeled bananas, peeled and cored pears, and whole strawberries on a large dessert platter. Spoon the fondue sauce into individual small bowls. Allow each person to spear chunks of fruit with a fork or toothpick, then dip into the chocolate fondue. You can also offer ½ cup finely chopped toasted almonds in another small bowl. Diners can roll the coated fruit in the nuts, if they like. Cubes of angel food cake can also be used as dippers.

Fancy Ice Cream Cake

Save this delight for truly special and very festive dessert parties. It is unusual, beautiful, and delicious—and it can be made several days ahead of time.

Homestyle Makeover

Each serving contains

	Before	After
Calories	463	289
Fat g.	13	7

24 ladyfingers (6 ounces), halved crosswise

2 quarts low-fat vanilla ice cream

1 can (6 ounces) frozen orange juice concentrate

1 can (16 ounces) unsweetened crushed pineapple

1 bag (12 ounces) frozen raspberries, thawed

1 tablespoon lemon juice

3 tablespoons chopped blanched pistachios

1 teaspoon almond extract

1 teaspoon rum extract

Fat-free whipped topping (optional)

12 whole strawberries (optional)

12 sprigs fresh mint (optional)

1. Line the bottom and sides of a 9" springform pan with the ladyfingers, cut side up. Set aside.

2. Place 1 quart of the ice cream in a large bowl. Microwave on medium power for 30 to 45 seconds or allow to stand for 10 minutes, or until soft enough to mix. Stir in the orange juice concentrate. Spoon over the ladyfingers. Cover tightly and freeze for 2 hours, or until firm.

3. In a blender, combine the pineapple (with juice), raspberries, and lemon juice. Blend until liquefied. Push through a fine strainer to remove the seeds. Pour into a freezerproof bowl and freeze for 2 hours, or until partially frozen.

4. Remove the pineapple mixture and ice cream mixture from the freezer. Beat the pineapple mixture lightly and spoon over the ice cream layer. Cover and place in the freezer for 2 hours, or until the pineapple mixture is solid.

5. Place the remaining 1 quart ice cream in a large bowl. Microwave on medium power for 30 to 45 seconds or allow to stand for 10 minutes, or until soft enough to mix. Stir in the pistachios, almond extract, and rum extract. Spoon over the pineapple layer. Cover tightly and place in the freezer overnight.

6. One hour before serving, place the pan in the refrigerator. To serve, remove and cut into slices. Garnish each slice with a dollop of whipped topping, a strawberry, and a sprig of mint, if using.

Makes 12 servings

Per serving:			
	289 calories	*7 g. fat*	*93 mg. cholesterol*
	108 mg. sodium	*53 g. carbohydrates*	*7 g. protein*

Menus

Party Menus

The hospitality of the American home is legendary. In colonial and pioneer days, visitors traveled for weeks or even months to arrive at their destinations. They weren't about to leave after an hour's visit. So, hosts competed to outdo each other in preparing a welcoming table. To this day, no compliment is greater than to be invited to dine in the home of a friend or relative.

Hectic schedules can make entertaining a challenge—but not an insurmountable one. Menus should be designed so that most of the dishes are prepared ahead of time, allowing you to spend the majority of your time with your guests.

When designing a menu for any occasion, it is important to balance the types of dishes served. The flavors should complement each other. Colors and textures should be varied. And, of course, the dishes should provide excellent nutrition so that all at the table may share meals for many years to come.

Dinner by Candlelight

This fine meal is as elegant for a romantic couple by the fireside as it is for eight in a formal dining room. The soup, rice, and green beans can be made in the morning and reheated at serving time. Make the cheesecake a day or two ahead—it actually mellows in flavor.

Cream of Tomato Soup 59

Rack of Lamb 274

Rice Pilaf 138

Green Bean Casserole 100

Cheesecake 327

Cocktail Party

Although we still refer to a casual gathering with beverages and finger-food appetizers as a cocktail party, the cocktails these days often take a backseat to sparkling waters, fruit juices, and fine wines. Depending on the size of your guest list and the amount of time you have, you may choose to serve all of these appetizers or a selected few. Most of these tasty tidbits can also be prepared well in advance.

Baked Artichoke Dip 45

Clam Dip 39

Fried Shrimp 195

Mexican Pinwheels 20

Pimiento Cheese–Stuffed Celery Ribs 19

Smoked Salmon Mousse 43

Spanakopita 46

Swedish Meatballs 50

Ladies' Luncheon

You will be both hostess and guest at this easy, do-ahead ladies' luncheon. The fish and tomatoes can be prepared in the morning and then baked just before serving. The popovers can be made well in advance and frozen.

Celery Victor 74
Stuffed Fillet of Sole 168
Roasted Tomatoes 133
Popovers 286
Lemon Meringue Pie 340

Lazy Weekend Brunch

How better to celebrate sleeping in than with a leisurely late-morning meal that won't bog you down for the rest of the day? The waffles can be made several days in advance and refrigerated or frozen. Both the fruit salad and the ingredients for the sausages can be mixed the night before serving, tightly covered, and stored in the refrigerator.

Fruit Salad 85
Crunchy Grain Waffles 291
Spicy Turkey Sausage Patties 242

Midwest Harvest Gathering

In farming communities, dinner was typically the midday meal and much more substantial than supper, which was served at the end of the day. This hearty meal combines some popular dishes from the Heartland for a fabulous party wherever you live.

Stuffed Pork Chops 270
Lemon Gelatin Fruit Salad 94
Succotash 120
Butterscotch Pudding 355

Sunday Supper

A meal this comforting is going to either stir up wonderful memories or create some. Gather the family around the table this weekend and taste how good a Sunday supper can be.

Carrot-Raisin Salad 75
Southern Fried Chicken 199
Mashed Potatoes with Gravy 128
Granny's Turnip Greens 121
Apple Brown Betty 343

Regional American Potluck

With the diverse ethnic makeup of America, what could be more fun than a potluck menu that combines various regional and international specialties? Use this menu as a starting point but, by all means, encourage the neighbors to bring their own dishes.

Hot Crab Dip 40

Warm Spinach Salad 82

Turkey Tetrazzini 240

Garlic Bread 298

Chocolate Fondue 359

fresh fruit

Tailgate Party

This meal is perfect for a tailgate party because the hearty soup and substantial Muffaletta sandwich will fortify football fans for an afternoon of rigorous cheering.

Corn and Vegetable Chowder 54

Muffaletta 148

Brownies 350

fresh fruit

Tex-Mex Time

Whether you call it Tex-Mex, Southwest, or Mexicali, the vibrant style of cooking from the states that border Mexico has swept the entire country. You can serve the bean dip and guacamole with baked tortilla chips before dinner as appetizers or make them side dishes with the enchiladas.

Gazpacho 57

Chicken Enchiladas 232

Refried Bean Dip 22

Guacamole 41

Rice Pudding 358

fresh fruit

Thanksgiving Feast

Everything on this menu, except the turkey, can be prepared in advance, which certainly helps eliminate a lot of last-minute confusion. This meal can be served in courses, as a buffet, or family-style with all of the food in serving dishes on the table. For die-hard traditionalists, replace the Sticky Date Pudding with Caramel Sauce with Pumpkin Pie (page 342). Or serve smaller portions of both!

Cranberry Gelatin Salad 95

Roast Turkey 238

Herbed Bread Dressing 134

Sweet Potato Casserole 130

Old-Fashioned Green Beans 101

Sticky Date Pudding with Caramel Sauce 357

Index

Underscored page references indicate boxed text or Cook's Notes.
Boldface *references indicate photographs.*

C

O

Oats
  Apple Brown Betty, 343
  Oatmeal-Raisin Cookies, **319**, 352
Okra
  Brunswick Stew, 198
  Fried Okra, 124
  Seafood Gumbo, 180
Olive oil, to enhance flavor, 10
Omega-3 fatty acids, <u>194</u>
Onions
  Apple and Sage Rock Cornish Hens,
    118, 244
  Barbecued Beef Sandwiches, 154
  Bean Burritos, 156
  Beef Stew, **229**, 255
  Beef Stroganoff, 256
  browning, 8–9
  Chicken Cacciatore, **114**, 204
  Chicken Potpie, 200–201
  Chili, 69
  Cornbread Stuffing, 135
  Corned Beef Hash, 258
  Creamed Onions, 122–23
  Diamond Jim's Special, 267
  French Onion Soup, **28**, 64
  Gazpacho, 57
  Green Bean Casserole, **37**, 100
  Hamburgers, **105**, 152
  Hash Brown Potato Casserole, 125
  Herbed Bread Dressing, 134, **215**
  Hungarian Goulash, **220**, 259
  Lamb Curry, 276–77
  New England Clam Chowder, 55
  Onion Dip, 42
  Potato Soup, 63
  Pot Roast with Vegetables, 248–49
  Roast Turkey, **215**, 238–39
  Scalloped Potatoes, 126, **221**
  Sloppy Joes, 153
  Spicy Braised Lamb Shanks, 275
  Split Pea Soup with Ham, 70
  sweating, to reduce fat in recipes, 11
  Sweet-and-Sour Pork, **226**, 272
  Swiss Steak, 252–53
  Warm German Potato Salad, 83
  Warm Spinach Salad, **32**, 82

Oranges
  Ambrosia, 87
  Duck à l'Orange, 245
  Fruit Salad, 85
Oven cooking bags, <u>237</u>
Oven-frying, 11, <u>243</u>
Overnight refrigeration, to enhance
    flavor, 10
Oysters
  Angels on Horseback, 47
  Devils on Horseback, <u>47</u>
  Hangtown Fry, 192
  Oysters Rockefeller Casserole, 190–91
  Oyster Stew, 67

P

Pancakes
  Buttermilk Pancakes, 290
  Light-as-a-Cloud Pancakes, 289
Paprika
  Chicken Paprika, **116**, 208–9
  Hungarian Goulash, **220**, 259
Parmesan cheese
  Baked Artichoke Dip, **26**, 45
  Chicken Divan, 206–7
  Eggplant Parmesan, 132
  Lasagna, **222**, 264–65
  Lobster and Broccoli Stir-Fry, 185
  Tuna Noodle Casserole, **109**, 176–77
  Turkey Tetrazzini, **217**, 240–41
  Veal Parmesan with Tomato Sauce,
    278–79
Parsley
  Beef Stew, **229**, 255
  Chicken and Dumplings, **113**, 202–3
  Cioppino, 178–79
  Herbed Bread Dressing, 134, **215**
  Lasagna, **222**, 264–65
  Roast Turkey, **215**, 238–39
  Seafood Gumbo, 180
Party Menus
  Cocktail Party, 364
  Dinner by Candlelight, 364
  Ladies' Luncheon, 365
  Lazy Weekend Brunch, 365

Roasting foods, <u>243</u>, <u>269</u>
Rock Cornish hens
    Apple and Sage Rock Cornish Hens,
        118, 244
Roquefort cheese
    Lettuce Wedges with Roquefort
        Dressing, 79

S

Sage
    Apple and Sage Rock Cornish Hens,
        118, 244
Salad dressings
    fat in, <u>93</u>
    as marinades, 8
    texture of, 11
Salads
    Ambrosia, 87
    Carrot-Raisin Salad, 75
    Celery Victor, 74
    Cobb Salad, **31**, 76
    Cranberry Gelatin Salad, 95
    Creamy Coleslaw, 77, **106**
    Creamy Potato Salad, 78, **105**
    Curried Chicken Salad on Greens,
        90–91
    fat in, <u>93</u>
    Fruit Salad, 85
    Lemon Gelatin Fruit Salad, 94
    Lettuce Wedges with Roquefort
        Dressing, 79
    Macaroni Salad, 84
    Salmon Mousse, 172
    Seven-Layer Salad, **33**, 80
    Shrimp Louis, 89
    Shrimp Rémoulade, 88
    Three-Bean Salad, 81
    Tomato Aspic with Artichokes, 92
    Waldorf Salad, 86
    Warm German Potato Salad, 83
    Warm Spinach Salad, **32**, 82
Salmon
    Poached Salmon, 171
    Salmon Croquettes, **108**, 173
    Salmon Loaf, 174

Salmon Mousse, 172
    Smoked Salmon Mousse, 43
Salsa
    Guacamole, 41
    Roast Chicken Tacos, 236–37
Sandwiches
    Bacon, Lettuce, and Tomato
        Sandwiches, 146
    Barbecued Beef Sandwiches, 154
    Bean Burritos, 156
    Chicken Salad Sandwiches, **103**, 142
    Club Sandwiches, 145
    Corn Dogs, 155
    Crunchy Grain Waffles, 291, **311**
    Egg Salad Sandwiches, 143
    Grilled Cheese Sandwiches, **30**, 151
    Hamburgers, **105**, 152
    Mexican Pinwheels, 20, **25**
    Monte Cristo Sandwich, 147
    Muffaletta, **104**, 148–49
    Quesadillas, 160
    recipes suitable as
        Curried Chicken Salad, 90–91
        Deviled Eggs, **23**, 44
        Hot Crab Dip, 40
        Meat Loaf, **221**, 260–61
        Peppered Steak, **228**, 251
        Pimiento Cheese–Stuffed Celery
            Ribs, 19
        Salmon Loaf, 174
    Reuben Sandwiches, 150
    Sloppy Joes, 153
    Tuna Salad Sandwiches, 144
Sauces. *See also* Gravies
    Fish and Fries with Tartar Sauce,
        164–65
    Halibut Amandine with Dill Sauce,
        175
    Pasta with Clam Sauce, 184
    recipes suitable as
        Butterscotch Pudding, **322**, 355
        Cheddar Cheese Soup, **27**, 65
        Cream of Mushroom Soup, 58
        Gazpacho, <u>57</u>
        Roquefort Dressing, <u>79</u>
    reducing and thickening, 9
    Spaghetti with Meat Sauce, **224**,
        266–67

peeling, <u>189</u>
Roast Chicken Tacos, 236–37
Roasted Tomatoes, **35**, 133
Seafood Gumbo, 180
Shrimp Louis, 89
Spicy Braised Lamb Shanks, 275
Swiss Steak, 252–53
Tomato Aspic with Artichokes, 92
Tortilla Soup, 61
Tuna Salad Sandwiches, 144
Veal Parmesan with Tomato Sauce,
   278–79
Tortillas
  Bean Burritos, 156
  Chicken Enchiladas, **218**, 232
  Mexican Pinwheels, 20, **25**
  Quesadillas, 160
  Roast Chicken Tacos, 236–37
  Tortilla Soup, 61
Trout
  Pan-Fried Trout, 167
Tuna
  Tuna Noodle Casserole, **109**, 176–77
  Tuna Salad Sandwiches, 144
Turkey
  Club Sandwiches, 145
  fat in, <u>243</u>
  Monte Cristo Sandwich, 147
  Roast Turkey, **215**, 238–39
  sizes and servings, <u>239</u>
  Spicy Turkey Sausage Patties, **117**,
    242
  Swedish Meatballs, 50
  Turkey Tetrazzini, **217**, 240–41
Turkey bacon
  Angels on Horseback, 47
  Bacon, Lettuce, and Tomato
    Sandwiches, 146
  Chicken Paprika, **116**, 208–9
  Club Sandwiches, 145
  Cobb Salad, **31**, 76
  Devils on Horseback, <u>47</u>
  flavor of, 5
  Granny's Turnip Greens, 121
  Hangtown Fry, 192
  Manhattan Clam Chowder, 56
  New England Clam Chowder, 55
  Old-Fashioned Green Beans, 101

Potato Soup, 63
Quiche Lorraine, 161
Seven-Layer Salad, **33**, 80
Warm Spinach Salad, **32**, 82
Turnips
  Beef Stew, **229**, 255
  Granny's Turnip Greens, 121
Turnovers
  Apple and Raisin Turnovers, 344

U

U.S. Department of Agriculture
          Dietary Guide for Americans, 4,
    <u>6</u>, <u>7</u>

V

Veal
  Spaghetti with Meat Sauce, **224**,
    266–67
  Veal Parmesan with Tomato Sauce,
    278–79
Vegetable(s). *See also specific*
    vegetables
  Beef Vegetable Soup, 71
  browning, 8–9
  Chicken Potpie, 200–201
  Cioppino, 178–79
  Corn and Vegetable Chowder, 54
  Gazpacho, 57
  Jambalaya, 188–89
  juice, to replace oil, <u>93</u>
  Lentil Vegetable Soup, 60
  Lobster Bisque, **29**, 66
  Manhattan Clam Chowder, 56
  Minestrone, 62
  Muffaletta, **104**, 148–49
  Pot Roast with Vegetables, 248–49
  Seafood Gumbo, 180
  Spaghetti with Meat Sauce, **224**,
    266–67
  Split Pea Soup with Ham, 70
Vinegar, for flavoring, 9

W

Waffles
  Crunchy Grain Waffles, 291, **311**
Walnuts
  Banana Bread, 282, **312**
  Chocolate Chip Cookies, **319**, 351
  Cinnamon–Sour Cream Coffee Cake,
      294, **314**
  Fruit Salad, 85
  Lemon Gelatin Fruit Salad, 94
  Pineapple Upside-Down Cake,
      330–31
  Velvet Cake with Seven-Minute
      Frosting, 328–29
Water chestnuts
  Sweet-and-Sour Pork, **226**, 272
Wax beans
  Three-Bean Salad, 81
White beans
  Classic Baked Beans, **34**, 98
Whole-wheat flour, <u>281</u>
Wild Rice
  Wild Rice Dressing, **118**, 139
Wine
  Beef Stew, **229**, 255
  Chicken Cacciatore, **114**, 204
  Cioppino, 178–79
  French Onion Soup, **28**, 64

Lobster Bisque, **29**, 66
Peppered Steak, **228**, 251
Pot Roast with Vegetables, 248–49
Spaghetti with Meat Sauce, **224**,
    266–67
Spicy Braised Lamb Shanks, 275
Swiss Cheese–Fondue Canapés, 21

Y

Yogurt
  Fruit Salad, 85
  Halibut Amandine with Dill Sauce,
      175
  Roasted Tomatoes, **35**, 133
  in salad dressings, <u>93</u>
  Tuna Noodle Casserole, **109**, 176–77

Z

Zucchini
  Crab Torta, 158–59
  Minestrone, 62
  Scampi with Spaghetti, 193
  Zucchini Bread, 283

Conversion Chart

These equivalents have been slightly rounded to make measuring easier.

VOLUME MEASUREMENTS

U.S.	Imperial	Metric
¼ tsp.	–	1.25 ml.
½ tsp.	–	2.5 ml.
1 tsp.	–	5 ml.
1 Tbsp.	–	15 ml.
2 Tbsp. (1 oz.)	1 fl. oz.	30 ml.
¼ cup (2 oz.)	2 fl. oz.	60 ml.
⅓ cup (3 oz.)	3 fl. oz.	80 ml.
½ cup (4 oz.)	4 fl. oz.	120 ml.
⅔ cup (5 oz.)	5 fl. oz.	160 ml.
¾ cup (6 oz.)	6 fl. oz.	180 ml.
1 cup (8 oz.)	8 fl. oz.	240 ml.

WEIGHT MEASUREMENTS

U.S.	Metric
1 oz.	30 g.
2 oz.	60 g.
4 oz. (¼ lb.)	115 g
5 oz. (⅓ lb.)	145 g.
6 oz.	170 g.
7 oz.	200 g.
8 oz. (½ lb.)	230 g.
10 oz.	285 g.
12 oz.(¾ lb.)	340 g.
14 oz.	400 g.
16 oz. (1 lb.)	455 g.
2.2 lb.	1 kg.

LENGTH MEASUREMENTS

U.S.	Metric
¼"	0.6 cm.
½"	1.25 cm.
1"	2.5 cm.
2"	5 cm.
4"	11 cm.
6"	15 cm.
8"	20 cm.
10"	25 cm.
12" (1')	30 cm.

PAN SIZES

U.S.	Metric
8" cake pan	20 × 4-cm. sandwich or cake tin
9" cake pan	23 × 3.5-cm. sandwich or cake tin
11" × 7" baking pan	28 × 18-cm. baking pan
13" × 9" baking pan	32.5 × 23-cm. baking pan
2-qt. rectangular baking dish	30 × 19-cm. baking pan
15" × 10" baking pan	38 × 25.5-cm. baking pan (Swiss roll tin)
9" pie plate	22 × 4 or 23 × 4-cm. pie plate
7" or 8" springform pan	18 or 20-cm. springform or loose-bottom cake tin
9" × 5" loaf pan	23 × 13-cm. or 2-lb. narrow loaf pan or pâté tin
1½-qt. casserole	1.5-liter casserole
2-qt. casserole	2-liter casserole

TEMPERATURES

Fahrenheit	Centigrade	Gas
140°	60°	–
160°	70°	–
180°	80°	–
225°	110°	–
250°	120°	½
300°	150°	2
325°	160°	3
350°	180°	4
375°	190°	5
400°	200°	6
450°	230°	8
500°	260°	–